Representations of Youth

The Study of Youth and Adolescence in Britain and America

Christine Griffin

Polity Press

Copyright © Christine Griffin, 1993

The right of Christine Griffin to be identified as author of
this work has been asserted in accordance with the
Copyright, Designs and Patents Act 1988.

First published in 1993 by Polity Press
in association with Blackwell Publishers

Editorial Office:
Polity Press
65 Bridge Street
Cambridge CB2 1UR, UK

Marketing and production:
Blackwell Publishers
108 Cowley Road
Oxford OX4 1JF, UK

238 Main Street
Cambridge, MA 02142
USA

↑ DAY

ISBN 0 7456 0279 7
ISBN 0 7456 0280 0 (pbk)

A CIP catalogue record for this book is available from the British
Library and from the Library of Congress.

Typeset in 10½ on 12 pt Times By Pure Tech Corporation, Pondicherry, India
Printed in Great Britain by Biddles Ltd, Guildford and King's Lynn

This book is printed on acid-free paper.

Contents

Acknowledgements

Writing this book has proved extraordinarily difficult, partly because this type of work does not combine easily with a full-time lecturing job in the distinctly embattled higher education system in Britain. There is something more involved, however, which stems from the dead hand that Thatcherism and the Reagan administration laid over critical intellectual and political work for much of the 1980s. It has been hard enough for many people to survive that decade, and it became increasingly difficult to sustain and develop any kind of radical analysis.

I am extremely grateful to all those who gave me support and encouragement in this project when I most needed it, and especially to Kum-Kum Bhavnani and Ann Phoenix for their unfailing faith in my ability to complete the manuscript. I have particular cause to value the patience of my editor at Polity Press, Michelle Stanworth, and also the advice of Gill Motley and Debbie Seymour. Kum-Kum Bhavnani, Bob Connell, Ann Phoenix and Beverley Skeggs read earlier drafts of the manuscript, and whilst I bear full responsibility for the final product, I am extremely grateful for their comments and their time.

Finally, this book deals with research about 'youth' in a 'First World' context, and it is worth remembering that for many children born outside Britain and the USA, simply reaching 'adolescence' remains a sign of survival against considerable odds. On a more optimistic note, I would like to dedicate the book to my sister Kate, who had her first child, Rhianna, in November 1992. This book is for both of them.

Abbreviations

AFDC	Aid to Families with Dependent Children
CCCS	Centre for Contemporary Cultural Studies, University of Birmingham, UK.
CIECEMG	Committee of Inquiry into the Education of Children from Ethnic Minority Groups
CP	Critical Pedagogy
GHQ	General health questionnaire
IDU	Illicit drug use
MSC	Manpower Services Commission
MSF	Minority school failure
NSE	New Sociology of Education
NUWM	National Unemployed Workers' Movement
OPEC	Organization of Petrol-Exporting Countries
ROSLA	Raising of the school leaving age
SAPU	Social and Applied Psychology Unit (University of Sheffield, UK)
TSW	Transition from school to work

1
Starting Points and Reservations: A Century of Adolescence: From 1880 to 1980

Once more the legend flourished that the number of years lived constitutes some kind of temperamental bond, so that people of the same age are many minds but a single thought, bearing to one another a close resemblance. The young were commented on as if they were some new and just discovered species of animal life, with special qualities and habits which repaid investigation. (Macaulay, 1923, p. 305)

Novelist Rose Macaulay was referring in the above quote to 'common sense' assumptions about British young people in the years following what came to be known as the First World War. The analysis presented in this book looks at the contemporary treatment of 'the young' as some 'just [re]discovered species', turning the investigative spotlight onto the work of youth researchers in Britain and the USA during the 1980s. One of the most striking aspects of this analysis is that whilst overarching conceptions of 'youth' do remain, young people are also represented as racialized, gendered and sexualized beings set in specific class positions within these research texts. Biological determinism, social constructionism and structural theories clash and intersect in the contradictory context of academic stories about 'youth' as a universal age stage, with certain groups of young people represented as particularly 'deviant', 'deficient' or 'resistant'.

The origins of this book are disparate. The most obvious impetus was the publisher's invitation to submit a proposal for a book 'about youth cultures' which would cover research from Britain and the USA. At this time (mid-1985), I was approaching the end of a research contract and facing (another) period of unemployment interspersed with part-time teaching and youth work. I expected to have plenty of time and not a great deal of money for the foreseeable future, so writing a book would solve the former problem if not the latter. As things turned out, I was lucky enough to get a full-time lecturing job at Birmingham University in the autumn of 1985. This helped on the financial front, but it put paid to the spare time. So what began as a book about youth cultural studies and the backlash against radical analyses during the first half of the 1980s eventually became an examination of youth research over the whole decade.

There is more to this book than a publisher's request and my expectation of an indefinite post as a government artist ('drawing the dole', for the uninitiated). Through the practice of youth work and research as a feminist throughout the 1980s, I became increasingly aware of the ideological role played by youth research in the construction and reproduction of academic 'common sense' about young people. Youth researchers, including myself, are involved in presenting interpretations of young people's lives, cultures and experiences. The institutions of academia, including access to publishing 'serious' texts like this one, provide us with a privileged 'claim to truth': an intellectual expert status about other people's lives. However 'radical' our intentions, academics can never completely overcome the voyeuristic element of research, nor the power imbalances between researcher and researched. This is not to deny the potential benefits of social research, but it is important to recognize the consequences of the authoritative voice which comes with the researcher's gaze. This is particularly relevant in youth research, where most research participants have minimal material, cultural or ideological 'power': their voices are frequently pathologized, criminalized, muted or silenced altogether.

In *Representations of Youth*, I have turned the spotlight onto youth research itself, especially those texts produced during the 1980s, to examine the causal stories and conceptual categories through which 'youth' and 'adolescence' have been constructed, represented and understood. The relationship between young people's experiences and academic 'common sense' about 'youth' is not straightforward. Youth research does not simply reflect aspects of young people's lives, nor does it merely *mis*represent their experiences, as though the latter were sitting around like the truth waiting to be discovered – or misunderstood. Youth research is more complex than this, given the ideological role it plays in constructing the very categories of 'youth' and 'adolescence', and in presenting stories about the origins of specific forms of youthful deviance or resistance.

This brings me to the third point of impetus for this book: anger and despair at some of the developments in British and North

American youth research during the 1980s, just as social and economic conditions for many young people were taking a dramatic turn for the worse. Research funding in the social sciences became increasingly difficult to come by, and many youth researchers either moved on to another research 'topic', or scrambled over each other in a return to more acceptable mainstream methods and perspectives. A rising chorus of voices could be heard challenging that radical strand of youth research which had presented a strong critique of mainstream youth studies during the 1970s.

I have used the term 'mainstream' to refer to the perspective which presents those causal stories which are used to justify hegemonic discourses around 'youth' and 'adolescence'. The 'radical' perspective has been formed through theoretical, political and methodological critiques of the mainstream, and both perspectives can be defined as sets of discourses rather than as distinct types of research or specific theoretical frameworks. Any one academic text may incorporate a combination of elements from the radical and mainstream perspectives. The mainstream perspective is positivist, empiricist and conservative, presenting itself as an apolitical and objective project. It is characterized by the tendency to investigate young people as both the source and the victims of a series of 'social problems', adopting the victim-blaming thesis in the search for the cause(s) of specific phenomena. The radical perspective has been more likely to adopt structuralist and post-structuralist analyses, and to deconstruct the association between young people and 'social problems', asking different questions and viewing research as part of a consciously political project.

The 1980s also brought a series of crises for youth research as the mainstream perspective attempted to deal with the critiques posed by radical youth cultural studies during the 1970s. Within the radical perspective, Marxist analyses were facing up to the diversity of youth cultural forms, challenges to a predominantly class-based approach, the arguments of feminist and radical Black, lesbian and gay scholars, and the questions posed by post-modernism and post-structuralist analyses (McRobbie, 1980; McCarthy, 1988). The various elements of contemporary western youth research were facing the crises posed by rising rates of youth unemployment for young people, and for the conceptual construction of youth as a transition into the adult world of waged work, marriage and parenthood. The decade of Thatcher and Reagan saw the rise of the 'New Right' on both sides of the Atlantic, and a resurgence of biological determinism which had profound implications for the treatment of 'youth' and 'adolescence' (Rose and Rose, 1986).

The primary focus on British and US youth research in this book reflects the overwhelming dominance of British and US approaches within academic 'common sense' about young people. I am sure that youth researchers in Canada, Australia, the Indian subcontinent, Africa, and across western Europe will be all too familiar with this form of academic cultural imperialism, and I have included some work from outside Britain and North America to illustrate this process. Youth researchers outside Britain and the USA are frequently compelled to use theories developed in these centres of western capitalism, which have minimal relevance to young people from different cultural and political contexts. Even within the UK/US nexus, many supposedly universal theories and models are not necessarily relevant to *all* young people in these societies (e.g. Mirza, 1992). The ideological force of British and US youth research during the 1980s was also strengthened by the political partnership between the Thatcher and Reagan administrations.

There are many thousands of publications which could be included within the sphere of 'youth research'. Almost all areas of academic endeavour have addressed the 'youth question', and many journals published at least one special issue on 'youth' or 'adolescence' during the 1980s. *Representations of Youth* does not present a quantitative content analysis of youth research, nor does it pretend to be completely exhaustive or 'representative' in the positivist sense. This is a critical analysis of academic texts and the discourses through which 'youth' and 'adolescence' were constructed during a specific historical period. Rather than focusing on one segment of youth research such as delinquency or youth cultures, I have selected texts from a wide range of academic disciplines, and from 'pure' and 'applied' areas, including psychology, sociology, education, cultural studies, clinical psychology and social work.

The decision to cover such a broad range of academic texts was deliberate. I wanted to examine the various ideological resonances of 'youth' and 'adolescence' in the disparate discourses of psychological and sociological research, and in a range of topic areas. In selecting texts for detailed analysis I have used two strategies which relied on a combination of breadth and depth. Texts were selected for their reflection of academic 'common sense' about young people, and for their representation of contradictory themes within both radical and mainstream perspectives. I have also looked for ideological 'gaps', conceptual omissions and silenced voices, since an examination of such absences can be just as revealing as the analysis of those themes which are represented.

The decision to examine a range of academic disciplines, especially across the disciplinary boundaries between sociology and psychology, was also deliberate, since specific academic disciplines have tended to operate in relative isolation. Since notions of 'youth' and 'adolescence' have tended to be shaped by sociology and psychology respectively, it is important to examine the discursive interplay between these two related but distinctly antipathetic disciplines. I have looked at the ways in which a psychological perspective might be mobilized within a sociological framework, or vice versa, especially since psychological understandings have dominated representations of 'youth' in general, and in the construction of certain young people as 'social problems'.

Representations of Youth reflects the diversity of contemporary youth research, without taking each study as a straightforward reflection of 'what young people are *really* thinking and doing' (Lather, 1990). It presents an analysis of the various discourses through which 'youth' and 'adolescence' have been constructed in academic texts. Embarking on an analysis of ideologies and discourses in the 1980s is a daunting prospect. The shelves of academic libraries and bookshops are well stocked with texts on discourse analysis, semiotics, ideology, social representations, poststructuralism and textual/linguistic analysis. The various theories contained therein are diverse, but most share one common factor: they are almost incomprehensible to all but the most dedicated reader. Hidden within the groves of 'subjectivities', 'interpellation' and 'signifiers' are some important and interesting arguments about the analysis and construction of ideologies and discourses. Even if I were to dismiss all these texts as elitist rubbish – which is not my intention – it would be impossible to 'do' a critical analysis of contemporary texts without addressing some of these ideas.

Despite undeniable reservations about theories of ideology and discourse, born of repeated problems in trying to understand them, I have struggled through the various approaches in search of those theoretical perspectives which can most usefully be applied to the changing discourses around 'youth' and 'adolescence' in contemporary academic texts. I have deliberately tried to avoid many of the more mystifying terms used in this literature whilst retaining some of the key arguments. My aim in this analysis is not to conduct an exercise in theoretical one-upmanship (*sic*), but to take a critical look at the ways in which 'youth' appeared on the academic agenda in the 1980s, highlighting the continued prevalence of the victim-blaming thesis in mainstream studies, examining the construction of 'crisis' (or crises) as a key element of radical and mainstream perspectives on youth, and signalling some of the major absences in both mainstream and radical analyses.

Representations of Youth has been shaped by many influences, and I want to mention three starting points for this analysis: Gramsci's notion of hegemony; the post-structuralist approach to the analysis of discourse; and feminist theories and practices.[1] In brief, Gramsci argued that in capitalist societies, the ruling class maintain control partly by coercion through state institutions such as the police and the judicio-legal system. They can also achieve hegemony (or dominance) through ruling by 'consent', but this consent is based on the mystification of existing power relations as natural and inevitable, and the concealment of opposition and oppression (Gramsci, 1971). Hegemony operates at the ideological level as well as the political and the economic, and struggles over the gaining of 'consent' through the ideologies of the New Right were the focus of considerable debate on the Left throughout the 1980s (Hall, 1988). Hegemony is concerned with the production and reproduction of forms of consciousness, as a form of domination which is imposed through a mixture of persuasion and coercion.

So contemporary youth research can be read in part as a reflection of hegemonic 'common sense' about 'youth' and 'adolescence': or all those meanings and values which academic researchers have tended to take for granted. This involves the construction of the age stage of 'youth' or 'adolescence' itself and distinctions between 'normal' and 'deviant' forms of adolescent behaviour with the associated family forms and cultural practices. Such notions are put together via a complex process of interaction between research funding agencies, academic career moves, research designs and techniques, publication of research 'results' – and the practices of young people and other adult groups with whom they are involved. 'Youth' is not a uniform category, and young people's material conditions and lived experiences are by no means identical, nor do they exist untouched by the arguments of youth researchers and policy-makers. Contemporary youth research can be seen as a contested terrain in which mainstream and radical perspectives jostle for position in the construction of dominant and oppositional discourses around 'youth' and 'adolescence'.

With the growing impact of post-modernism, feminism and post-structuralism on radical analyses during the 1980s, the Marxist concept of ideology and Gramsci's notion of hegemony came under considerable critical scrutiny (e.g. McRobbie, 1991). In this analysis I have retained what may appear (to some) an unfashionable use of concepts such as ideology and hegemony alongside an examination of discourses which is informed by materialist feminist versions of post-structuralism (e.g. Roman et al., 1988). The latter approach has proved useful in its capacity to appreciate the ways in which specific discourses and discursive configurations can construct, marginalize, silence and reproduce certain concepts and arguments within particular structural relations of domination. Although *Representations of Youth* is a critical analysis of discourses rather than ideologies, I have tried to show how specific discourses operate in the ideological domain. The discourses discussed in this book make certain arguments, institutions and practices possible, whilst precluding or obscuring others (Parker, 1989). For me, it is power which provides the link between discourse and ideology.

Rather than identifying specific discourses as either dominant *or* subordinate, I have viewed discourse as 'a system of statements which constructs an object. This fictive object can then be reproduced in the various texts written or spoken within the domain of discourses (that is, within the expressive order of society)' (Parker, 1989, pp. 61–2). The analysis of discourse reveals those sets of rules and practices through which power is legitimated. Discourses are governed by rules that determine what can be said and how it can be said (Newton, 1990). This concerns both what is apparent in the text and what is obscured, and the ways in which texts organize what Dorothy Smith has termed the 'relations of ruling' in contemporary society. She uses discourse, in an approach which draws on Foucault's work: 'to identify those distinctive forms of social organization that are like conversations mediated by texts and are carried out by and co-ordinate subjects situated in multiple local sites and organizational jurisdictions' (D. Smith, 1991, p. 159).

In this analysis I examine some of the ways in which discourses have been used in contemporary youth research, focusing on sets of rhetorical connections through which certain arguments about (certain groups of) young people are produced, and through which (certain groups of) young people are represented as deviant, deficient, perverted or resistant. I look at how these discourses have coincided in particular texts, especially in the context of constructed crises around youth during the 1980s. I also consider the mobilization and transformation of discursive configurations within and between radical and mainstream perspectives. I have adopted Kum-Kum Bhavnani's use of the term 'discursive configurations' here, since I am concerned to examine the ways in which arguments and ideas are given shape in youth research texts through specific discourses which are 'embedded in social relationships of structured domination and subordination' (1991, p. 181).

My debt to feminism is rather different, and cannot be traced solely to the influence of specific texts nor to a clear-cut theoretical position. The contemporary feminist movement has generated a broad range of analyses and actions, adopting a critical view of the relation between theory and practice (Christian, 1988). Much feminist debate has never been published in academic texts, despite the embattled expansion of Women's Studies courses and feminist publishing initiatives (e.g. *Outwrite*, 1988). In order to encompass this diversity within and between feminisms, I have used Barbara Smith's definition of feminism as 'the political theory and practice that struggles to free *all* women' (1982, p. 27, original emphasis; see Griffin, 1989).

So as a feminist analysis, this text is not 'just' concerned with sex, gender and sexuality, but also with 'race' and ethnicity, class, nationality, dis/ability and age relations. This produces an analysis of the ways in which these sets of power relations interact, working against and with each other in different contexts, without necessarily viewing any *one* set of power relations as always overdetermining in all periods and all conditions. Power is not an innate capacity, nor is it an idiosyncratic characteristic of particular individuals. Power operates in the context of social structures, cultural and ideological practices. Ideologies are constructed through relations of power and dominance, which are also disputed and contradictory. As an ideological category and a social condition, 'youth' is not uniform, but it is seldom invested with significant power, especially compared with those groups of adults who have varying degrees of authority over young people's lives, from parents and teachers to employers and academic researchers. This feminist analysis will examine the construction and dis/empowerment of 'youth' and of specific groups of young people in different strands of youth research.

Throughout the process of writing this book, I experienced continual doubts and reservations about the relevance and value of such a project for young people in the 1980s and 1990s. A little voice in my head kept repeating that yet another book about academic youth research was surely the last priority at the end of this disastrous decade. Yet it is precisely *because* academic texts and research reports have had such a significant impact in shaping government policies and popular 'common sense' around youth that I continued to struggle with the analysis. I hope to make new points and arguments, shifting the focus of language and debate. This entails a move away from the pretence of an 'apolitical' analysis; away from the foregrounding of class at the expense of 'race', gender and sexuality; and away from the presentation of 'youth', or specific groups of young people, as the 'problem'. It involves questioning the dominant practices, language, policies and values of the adult world, and especially those of academic youth research texts operating from the mainstream perspective.

Academic youth research has provided a source of employment, career advancement and kudos for hundreds, if not thousands, of educated adults since the 1880s, when G. S. Hall was credited with the 'discovery' of adolescence, and I would not exempt myself from this phenomenon. As with all research work, my critical perspective is not value-free, nor does this pretend to be an atheoretical or apolitical text: such a project would be neither possible nor desirable (Spivak, 1987). Research is never neutral territory, but the political nature of youth research has been especially significant in the 1980s.

Writing in the classic radical text on youth cultures from the 1970s, *Resistance through Rituals*, John Clarke and his colleagues argued that 'youth' can serve as a metaphor for dealing with crises in society (Clarke et al., 1975). Whilst Clarke and his colleagues were most concerned with the ideological significance of youth in the social class relations of capitalist societies, my interest is in the operation of racially structured capitalist patriarchies (see Bhavnani, 1991). 'Youth' is still treated as a key indicator of the state of the nation itself: it is expected to reflect the cycle of booms and troughs in the economy; shifts in cultural values over sexuality, morality and family life; and changes in class relations, concepts of nationhood, and in occupational structures. Young people are assumed to hold the key to the nation's future, and the treatment and management of 'youth' is expected to provide the solution to a nation's 'problems', from 'drug abuse', 'hooliganism' and 'teenage pregnancy' to inner city 'riots'. The everyday operations of international capitalism or patriarchal power relations are seldom represented as the source of such 'social problems'. The young are assumed to hold the key to the nation's future: if official levels of unemployment rise or the incidence of violent crime increases, this can be attributed to 'problem youth', and a whole series of 'respectable fears' have been dealt with in this way (Pearson, 1983).

As with gender, sexuality, 'race' and nineteenth-century assumptions about class, 'common sense' ideas about age stages in general and youth in particular are founded on biological determinism. Since the onset of puberty is taken to be the key defining feature of adolescence, the category is almost immune from effective challenge or deconstruction, since the biological domain is assumed to be inherently 'natural', inevitable and irrevocable (Haraway, 1989). There are some undeniable physical and physiological variations between children, young people and adults, but western cultural traditions from the latter half of the nineteenth century have enshrined the 'biological' as separate from and dominant over the 'social': as involving a set of more basic determining factors (Riley, 1978). One legacy of this distinction is that we have come to view certain phenomena as immutable and universal, since they are assumed to have their true roots in a biology which is static and unchanging.

Some feminists initially rejected the arguments of biological determinism in favour of social constructionist analyses of gender development, since the former reproduce 'common-sense' notions about women's 'natural' destiny as wives and mothers, and men's 'naturally' aggressive sexuality. By the mid-1980s, other feminists were calling for a reassessment of the nature–nurture dichotomy on which the distinction between the biological and the social is based (e.g. Sayers, 1982; Birke and Vines, 1987). Rather than presenting social constructionism as a replacement for biological determinism, this approach set out to develop a feminist revision of the biological domain. In order to do this, 'common-sense' constructions of the biological as the inevitable and irrevocable basis on which the more malleable and dynamic social domain is based must be deconstructed. It is no longer possible to represent the biological as 'natural', as New Right ideologies have attempted to do, but neither can radical analyses ignore our biological selves, or 'locate [them] within the rhetoric of social construction' (Birke and Vines, 1987, p. 555, my insertion). This more dynamic vision of the biological would represent biological processes and experiences in a transformative way with implications for our understandings of gender, sexuality, 'race', class and dis/ability (Haraway, 1989).

New Right ideologies ensured that the nature–nurture dichotomy retained its force throughout the 1980s (Rose and Rose, 1986). One of the most powerful elements within hegemonic discourses around youth is the continuing importance of biological determinism and the onset of puberty as the defining moment of adolescence. Youth becomes a unitary category which is distinct from and preliminary to adulthood and maturity. It seems impossible to imagine a society in which the phenomenon of adolescence does not exist. After all, we were all young once, so surely this *must* be a natural and universal phenomenon?

My main interest is the ways in which the biological domain is constructed as privileged over the social, historical and economic realms in most mainstream academic narratives about 'youth' and 'adolescence'. So *Representations of Youth* begins not in 1980, nor even 1950, but in the 1880s with the 'discovery' of adolescence, the concept which has had such a profound effect on ideologies around youth. Tracing the origins of the concept of adolescence, however briefly, is a salutary experience. We begin to uncover some connections with discourses in contemporary youth research. This is more than 'merely' a history of ideas: the seeds of most twentieth-century adult-sponsored institutions for young people lie in the developing concept of adolescence. The latter had a range of material and institutional consequences, and traces of nineteenth-century discourses on adolescence can be found in the contemporary Youth Service, the education system, apprenticeships and training schemes, child-rearing conventions and practices, the juvenile justice system, the youth job market, as well as in the priorities of contemporary youth research.

The Discovery of 'Adolescence'

American psychologist G. Stanley Hall is usually credited with the 'discovery' of adolescence, but his influential two-volume text on adolescence merely synthesized a range of themes, assumptions and arguments in late nineteenth-century western ideologies around education, sexuality, family life and employment (G. S. Hall, 1904). 'Adolescence' was not simply a product of Hall's idiosyncratic ideas as an influential North American psychologist, nor did this represent an essential truth about 'youth' which was discovered by Hall via the techniques of scientific psychology. Hall's work reflects a particular combination of discourses around 'race', sexuality, gender, class, nation *and* age which were very much rooted in a specific historical moment.

Pre-industrial European societies made no clear distinction between childhood and other pre-adult phases of life. There was no concept of adolescence, nor of any clear physiological boundary at puberty. The main age stages, childhood, youth and adulthood, were not strictly defined by chronological age, but in terms of dependence and separation from the family of origin (Ariès, 1962). John Springhall and others have argued that the concept of adolescence emerged mainly as a result of capital's demand for a cheap and youthful labour force, with the ideology of adolescence forged by fundamental changes in *class* relations (P. Cohen, 1986; Walvin, 1982; Springhall, 1986). The coincident development of a muscular Christian form of masculinity also marked a significant transformation within *gender* relations and the management and construction of young people's sexualities. This operated in a colonial context, playing a crucial role in preparing elite Anglo-European males for positions of imperial power and in racializing notions of 'normal' adolescence.

This new form of muscular Christianity shaped dominant constructions of femininity as well as masculinity, particularly through discourses around sexuality. The earlier model of the Latin school was akin to a monastery: women and 'the feminine' were to be avoided as potential sources of temptation for masculine (hetero)-sexuality. The new public school, following Arnold's regime at Rugby, was modelled on a military institution, associating women and the feminine with weakness and fragility, and men and masculinity with strength and virility (Gillis, 1974). So the 'discovery' of adolescence coincided with the emerging cult of heterosexual masculinity; with the determined avoidance (especially by elite males) of all things 'feminine', and with the construction of 'homosexuality' as a new judicio-legal category which was synonymous with sexual deviance, evil and pathological sickness (Weeks, 1981; Faderman, 1981). According to Kett, the mid-nineteenth-century concept of adolescence was 'in its crudest form an embodiment of Victorian prejudices about females and sexuality' (1977, p. 143).

Most of the changes in young people's lives which laid the foundations for the 'discovery' of adolescence occurred in the second half of the nineteenth century with the onset of industrialization. Domestic industries in Britain gradually declined after the 1830s as cities expanded with the growth of factory production and mechanization. Working-class families were fragmented by migration to cities and inter-generational conflicts as young people entered factory work. Many fifteen- to twenty-five-year-olds moved into cities and stayed, working in the expanding manufacturing industries. Apprenticeships were the main regulatory device for young men in traditional crafts. The factory system also improved the conditions of young working-class women's lives to some extent, although not always enough to live as independent single women (Pinchbeck, 1930).

Distinctions between dependent childhood, semi-dependent youth and independent adulthood blurred as young people stayed longer in the parental home, leaving to set up independent households on or after marriage, with young women often moving from the authority of the father to that of the husband. Sentimental ideas about children in a modern family of individuals, as opposed to a collective of mini-adults and adults, did not emerge until the late nineteenth century, when attitudes to children became increasingly sentimental and individualized (Walvin, 1982).

Changes in the education system played a major role in shaping the emerging ideology of adolescence, and as the century progressed, classical and formal education became increasingly essential as a means of entry to the professions for the sons of the middle classes. It also became increasingly expensive, posing particular financial problems for bourgeois parents, who were eager to get 'value for money' as far as their sons' education was concerned. Daughters of the privileged classes seldom had any formal education, remaining in the parental home until marriage, which was assumed to be their destiny and primary 'career'. For the children of working-class parents, such considerations were scarcely relevant as the demands of waged labour and domestic work took precedence over their educational needs (Humphries, 1981).

The ideology of adolescence lay at the heart of an interaction between class, 'race', gender _and_ age relations. This ideology had important cultural and commercial connections across the Atlantic. There were many similarities in the processes of industrialization, urban migration, and changes in the education system, but there were also some important differences between the USA and Britain. The end of the nineteenth century was a distinctive era for young Americans. There were a series of mass migrations from rural to urban areas; intense Evangelical moralism and continuing cycles of revivalism; and an increase in commercial employment opportunities. For enslaved and disenfranchised African-Americans, these years marked an increase in Abolitionist activity, and the gradual overthrow of slavery in its 'official' form (Davis, 1982).

In North America, the experience of colonization and the slave system were 'closer to home' than the British history of exploitation in parts of Africa and the Indian subcontinent. Following the War of Independence the construction of a unitary American national identity assumed even greater urgency, and the diverse cultural traditions of the American 'melting-pot' after the Civil War were to be united into *one* national identity, in which immigrant, Catholic, Jewish, working-class, Native American, South American and African-American cultures came to be defined as inferior to the WASP norm. The emerging ideology of adolescence made use of 'racial' themes which were based on assumptions about the supposedly natural superiority of Anglo-Saxon white European 'stock' (Kett, 1977). The apparently universal nature of adolescence provided an illusory uniformity at a time when the construction of a united national identity and culture was of paramount importance for the Union.

The seeds of the 'discovery' of adolescence could also be identified in the sphere of religious practices, particularly during the cycles of Evangelical Revivalism. Religious conversion was seen as the pinnacle of youthful idealism, and a mark of the transition to adulthood, with discourses sharply differentiated according to gender. Conversion narratives for young men were filled with the rhetoric of decision-making, whilst in those for young women stories of piety, submission and humility predominated. Religious conversion (in the Evangelical Protestant context) was the ideological counterpart of puberty in later nineteenth-century discourses around adolescence and the transition to adulthood. By the mid-nineteenth century, scientific and medical discourses were replacing religious and spiritual themes in defining the boundaries of 'adolescence'.

A further similarity with conditions in western Europe, apart from the emergence of the North American high school and college system for the children (mainly the sons) of the upper and middle classes, was the 'moral panic' over the urban poor, which focused

on young working-class, immigrant and African-Americans, particularly young men in street gangs (Kett, 1977). Social reformers
used a wide range of strategies to 'protect' and 'civilize' urban
working-class youth groups, in which religion played a central role.
Adult-sponsored institutions for the regulation of young people
became increasingly professional from 1900 onwards. These professional (predominantly white, male and middle-class) workers
used the new concept of adolescence to define normality. Young
people (especially poor and working-class groups) could be labelled
as deviant and pathological whenever their experiences or attitudes
seemed to differ from the idealized image of the 'normal adolescent'. This was reflected in the alliance between academic psychology and social reformers found in the work of G. Stanley Hall.
Hall represented unspontaneous young white middle-class males
as normal, with exteriors of conformity and confidence hiding a
turmoil of emotion, sexual confusion and self-doubt.

G. Stanley Hall and the Role of Psychology

For Hall and his peers, adolescence was defined as a physiological
stage triggered by the onset of puberty. Hall saw adolescence as
a process of becoming and a period of transition, drawing on
earlier notions about spiritual conversion which presented adolescence as the key period of universal religious awakening (G. S.
Hall, 1904). For Hall, the origins of religious conversion lay in
the physiological changes at puberty: sexual awakening and the
transition to 'normal' adult genital heterosexuality. Hall shifted
the emphasis from the spiritual and the religious realm to the
sexual and the biological domain via this metaphor of religious
conversion. His work allowed young people to be dealt with not
in the religious sphere, but in the emerging profession of medicine,
particularly through its psychological manifestations. Reduced
economic circumstances compelled Hall to make links with the
non-academic child-study movement during the 1890s, populariz-
ing psychology, and giving a gloss of academic respectability to
the activities of the child and youth savers (Ross, 1972).

Hall attempted to blend Christian theology with his own brand
of genetic psychology. As a result, his work was riddled with
contradictions, reflecting a combination of liberalism and re-
pressive ideas; militarism and the advocacy of freedom; and an emphasis on the roles of instinct *and* environment. The exceptionally

broad scope of Hall's work contributed to its ideological influence, since his texts incorporated diverse and opposing discourses on adolescence. It was through the inclusion of such contradictory elements that Hall's texts were able to make the ideological transition from the religious to the medical and scientific spheres.

Hall borrowed the pre-Darwinian law of recapitulation from biology, applying it as literally as possible to his psychology of adolescence. The earlier version of recapitulation theory, or the 'Great Chain of Being', had provided a justification for slavery, imperialist exploitation and colonial expansion. It constructed a developmental progression from non-human animal species such as the chimpanzee or the gorilla, through the supposedly 'primitive' and 'barbaric' Africans, more 'civilized' Asians, to the white European 'races' who were set up as the pinnacle of civilized life (Haraway, 1989). This also operated in class and gender terms, so that men were higher in the evolutionary scale than women, the aristocracy over the bourgeoisie, with the labouring poor and the destitute at the bottom of the heap. Hall adapted this 'law' to a life-stage model of the move from birth, through childhood and adolescence, to the fixed point of maturity at adulthood (the prime of life for upper-class males), and down again to old age (the second childhood). Infancy, childhood and adolescence were likened to earlier prehistoric cultures, a time when we were supposedly at the mercy of our most basic impulses, and to contemporary 'primitive' societies.

The origins of puberty lay in inherited biological impulses which initiated a period of 'storm and stress', characterized by alternating and opposing emotions. Adolescence was represented as a stressful and distressing time for everyone, and this hormonal turmoil set adolescents apart from the stasis of the 'mature' adult world. Hall advocated a contradictory mixture of freedom and control: freedom would allow adolescents to discover their potentialities, and control would be necessary to establish order and self-discipline. Such self-control was particularly crucial for the suppression of sexual impulses.

Hall argued that 'normal' sexuality appeared first at puberty, and that this took the form of genital heterosexuality. Hall drew on his own version of Freudian psychoanalytic theory to propose that adolescents should be able to sublimate their sexuality in order to establish self-control. One of his main concerns was the need to control masturbation, especially amongst young men. Hall

still saw masturbation as a potentially dangerous v
entirely 'natural' phenomenon, but he did eschew
previous generations, calling for frank and open d
subject with young people. Homosexuality, esp
young men, was also a potential danger which hau ..
and channelled into 'normal' adult heterosexual relationsmp.,
preferably within monogamous marriage.

Hall had little to say about lesbian relationships, although he
did not deny the existence of female sexuality altogether. Hall felt
that sublimation was easier and more 'natural' for young women,
since women were defined as less active sexual agents than men.
Women's primary destiny was motherhood, since they had to
ensure the survival of the 'race'. So Hall placed less emphasis on
the need to ensure female chastity, concentrating his concern on
maintaining young women's physical health for their ultimate
destiny as mothers. The establishment of a regular menstrual cycle
was especially crucial, since this was assumed to ensure the later
ability to bear children.

Hall also combined contradictory elements in his treatment of
'race' and eugenics during frequent public speeches in 1910 and
1911, when the American eugenics movement began to emerge.
Like many of his peers, Hall was worried that the Anglo-Saxon
middle class was committing 'race suicide' as a result of the declining birthrate, although he did not share some of the more un-
pleasant genocidal views of the extreme eugenicists. His concern over
young women's childbearing capacities was addressed primarily to
the European upper and middle classes.

Hall's treatment of social class is clearest in his approach to the
theory and regulation of 'delinquency'. His studies of lies, fears
and anger focused on 'adolescent faults and vices' which Hall
presented as inherited adjustments to an earlier 'savage' past. Such
behaviours were inappropriate to modern industrial civilization,
although boys in particular should be allowed some 'vicarious
cathartic expression' in the form of lies, truancy, swearing and
fighting. Here again, Hall managed to combine opposing
approaches, developing a social theory of adolescent delinquency
and criminality which retained elements of Lombroso's theory of
hereditary degeneracy (Hollin, 1989).

Hall's work fitted well within the context of nineteenth-century
scientific psychology: indeed it played a key part in constructing
the discipline as an expanding academic enterprise (Rose, 1977).
Whilst Hall's two-volume opus is now seldom read, his name is

still cited in many contemporary texts as the 'discoverer' of adolescence. It is the key ideological role played by Hall's work in the 1880s, and the continuing influence of these discourses in the 1980s, which lead me to examine the particular impact of G. S. Hall and of psychology in shaping the ideology of 'adolescence'.

From 1880 to 1980: The Story Continues

Since the 1880s, dominant ideologies about 'youth' and 'adolescence' have been characterized by a series of tensions and realignments between biological determinism and social constructionism, with the storm-and-stress model providing a recurrent element in psychological and sociological texts. Research about 'youth' and 'adolescence' is an amorphous and sprawling body of work which has engaged in repeated attempts to assess and reassess itself, often striving to impose a coherence on the diverse set of theories and empirical studies which I have termed 'youth research'. In recent years this project has drawn on texts from the social history of youth, although the latter has so far focused mainly on young white males. We do not yet have a social history of young people which is more than partially relevant beyond the confines of this group (see Dyhouse, 1981, and Brady, 1987, for exceptions). In the absence of a more developed social history of young people, what follows is a necessarily brief and partial account of the years since the 1880s, with a bias towards those events which do *not* appear in current historical work. It is worth repeating here that what was happening to young people in western industrialized nations was and is not necessarily equivalent to the concerns and 'findings' of youth research, although the two are inextricably related. During the period immediately following G. S. Hall's 'discovery' of adolescence, the First World War decimated a generation of young men, mainly, but not entirely from western Europe. The 'roaring twenties' saw a widespread moral panic over youthful female sexuality on both sides of the Atlantic, represented in studies of working-class female prostitution and serialized novels. The mainly white and upper-class female 'flappers' of the period were constructed as the focus of this panic during a time of increasing independence for some groups of women (Kett, 1977).

The 1930s brought severe economic depression to most western nations, and unemployment and poverty to the majority of working-class people. The decade also brought the spread of fascism in

Europe, with Nazism coming to power in Germany. The Second World War marks the 1940s like a running sore, sending another generation of young and not-so-young men into battle, and affecting the lives of civilians on a massive scale, including the largely unrecognized but ubiquitous war crime of rape (Strange, 1983). Few contemporary social historians of youth dwell on the 1940s, yet the foundations of the 1960s counter-culture were emerging in African-American urban life. The 'Harlem Renaissance' saw the emergence of the many African-American cultural forms from which the youth groups of the 1950s and 1960s drew so much of their inspiration (Tyler, 1989). In addition, moral panics over Frank Sinatra's young female fans meant that 'Sinatrauma' pre-dated 'Beatlemania' by some twenty years (Shaw, 1968; Griffin, 1987). The end of the 1940s saw the emerging period of 'recon-struction' and early attempts to deal with the terrible legacy of the Holocaust.

The 1950s figure heavily in historical work on (white, working-class, male) 'youth', with liberal references to Teddy boys and rock and roll in most radical analyses of youth subcultures (Springhall, 1986). The 1950s also saw a reassertion of women's 'ideal' role in the home and at the centre of (nuclear) family life, and the ideology of domesticated femininity took on a new strength as women were forced out of 'men's jobs' in factories, shipyards and on the land to make way for the returning male labour force after the Second World War (Summerfield, 1984). The implications of these changes for young women were scarcely mentioned in some of the academic texts of the time (e.g. Hoggart, 1957).

In the USA, the 1950s saw the emerging Civil Rights movement politicize a generation of African-American (and some white) young people, encouraged by the anti-colonial movements in the Indian subcontinent and Africa. This combined with the cultural impact of the Harlem Renaissance years to lay the foundations for the 'counter-culture' of the 1960s and 1970s, as well as shaping the political activities of the period. For many contemporary youth researchers, the 1950s marked the development of 'the first dis-tinctive post-war youth subcultures' (Springhall, 1986, p. 190). In Britain, this usually referred to the culture of the 'Teddy boy', an import from North America, and in the USA Parsons had already speculated on the emergence of distinct 'youth cultures' during the immediate post-war period (Parsons, 1942; Brake, 1984).

Adolescence has been defined via an uneasy mixture of the biological and the social, with biology positioned as the major determining element, and puberty onset defined as the starting point of adolescence. The biological dimension generally refers to the development of 'normal' genital (hetero)sexuality, reproductive capacity (especially for young women) and/or more generalized hormonal surges. In practice, the identification of puberty onset is notoriously difficult to define, especially in young men (Muuss, 1968). The age of menarche is usually taken as the agreed criterion for young women, but there is not necessarily a neat transition into (or out of) menstruation (Ussher, 1989). The latter is not a solely physiological process of course, since physical maturation and menarche are closely associated with nutrition levels (Laslett, 1971). The social dimension of youth/adolescence often appears at its end-point, referring to economic transition points such as entry to the job market, and/or to marriage and independence from the family of origin (Springhall, 1986). This places those who are not in a 'normal' heterosexual marriage relationship, or outside full-time permanent employment, for whatever reason, in a difficult position: they are effectively denied access to 'mature' adult status (Willis, 1984).

We can still see this uneasy combination of the biological and the social in contemporary psychological and sociological texts on adolescence and youth (e.g. Marsland, 1986). Contemporary crises over 'youth' are frequently attributed in the mainstream literature to a mismatch between the biological and social boundaries of this age stage. American sociologist Jerold Starr, in his review of 'American youth in the 1980s', defined adolescence in terms of just this type of 'discrepancy' (Starr, 1986).

Some of the main discourses in G. S. Hall's work are evident in texts using the psychoanalytic perspective, and the latter is frequently cited as a key theoretical influence in the contemporary psychology of adolescence (e.g. Coleman, 1980). Hall was the first academic psychologist to invite Sigmund Freud to the USA, incorporating his own version of Freud's ideas into his 'genetic psychology'. However, it was Sigmund's daughter Anna Freud who presented a more detailed conceptualization of the psychology of adolescence. For Anna Freud, adolescence was constructed as a period of inevitable psychic turmoil and vulnerability. Rather than merely repressing sexual desire *or* expressing it in order to overcome sexual repression, she stressed the need to achieve a balance between control and satisfaction. Adolescence is defined around puberty and the path to 'normal' heterosexuality, in which certain elements such as rebellion and disengagement from the family of origin are presented as universal and even ahistorical phenomena. According to this perspective, the source of such changes and the means of dealing with them are to be located in the individual adolescent, or perhaps within their families of origin (Blos, 1962). The influence of the psychoanalytic perspective in framing the psychology of adolescence has not been without its critics (Gallatin, 1975). The supposedly universal nature of adolescence has been questioned since the psychoanalytic framework rests on a male-specific theory, and the biological determinism of the storm-and-stress model has also come under considerable critical scrutiny (Coleman, 1980).

A series of texts published between the late 1940s and the late 1960s are frequently cited as shaping the contemporary psychology of adolescence (e.g. Adelson, 1964; Erikson, 1951, 1968).[2] When these texts are cited by contemporary youth researchers, it is sometimes with approval (e.g. Marsland, 1986), and sometimes with approbation (e.g. Allen, 1968). In sociology, the works of Parsons (1942), Eisenstadt (1956) and Mannheim (1952) are usually mentioned as examples of key theoretical texts in post-war youth research. Several pieces of empirical work, such as Hollingshead's *Elmtown's Youth* (1949), Douvan and Adelson's *The Adolescent Experience* (1966) and Margaret Mead's *Coming of Age in Samoa* (1928) are also presented as 'landmark' studies in the sociology of youth.

These texts do not present a coherent development of ideas which move in a linear progression towards a unitary conceptual position on youth and adolescence. Tensions between the biological and the social domains are evident throughout the various definitions of youth and adolescence, as are diverse perspectives on the storm-and-stress model. Erikson juggled with biological and social elements in a gender- and class-specific theory which pathologized various forms of behaviour as 'deviant' (e.g. 'young homosexuals, addicts and social cynics'). Successful socialization into a mature adult involved the internalization of a conflict-free set of social values and behaviours which could then be presented as universal and ahistorical due to the biological determinism of the storm-and-stress model of adolescence (Erikson, 1968).

For Erikson, adolescence came to signify *both* key physiological changes *and* the development of a 'separate' independent adult identity. The process of identity formation, and the nature of 'normal' adult behaviour to which individual adolescents should aspire were defined as having their 'natural' origins in hormonal and other physiological changes at puberty. Erikson's theory defined adolescence as a key moment of formation for that construction which has been central to mainstream psychology: the notion of the unitary individual subject (Venn, 1984). As with the psychoanalytic perspective, Erikson's work has come in for considerable criticism, but the 1980s saw a number of attempts to 'rescue' all or part of Erikson's theory for use as a potential means of dealing with a perceived crisis in youth research (see chapter 3).

The history of youth research after G. S. Hall's 'discovery' of adolescence was one of gradual and then explosive expansion. The psychology of adolescence was well established amongst psychologists and educationalists by the mid-1920s, but it was only after Margaret Mead's *Coming of Age in Samoa* (1928), and Frederick Thrasher's study of Chicago youth gangs in *The Gang* (1927) that the sociology of youth began to develop. What Murdock and McCron (1975) have called 'the gang theme' has occupied a central place in sociological approaches to 'youth', and in practice this could more accurately be termed a 'gang of lads' model (Griffin, 1988).

The universalizing discourse of the storm-and-stress model submerged relations of sex/gender, 'race' and class behind the raging hormones theory of adolescence, but the latter was to be challenged in the period following the Second World War. The late 1940s saw the publication of August Hollingshead's influential study *Elmtown's Youth* in the USA (Hollingshead, 1949). Hollingshead argued that class position was the main determinant of social behaviour amongst Elmtown's young people: he emphasized the importance of the social over the biological in young people's lives, and hence in the definition of 'youth' itself.

During the 1950s and 1960s, the mainstream sociology of youth was obscuring the potential importance of class, and the psychology of adolescence was bringing adolescence out of the sphere of education and towards the medical arena of psychiatry and clinical psychology (Muuss, 1968). By the 1960s, adolescence was established as both a 'natural' phenomenon, *and* a source of potential problems for all young people as a result of the biologically based storm-and-stress model. Through the 1950s and early 1960s, 'youth' became an increasingly common focus for academic concern through debates about young people's perceived 'overconformity', 'teenage consumerism', and young people's apparent *refusal* to conform, as in research on 'juvenile delinquency'. Young people were seen as simultaneously malleable and obstinate, a danger both to themselves and to others. Individual adolescents or specific groups of young people were presented as social problems, and as either actually or potentially capable of terrible upheaval and trauma for 'society' (Conger, 1979). It was against this mainstream perspective that 'radical' analyses of youth sub/cultures developed during the late 1960s and 1970s in an attempt to bring social structures and especially class relations (back) into the theoretical framework of western youth research (Mungham and Pearson, 1975; Hall and Jefferson, 1975). Radical analyses which examined class, sex/gender, 'race' *and* age relations did not begin to appear until the late 1970s and into the 1980s.

The history of youth research is inextricably related to the history of young people themselves. It has also provided a history of adults' preoccupations and panics – at least over certain groups of young people, and by certain groups of adults. Youth/adolescence remains a powerful cultural and ideological category through which adult society constructs a specific age stage as simultaneously strange and familiar. Youth/adolescence remains the focus of adult fears and pity, of voyeurism and longing. Despite the continuation of earlier arguments, there has also been something specific about the academic concern over 'youth' in the 1980s: most notably the crisis over mass youth unemployment and the realignment within and between radical and mainstream perspectives in youth research. It is this combination of apparently new and old debates, the tension between the 'biological' and the 'social' domains, and discussions of the relationship between culture, structure and agency which are dealt with in this book.

The following five chapters are organized around key 'sites' such as education and training, unemployment and the job market, leisure, family life and sexuality, and each chapter incorporates a range of research areas. In some cases it is obvious that research on specific areas or issues will fall within a particular chapter, whilst in other cases the association is more problematic. Studies of 'teenage pregnancy', for example, incorporate a range of elements which relate to family life, sexuality and education. Wherever possible, I have let the predominant causal stories and narrative forms through which texts are constructed dictate the latter's place in the analysis, so research on 'teenage pregnancy' is mainly (although not entirely) covered in chapter 6, on family life and sexuality.

Chapter 2 concentrates on the mainstream sociological tradition of research on education and the 'transition from school to work' (TSW), and the series of discursive shifts which occurred as this perspective attempted to deal with the various radical critiques which have been termed critical pedagogy or the new sociology of education (CP/NSE). This chapter examines the ways in which elements of the radical and mainstream perspectives struggled to come to terms with the meanings of education for young people at a time of rising youth unemployment, with expanding New Right ideologies constructing education as a forum for the interplay of competitive individualism, enterprise and monetarist economic forces. This chapter also considers the research on government-sponsored youth training programmes which burgeoned during the 1980s in Britain and the USA, since such programmes played a key role in dismantling the boundary between the education system and the youth labour market.

Chapter 3 considers the crisis (or crises) posed by rising youth unemployment for both radical and mainstream research, examining the ways in which this crisis was constructed by texts operating from both perspectives. The chapter develops the analysis presented in chapter 2, identifying some of the key discourses and narrative forms through which young people, and especially unemployed working-class young men, were represented in a range of research texts. Chapter 3 also considers the various challenges posed to the (white working-class) male norm which pervades research on youth unemployment by feminist and other radical analyses, and the use of the discourse of resistance in such texts.

Chapter 4 considers the related spheres of youth, crime and 'delinquency', and the processes through which certain young people (especially young men) come to be represented as 'deviant' or 'delinquent' are examined in relation to critiques from feminist and radical Black scholars. Once again, there are some connections with previous chapters, as the main discourses involved in the construction of 'delinquent youth' revolve around the clinical and medical domain, relying on notions of deficiency and deprivation, rebellion, (sexual) deviance and disaffection. Chapter 4 goes on to trace the impact of radical subcultural analyses, resistance theory and feminist work on research about youth, crime and 'delinquency'.

Chapter 5 focuses on the threat posed by 'unstructured free time' in mainstream research on young people and leisure. It examines the male focus in most definitions of 'leisure' (and 'work'), and the challenges presented by rising youth unemployment to the key discursive configurations in the mainstream perspective on young people's use of leisure. The chapter ends by considering the arguments of feminist and other radical analyses as challenges to the 'gang of lads' model, and to the discourse of resistance which pervaded the youth subcultures research of the 1970s. By the late 1980s, many radical analyses of young people and leisure drew on discourses of defence and survival rather than resistance.

Chapter 6 looks at the 'private' spheres of family life and sexuality, which unlike education and training, the job market and leisure, have usually been feminized in most youth research studies. The key discourses in mainstream analyses are considered alongside those which predominate in radical research. This chapter examines mainstream analyses which represent 'youth' as a transition to 'normal' adult status through heterosexuality, marriage and parenthood (in that order). Key issues concern panics over 'teenage pregnancy', 'adolescent homosexuality', HIV and AIDS. Radical analyses are considered in relation to debates over the relationship between culture, structure and agency, as well as those radical analyses which questioned the primacy of class-based structural theories. Some of those voices which are absent or silenced in both radical and mainstream analyses are also considered, including the relative dearth of radical analyses on the experiences of young lesbians and gay men.

The final chapter summarizes the key arguments presented in this book, looking at the main transformations in discourses around 'youth' and 'adolescence' as reflected in British and American research texts of the 1980s. Focusing on the related panics over 'teenage pregnancy' and the 'Black underclass',[3] the chapter ends by considering some of the key issues for radical youth research as it moves into the 1990s in relation to the three 'starting points' for this analysis mentioned above.

Referring to the long-established tradition in Anglo-European scholarship of constructing the Orient as exotic and Other, Edward Said quoted Marx: 'they cannot represent themselves; they must be represented' (Said, 1978, p. xiii). This argument could equally be made with respect to the treatment of young people in academic research: 'youth' is/are continually being represented as different, Other, strange, exotic and transitory – by and for adults. Youth research which operates from the radical and mainstream perspectives has told different stories of transition and threat about (certain groups of) young people. The gaze of the researcher is generally voyeuristic, invested with a magisterial authority which can decide who is deviant, deficient, perverted and/or resistant. Mainstream analyses in particular are replete with origin stories about specific 'social problems' which implicate individual young people, their 'deficient' family forms or cultural backgrounds.

Young people may refuse to fit within the shifting categories of dominant discourses, creating their own negotiations of increasingly oppressive conditions which adult researchers can follow only inadequately and intermittently, never really catching up. There is no sharp and irrevocable separation between young people's experiences and ideologies about 'youth', but there is a sense in which adult academics (including myself) can never 'know' what it meant to be young in the 1980s. This has not prevented us from speaking for and about young people in a massive and growing research literature, and it is the latter which provides the focus for this book. The central theme of *Representations of Youth* is not 'what it meant to be young in the 1980s', but the diverse ways in which youth research texts represented 'youth' and 'adolescence' during a decade of political crisis and change.

Notes

1 Each of these three 'starting points' is a mass of internal contradictions and debates. The three areas coexisted in a difficult and abrasive proximity in radical analyses throughout the 1980s, and I am not striving to attain a magical synthesis between them.

2 See P. Cohen (1986) for a fuller analysis of the varied constructions of 'adolescence' and 'youth' represented within these texts.

3 'Black' is used in Britain as a political term when referring to 'the common experience of racism directed at non-white peoples' (Bhavnani, 1992, p. 1). In the USA, 'Black' usually refers specifically to African-Americans, and 'people of colour' is the more commonly used term which is equivalent to the term 'Black' in the British context. Throughout this text I have generally used American terminology when referring to US texts, and British terminology in references to British texts. I have specified which group of people are being referred to in each case, for example 'Asian' in the British context usually refers to people from the Indian subcontinent, whilst in the US context, 'Asian' is more often used to mean people of south-east Asian origin or descent. I have used the terms 'white', 'Anglo-European' or 'WASP' (white Anglo-Saxon Protestant) when referring to those peoples who benefit from racism, differentiating between groups of 'white youth' where relevant.

2
Schooling for the Scrap Heap: Research on the 'Transition from School to Work'

That's one thing the Tories have over you [face to camera]. They want to keep you stupid. They want to keep you down. If you can't beat this system intelligently you never will. (John Lydon, 'Def-2' youth programme, BBC2 TV, April 1989)

The 1980s now means pressure for all youth in attaining exam results . . . but there's no stopping there, next it's on to University to obtain a degree and finally out into the wide world to make a million! (School student's response to the question: 'What's it like to be young in the 1980s?', Birmingham University Open Day, April 1988)

This chapter examines the treatment of youth in research on education and entry to the job market, sometimes referred to as the 'transition from school to work' (TSW). This literature is relatively fragmented, since research on the TSW has tended to deal with relatively discrete areas, such as the final years of compulsory schooling; entry to full-time employment; training and vocational education; or youth unemployment. Such research has been less inclined to devote equivalent attention to young people's family lives, sexualities or leisure activities in relation to the move from school to the job market, although there are exceptions here (e.g. Wallace, 1987; Borman, 1988). Research on the TSW has had close links with the construction of government policies in education, training and employment: research has frequently been commissioned to address specific questions, usually generated by government departments. This relationship between policy and research has been overlaid by the disciplinary boundaries between psychology, sociology and educational research. Although I have referred to research on the 'TSW' as a shorthand term, it is important to emphasize the fragmentary nature of this literature. As this chapter will demonstrate, research on the 'TSW' has shown considerable variation in both discursive form and content.

Research on the TSW has been concerned with one Big Question: the incidence and explanation of inequalities in the move from full-time education to waged work (Murphy, 1989). The 'TSW' has usually been treated as a potential, even an inevitable problem for unqualified working-class young people. Whilst a degree of disturbance is expected, any apparent absence of a smooth and linear transition from full-time education to full-time employment has usually been treated as a cause for academic concern (Finn, 1987). The ideal model here is the career pattern which is far more readily available to white and middle-class young men, with a smooth shift into an unbroken pattern of full-time employment. Since 'adolescence' is assumed to be a universal period of adjustment and change, those who do not fit this pattern are expected to adjust to the demands of the job market if a smooth transition is not made (Coleman and Hendry, 1990).

The impact of unemployment was a recurring theme in most areas of youth studies during the 1980s, and research on the TSW is no exception (King, 1984). Chapter 3 deals with those texts in which youth unemployment plays a central narrative and explanatory role, whilst this chapter looks at those studies which have focused on the final years of schooling, entry to the job market, youth employment, training and vocational education. It is impossible to provide a truly exhaustive picture of this vast field: my intention is to highlight the main discourses and conceptual strategies through which research on the TSW negotiated the ideological and political conditions of the 1980s.

Emerging from the Shadows: Research on the TSW after the Second World War

The period since the Second World War has seen considerable academic and government interest in the TSW for working-class young people, emphasizing a contradictory combination of the need for conformity to traditional values and the reconstruction of a new and more egalitarian society. Relatively less attention has been devoted to white middle-class young people: this group usually acts as the invisible norm against which other school leavers are judged. As manufacturing industries moved into post-war boom, there was a need for a relatively cheap, unskilled labour force which made working-class school leavers (and married women) an attractive proposition for employers. In Britain, this period of relative labour shortage led to a series of active recruitment programmes in the Indian subcontinent and the Caribbean to fill vacancies in the expanding public sector (Sivanandan, 1982). The USA did not experience quite the same transformatory push to create 'a home fit for heroes' which, however short-lived, laid the foundations for the British welfare state.

Official concern over the role of 'adolescent workers' was reflected in the commissioning of research which was intended to inform the policies of successive post-war governments. This was especially prevalent in Britain given the expanding role of the state in education and welfare provision. Discourses concerning the 'wasted abilities' and 'problem attitudes' of working-class school leavers have pervaded mainstream research on the TSW since the 1950s (Maizels, 1970). The period after the Second World War also saw a series of panics over the impact of North American mass culture on British young people (e.g. Hoggart, 1957; Veness, 1962).

By the mid-1960s, sociological studies of the TSW began to develop a more critical and explicit analysis of class inequalities, moving towards an examination of the structural nature of the education system and the job market (Little and Westergaard, 1964). The 'wasted potential' of unqualified working-class young people remained a major theme, but there was considerable concern that this group were receiving inadequate preparation for their entry to the full-time job market (M. Carter, 1962, 1966). This shift towards structural analysis was most marked in sociological research, although the biological determinism at the heart of ideological constructions of adolescence still retained much of its force in mainstream analyses, such as Joan Maizels's study of London school leavers during 1965. In this text social structure, via social roles, was assumed to constrain the expression of the 'true' individual via a block on young people's creative energies. For Maizels, it was the bio-psychological construction of individuality which provided the 'true' foundation for young people's experiences of the TSW (Maizels, 1970).

Maizels's perspective was of the 1960s, but David Ashton's early work paved the way for the mainstream British sociological research of the 1970s. Ashton called for a shift from the individual focus of the occupational choice literature toward the more 'societal' or 'experiential' perspective of the US symbolic interactionists, drawing on the work of Nobert Elias (Ashton, 1973). Although he constructed the TSW as a process set in its social context, rather than as a series of individual decisions, Ashton's primary focus was still on young white working-class men and the operation of social class differentials.

In the USA as in Britain, research on the TSW has maintained close links with government policy and policy-makers. Many empirical studies in the USA are financed by federal government agencies, often with the aim of developing specific policy recommendations (e.g. Borman and Riesman, 1986). The US literature also focused academic and government concern on working-class and 'minority' school and college leavers, the most mobile sector of the country's labour force. The relatively high job turnover amongst this group was constructed as a social problem which could be attributed to various 'inadequacies' in the characteristics, attitudes and abilities of these young people. Mainstream research examined school leavers' apparent lack of 'employability', inadequate preparation for the disciplines of waged work and poor attitudes towards employment (Jencks, 1973). As in the UK, a more structural set of explanations developed in sociological and economic research, which examined questions such as the effects of region, residence in rural or metropolitan areas, or shifting local job opportunities and discriminatory practices in education and the labour market.

Throughout the 1970s sociological analyses became increasingly polarized into mainstream research on the 'TSW' and more 'radical' youth cultural studies. The former looked at those potentially disaffected working-class young people who were assumed to have difficulty in moving smoothly from school to the job market, such as 'job changers' and 'the careerless' (e.g. Ashton and Field, 1976; Stephenson, 1979). By the mid-1970s, Marxists were using the youth cultural framework to stress the *class* element of such transitions, emphasizing the importance of economic, structural and cultural relations in capitalist societies (Willis, 1977). From this radical perspective, working-class (white, male) young people were not represented as the 'inadequate' and 'deficient' sources of various 'social problems' or social inequalities, but as the originators of collective cultural resistances to oppressive and predominantly class-based conditions of structural subordination. The biologically determined inevitability of adolescent trauma was questioned by some mainstream sociologists as well as within the radical analyses of Marxist youth cultural research (P. Cohen, 1986). Research on the TSW entered the 1980s attempting to deal with the challenges posed by rising youth unemployment and by radical analyses, striving to find a 'balance' between the individual, social/cultural and structural elements of academic explanations for young people's entry into the job market.

Research on the 'TSW' during the 1980s: Continuities and New Developments

Research and policies around the TSW entered the 1980s in a state of crisis which was mainly attributed to the rise in youth unemployment levels. Carol Varlaam made these concerns explicit in the introduction to her edited text *Rethinking Transition*, looking back to the early 1970s when nearly 75 per cent of British sixteen- to nineteen-year-olds were officially employed, and of these one fifth were in jobs with some training and further education (Varlaam, 1984). Youth unemployment levels were relatively low in the British job market at this time, and employers were having difficulty in recruiting sufficient numbers of school leavers. In the education sector, the raising of the school leaving age (ROSLA) from fifteen to sixteen which took effect in 1972/3 was the focus of considerable debate, since it effectively prevented thousands of young people from entering the full-time labour market (Finn, 1987).

The US situation was broadly similar, with a few notable differences. One of the most important was the decline in the proportion of young people employed as farm labourers since the 1950s, due to growing mechanization and the consolidation of individually operated farms. This had a marked effect on young African-American men in the rural South, especially since there was no compensating increase in low-skilled non-agricultural work. The second key post-war change was the decrease in the number of young women of colour employed in domestic service. The situation changed fairly rapidly during the 1970s as the Organization of Petrol-Exporting Countries (OPEC) declared a sharp rise in the international price of oil in 1972/3, upsetting (though not removing) the long-standing exploitation of 'Third World' economies by western industrial nations. In addition, manufacturing industries introduced a range of 'new technologies' in an attempt to improve productivity and reduce labour power. The number of young people of school leaving age peaked between the early 1970s and the early 1980s, with increasing numbers of young people and women entering the job market.

For Varlaam and many other youth researchers, these factors were seen as the prime cause of increases in British and North American unemployment, and especially the rises in long-term youth unemployment during the late 1970s. Such developments brought discussions of rising youth unemployment and the TSW into the centre of academic and political debate in many western industrial nations by the end of the 1970s. Whilst youth unemployment was treated as the main problem, this masked a set of more complex political, ideological and structural changes connected with the rise of the New Right on both sides of the Atlantic.

Building the Scrap Heap: The Rise of the New Right

It would be a mistake to assume that youth research in the 1980s underwent a sudden change sometime between 1979 and 1980: a series of gradual ideological and political shifts might be nearer the mark. In one sense the tendency to do our thinking in decades can be misleading, but 1979/80 *did* mark something of a watershed, with electoral victories for those bastions of the New Right, Margaret Thatcher and Ronald Reagan. During the 1980s, increases in youth unemployment levels, changes to the education system and the British welfare state (amongst other developments) came to be associated with the ideologies and practices of the New Right in Britain and the USA (S. Hall, 1988; McLaren, 1989). The emergence of New Right ideologies have been traced to the mid-1970s, with their origins further back in a reaction against the so-called 'permissive society' of the 1960s, the American Civil Rights movement of the previous decade, and the egalitarian post-war ideals of the late 1940s (Hall and Jacques, 1983).

As Steven and Hilary Rose have argued, New Right ideologies 'have a specific theoretical commitment to a view of human nature which is firmly grounded in biology' (1986, p. 47). This 'new' biological determinism straddled the spheres of academic respectability and popular 'common sense'.[1] New Right ideologies do not necessarily rest on biological discourses alone, but on a combination of bio-psychological and social/cultural discourses in which the biological element is usually presented as the most fundamental. The ideological moves around 'race' which characterized both Thatcherism and Reaganism (in different ways) meant that a combination of bio-psychological and social/cultural discourses shaped popular and academic 'common sense' and government policies around 'race' and racism, nation and nationality during the 1980s (Anthias, 1990).

In the USA, emerging New Right ideologies also operated to reassert the influence of biology in determining human behaviour. The New Christian Right presided over an ideological shift against the 'permissiveness' of the 1960s, which was itself characterized as 'a youthful fling with self-indulgence' (Gary Bauer, US Under Secretary of Education, quoted in *Education Week*, 1986). This 'new' conservatism produced a range of school reforms which at first silenced liberal/left voices of dissent. This initial silence can be attributed in part to the audacious ways in which the New Right adopted liberal/left arguments, transforming the latter in subtle ways to fit within their own political framework (Hall and Jacques, 1983).

Radical educational researchers represented the impact of the New Right in education as a disastrous attack on American democratic traditions, in which schools are to be held responsible for a wide range of the nation's problems, from the trade deficit to the supposed breakdown in family morality, and which provided a firm basis for a boom in Christian fundamentalism (McLaren, 1989). Apart from defining what New Right ideologies are *against*, recent educational reforms have also indicated what they are *for*: specifically a return to a mythical but ideologically powerful notion of 'traditional' education; and an emphasis on the demands of the market-place. Academic success is to be defined almost exclusively in terms of attaining certification for 'marketable' skills in a supposedly 'free' market, re-emphasizing existing practices such as 'streaming' or 'tracking' students according to their 'academic ability' (Wolpe and Donald, 1983).

In Britain, the era of the New Right also saw a reassertion of inequalities around class, 'race', gender and sexuality as education was represented as a market-place founded on 'enterprise', competition and the wealth and wishes of parents (Ball, 1990; P. Brown, 1989). The USA entered the 1980s with many of its citizens experiencing a worse standard of living than thirty years previously. Severe cuts in social and welfare programmes and in public housing projects, and rising poverty levels, produced a situation in which young people, and especially working-class young people and young people of colour were suffering more than at any time since the Second World War (Center on Budget and Policy Priorities, 1986).

The other means by which British and US governments intervened in the TSW for young people during the 1980s was through

the expansion of government-sponsored youth training programmes (Griffin, forthcoming). The vast array of youth training
schemes which appeared on both sides of the Atlantic share a
number of common features. They emerged from official concern
over 'mismatches' between the supply of unskilled labour and
demand for skilled workers, and over perceived inadequacies in
'disaffected' school leavers as prospective employees. The main
element which differentiates US schemes from British programmes
is money: the former have received proportionately higher levels
of government funding, whilst many of the latter were set up in
the 1980s as a series of temporary measures which saw a period
of rapid expansion during the decade. This disparity was especially
marked during the early 1980s until a series of US government
cutbacks and the expansion of UK schemes under Thatcher's
government narrowed some of the gaps between British and North
American provision (Bresnick, 1984; G. Cohen and Nixon, 1981).
Despite these differences, the British and North American youth
training sectors have both had a considerable impact on the TSW
for young people and on youth research in this area.

Constructing the 'Problem' and Blaming the Victim(s)

A central element in mainstream sociological and psychological
youth research is the 'blaming the victim' thesis which can be allied
to biological determinism or to a social constructionist perspective
(Ryan, 1969). This thesis operates to apportion blame for conditions of exploitation and oppression to those who occupy subordinated positions, whether this is attributed to the supposedly
'inadequate' characteristics of individuals, 'deviant' family forms
or 'deprived' cultures. Michael Carter, for example, identified
unemployed young Black Britons (whom he referred to as 'col-
oured children') as the main cause of 'racial strife' (1966). The
victim-blaming thesis has not been confined to periods of economic
recession, but it was particularly well suited to the ideological
terrain of the New Right.
   According to this thesis, individual young people (especially if
they are working-class and/or Black) are assumed to lack 'appropriate' skills or attitudes suitable for the disciplines of waged work.
Such 'deficiencies' are frequently attributed to their peer or family-
based cultural backgrounds, which are generally constructed in
overwhelmingly negative terms (e.g. Goodwin, 1980). Practices

which have traditionally served as means of survival for working-class young people during periods of recession are presented as dangerous phenomena which need to be eradicated at all costs. The potentially damaging effects of structural inequalities in the job market are rendered invisible in such analyses.

The victim-blaming thesis rests on the construction of specific 'social problems' which must be explained via a set of origin stories in which the individualizing discourse takes centre stage. Brian Becker and Stephen Hills for example, applied the findings of psychological research to the sociological literature on dual labour market theory (1981). Like many mainstream analyses, Becker and Hills used data from one of the many US National Longitudinal Surveys: in this case interviews with 230 young men who were aged between sixteen and nineteen in 1967, and who were then recontacted and reinterviewed in 1975. Becker and Hills selected the attitudinal construct locus of control 'to examine the role of personal motivation and initiative in . . . labour market experiences' (p. 60). This measure uses a series of forced choice questions to divide people into 'internals' and 'externals' in terms of how they explain events.

Becker and Hills proposed that greater 'externality' in locus of control (i.e. the attribution of events to external causes) was associated with lower employment rates, and that young African-American men were more likely to be 'externals' than their white counterparts. The notion that these young men might have become 'discouraged workers' as a *rational* response to the experience of racism in the job market was not on Becker and Hills's agenda. They concluded that a potential solution to 'the seemingly intract-able differences in black and white unemployment rates' might be provided by 'remedial manpower programs that may positively influence individual attitudes' (p. 68), specifically the attitudes of individual young African-American men. The construction of the problem defined the nature of the solution, which lay at the level of the individual subject.

Becker and Hills did not blame young Black men outright for creating their own unemployment, nor did they attempt to deny the incidence of 'premarket or current labor market discrimination' (p. 62). Their argument was more subtle. 'Race' and racism were not presented as the main topic of research in their study. This theme appeared as almost incidental to the more 'general' concern with individual attitudes and labour market activities, at least for young working-class men, and the gender-specific nature of the study was not seen as a potential problem for the general relevance of the analysis. Becker and Hills's text removed any other potential agents such as employers or government policies from the scene, shifting attention onto the 'victims', and especially to young African-American men's perceptions of themselves as victims of 'labour market discrimination': the terms 'racism' or 'racial discrimination' were not used.

Blind racism

Even when mainstream research has recognized unemployment amongst young people of colour as 'a major social problem', many academics have still been reluctant to identify racism as a key element in their analyses. Paul Osterman's text *Getting Started* for example, examined youth unemployment in the context of the youth job market from an economic and sociological perspective (Osterman, 1980). It is revealing to compare Osterman's text with the Becker and Hills article. Both were published in the early 1980s, operating from a mainstream perspective, and both texts brought a psychological approach into an area which was usually dominated by sociological and/or economic analyses. Both shared an explicit focus on entry to the youth labour market; and both texts took African-American (male) youth unemployment as a major theme, although only Osterman acknowledged that this male focus could limit the value of his analysis.

Whilst Becker and Hills concentrated on individual motivation and initiative, Osterman turned his attention to the structure of the youth job market. Osterman did not deny the role of 'young people's behavioral characteristics' in determining their marginal position in the job market, arguing that 'the modern economic structure permits the expression of characteristic adolescent patterns' (1980, p. 150). Whilst Osterman's text paid considerable attention to social or structural explanations of youth un/employment problems, he described 'psychosocial' adolescent behaviour patterns as the 'deeper foundation' behind specific economic and social systems, shifting from the sociological term 'youth' to the psychologized category of 'adolescence' in presenting these two sets of explanations.

Osterman argued that the characteristics of the British and US youth labour markets are remarkably similar, viewing high youth unemployment not as a transitory or pathological phenomenon, but as integral to the logic of the youth job market. Although his study pointed towards the need for major structural changes, Osterman shied away from drawing this conclusion, since the marginality of the youth job market has been 'created to protect the jobs of adults' (p. 153). Major intervention would be 'technically difficult and politically impossible', so government-sponsored youth training programmes could be introduced as the solution to the problem of working-class youth unemployment and underemployment. Osterman recommended that 'the goal of substantive policy should be to identify the youths who are having difficulty making the transition from moratorium to settling down behavior. These are the youth for whom the *natural* process is not working and who need help' (p. 153, added emphasis).

The use of terms like 'natural' and 'settling down behavior' in Osterman's text, rather than 'conditions' or 'social positions', signals an implicit debt to the biological determinism in the literature on the psychology of adolescence. This brings Osterman's analysis closer to that of Becker and Hills than one might at first suspect. These two texts illustrate the subtle and diverse forms taken by the victim-blaming thesis in the mainstream research of the 1980s, and the important role played by the biological discourse in shaping the construction of the individual adolescent subject. Once the 'problems' to be investigated had been constructed, researchers could move on to a search for causes and explanations.

Education and the TSW: Searching for the Causes of 'Academic Underachievement'

The study of 'academic underachievement' has provided a major focus for research on education and entry to the youth job market. This has concentrated on relatively unqualified working-class school and college leavers, and especially on young people of colour. In the USA, this literature is usually constructed around explanations for 'minority school failure' (or 'MSF': R. P. McDermott, 1987), or 'educational disadvantagement' (Murphy, 1986). In Britain, the term 'underachievement' is more commonly applied to working-class students, and the apparent 'underachievement' of Afro-Caribbean students is frequently compared with the supposed 'overaspirations' of their Asian peers.[2]

Academic studies within the mainstream perspective search for the cause(s) of specific 'problems', with individual, social/cultural and structural explanations jostling for position in texts which adopt the narrative form of the detective story. The genetic deficit model was one of the most pervasive explanations for the relatively low academic achievement of working-class students until the

1960s, to be replaced by the cultural deficit model of deprivation theory. 'Failing' students were represented as unfortunate
victims of inadequately stimulating family lives and/or cultural
backgrounds as the language of 'cultural deprivation' and 'social
disadvantage' replaced that of inherited genetic deficiencies. 'Normality' was defined in terms of white middle-class linguistic and
cultural practices and family forms. These various cultural deficit
models did not pass without criticism for their ethnocentrism,
racism and the tendency to blame working-class and 'minority'
young people for their relatively low academic achievements (Trueba,
1988).

A later sociolinguistic explanation proposed that cultural differences in communication style between teachers and students
inside school provided an important influence on low school
achievement and the self-esteem of working class and 'minority'
young people. This explanation adopted a form of cultural relativism which did not assign blame to teachers or students, whilst
sidestepping the question of power relations through which cultural differences were inscribed (Iadicola, 1981).

Continuing evidence of inequalities in the US education system
despite the educational reforms of the 1960s and 1970s brought a
surge of structural and cultural explanations for MSF during the
late 1970s. Originating in criticisms of mainstream research, John
Ogbu's work exemplifies the dilemma facing US youth research
on MSF in the 1980s with its attempt to negotiate structural and
cultural models.[3] Operating at the junction of education and
anthropology, Ogbu located the causes of MSF outside the school
in the unequal access to employment for 'minority' and white
working-class young people. Experiences of unemployment and
underemployment are communicated to subsequent generations of
working-class young people and young people of colour by their
parents in the form of a 'cynical' approach to the TSW (Ogbu,
1987). Ogbu argued that 'minority' students could be viewed as
members of 'castelike' groups who have resided in the USA for
generations in situations of oppression. He distinguished such
groups from those 'minority groups' which had recently migrated
to the USA, such as south-east Asians and the Punjabi community on the West Coast. The 'optimistic' approach of the latter
groups was contrasted with the more 'fatalistic' perspective of
earlier immigrant communities. Ogbu's distinction between 'host'
and 'immigrant' groups includes Native American peoples in the
latter group, in that he cited 'American Indians, black Americans,

and Native Hawaiians' as examples of *'castelike or involuntary minorities* who were *originally brought into US society involuntarily* through slavery, conquest or colonization' (p. 321, original emphasis). The common history of conquest and colonization is the key element here, since the process of US colonization has enforced an 'immigrant' status on a diverse group of Native Americans.[4]

Ogbu's argument was less structural than cultural, although he did acknowledge the force of racism and other systematic inequalities. Ogbu concentrated on blocked communication processes and conflicting cultural values, especially between the dominant WASP US culture and 'immigrant' cultures. He viewed the cultural values and practices of 'minority youth' and their families as a relatively pragmatic response to the poverty and racism of US society, yet his analysis can seem to paralyse them in a condition of inevitable oppression (Erickson, 1987).

Working from a radical perspective, R. P. McDermott argued that regardless of the analysis presented, 'MSF' research serves to construct 'minority' young people as the source of the 'problem', whereas for radical scholars the *real* problem lies in a society which maintains and sanctions poverty, racism and systematic inequalities, and in which we are all implicated (1987). McDermott preferred to examine the construction of academic success and failure, rather than their assignation to specific individuals or groups, or possible reasons for the unequal distribution of 'academic underachievement'. Moll and Diaz reinforced this point, arguing that 'we do not need to explain which kids [sic] do or do not learn at school. We need to explain why we have organized such an elaborate apparatus for pinpointing the failures of our children, when we could put all that energy into organizing more learning' (1987, p. 363). This refusal to engage in the search for the causes of MSF was less a rejection of Ogbu's work than an argument that mainstream researchers were asking the wrong questions and were therefore likely to find only a limited and inadequate set of answers. These critical texts were advocating a shift away from research on the academic performance of (specific) young people towards analyses of how the education system and labour market operated in a much wider social and political context.

British research texts defined the 'problems' under investigation in rather different terms, but these were also characterized by a search for the causes of MSF (or 'academic underachievement') and the tendency to avoid an overt focus on racism and other structural inequalities (Lawrence, 1982). The Rampton and Swann Reports are examples of the close but uneasy association between academic research and government policy in this respect; the focus on 'race differences' with minimal reference to class or gender; and the search for the causes of 'academic failure' in cultural difference and 'deficiency' rather than structural inequalities (Brah and Minhas, 1985). The Rampton Committee was set up in 1979 to examine 'the educational needs and attainments of children from ethnic minority groups taking account, as necessary, of factors outside the formal education system relevant to school performance, including influences in early childhood and prospects for school leavers' (Committee of Inquiry into the Education of Children from Ethnic Minority Groups, Press Notice, 14 July 1981). When some Black members of the committee attempted to examine the role of racism more centrally, the newly elected Tory government replaced Rampton as chairman with Sir Michael Swann. The supposedly damaging influence of 'deprived' Afro-Caribbean families was moved forward in the analysis at the expense of 'racial discrimination'. The Swann Report, published in 1982, focused on the apparent 'overaspirations' of Asian students, managing to minimize the role of racism even more than the earlier Rampton report. Black family forms and cultural practices were defined as the causes of the 'problem' posed by young Black Britons. Government intervention had reinstated the central place of the victim-blaming thesis, pathologizing Afro-Caribbean and Asian family forms and cultural practices (Demaine, 1989).

The bitter irony of this literature is that Black school leavers are condemned for poor academic performance or aspirations (usually termed 'underachievement') *and* for high levels of achievement or aspirations (termed 'overaspiration'): they cannot win. Different groups are played off against one another in classic examples of the divide-and-rule strategy. Although there is evidence that white and Black working-class young people can and do distinguish between jobs they *want* (or aspire to), and those they *expect* to get, such students continue to be castigated for their 'unrealistic aspirations' (Griffin, 1986). None of these texts addressed the specific position of young Afro-Caribbean women in Britain, who have generally managed to gain reasonable qualifications with a markedly pro-academic (if not pro-school) ethos, only to face considerable difficulty in obtaining suitable employment (Mirza, 1992). The search for the causes of MSF and related 'social problems' continued throughout the 1980s and into the 1990s, producing a range of proposals about the 'treatment' of such 'problems'.

Truancy, Dropout and Pushout: Discourses of Education, Correction and Treatment

Studies on 'truancy' or 'school dropout' also addressed the implications of MSF or 'academic underachievement' for young people's subsequent experiences in the labour market. 'Truancy' and 'dropout' are more usually identified as causes of MSF or 'academic underachievement' in the mainstream literature. Explanations for and solutions to MSF and 'academic underattainment' have usually been confined to the educational sphere, whilst 'truancy' and 'school dropout' have also been defined as requiring various forms of 'treatment' or 'correction' in the context of the clinical and criminological domains. US educationalists generally refer to 'dropout' and 'academically marginal youth', whilst in Britain the more common terms are 'persistent non-attendance', 'suspension' and 'educationally-at-risk' respectively. Radical analyses have adopted terms such as 'pushout' rather than 'dropout', in order to emphasize the agency of educational institutions as opposed to 'alienated' individual students (e.g. Garibaldi and Bartley, 1987).

The renewed panics over school 'dropout' during the 1970s and 1980s coincided with a rise in youth unemployment. This affected precisely those groups who were most often identified as 'at-risk' or 'marginal': working-class young people, young people of colour, young men and inner city residents. In previous years a pool of low-paid, unskilled jobs had tended to 'mop up' such young people and provide a relatively smooth transition into 'adult' jobs. This pattern of job availability was less pervasive in the 1980s, so increasing numbers of young people became trapped in part-time and temporary jobs or long-term unemployment (see chapter 3).

The literature on 'truancy' and 'dropout' is characterized by considerable confusion between and within theoretical perspectives, with a concerted search for the causes of 'school dropout' in a series of texts which juggle individual, social/cultural and structural explanations (Hartnagel and Krahn, 1989; Stevenson and Ellsworth, 1991). The definition of terms like 'academic marginality' or 'educationally-at-risk' incorporates various dimensions of 'deviance' which are usually measured in quantitative terms.

Alpert and Dunham, for example, defined 'academic marginality' in terms of a 'dropout profile' constructed by the Dade County School System in Florida. This identified young people with sporadic school attendance, extremely low grade averages and low achievement scores as 'academically marginal', using a combination of non-attendance and academic performance measures (Alpert and Dunham, 1986). Mainstream approaches to 'the school dropout problem' in US youth research have attempted to identify those demographic factors associated with dropping out, examining the implications of 'academic marginality' for young people's subsequent employment and criminal histories, in an attempt to predict those individuals or groups most 'at risk' of dropping out. Most of this literature has paid minimal attention to the equally important question of why some of these 'academically marginal' young people stay *in* school.

Alpert and Dunham argued that misbehaviour in school; the view of school as relevant to getting a job; perceived success in school; parental monitoring of young people; and the proportion of young people's peers who had 'dropped out' were all predictive of whether a student stayed on or dropped out of school (Alpert and Dunham, 1986). Their article begins with a quote from the 1984 report of the Dade County Grand Jury to the effect that young Blacks in the inner city constituted a disproportionately large number of the school 'dropout' population. Yet Alpert and Dunham devoted negligible attention to the nature and origins of inner city poverty and racism, constructing 'school dropout' as a relatively uniform phenomenon. They mentioned neither the gender nor the ethnicities of their respondents, thereby obscuring any variations in the treatment of different school students (see Rumberger, 1987).

Mainstream texts on 'school dropout' are constructed around three key discourses: that of education and training, the clinical discourse and the discourse of disaffection. The discourse of education and training represents MSF and 'dropout' as products of mismatch or blocked communication in young people's perception of the relevance and value of education: solutions would therefore involve changes in the value systems and educational practices of individual students and their teachers (e.g. Alpert and Dunham, 1986). The clinical discourse uses terms such as 'school phobia' and 'school refusal' to denote 'deficiency' or 'deprivation' which is frequently located in young people's family forms or cultural backgrounds (e.g. Bryce and Baird, 1986). In this case, therapeutic interventions are usually advocated, in that such 'marginal' young people must be 'treated' by mental health professionals (e.g. Leone, 1990). The discourse of disaffection criminalizes 'marginal youth' through the concept of delinquency, advocating punishment, rehabilitation or correction by social workers, probation officers and the institutions of policing (Muncie, 1984; see chapter 4).

These discourses also pervade official texts on youth training, which is represented as a form of education, therapy and correction through what Philip Cohen has termed 'lifeskilling ideology' (1982). All three discourses rest on a distinction between those young people who are defined as 'academically marginal' (or as *at risk* of marginal status) and their 'normal' peers. Once the notion of marginality is in place as a characteristic of specific individuals rather than an inevitable consequence of the competitive education system, researchers can launch into the hunt for the 'causes' of this phenomenon in order to present suggested solutions to the 'problem' under investigation, just as they have searched for the 'causes' of youth unemployment.

Into the Job Market: Searching for the Causes of Youth Unemployment

The counterpoint to mainstream educational research on MSF, 'underachievement' and 'overaspiration' can be found in studies of the entry to the job market for young people. Once again we find the construction of specific 'problems' which are then individualized in the search for causes, thus providing the basis for the victim-blaming thesis. The concept of 'employability' is one of the more pervasive and long-standing elements of this literature, in which the onus is placed on young people to develop adequate skills in order to find and keep jobs (e.g. Wilson et al., 1987). A considerable research literature has emerged to demonstrate the validity of this argument, most of which has accepted the conditions under which specific qualities have come to be defined as desirable 'employability skills', devoting minimal attention to employers' hiring and firing practices or the distribution of labour market opportunities (see Borman and Riesman, 1986 for critique).

As youth unemployment levels rose steadily during the late 1970s and into the 1980s, the tendency to allocate blame for unemployment or frequent job changing to young people was undermined, but the assumptions underlying the concept of 'employability' did not disappear altogether. Mainstream research shifted away from a search for the causes of frequent job changing or 'disrupted' entry to the labour market, to a search for the causes of youth unemployment and underemployment, especially amongst young working-class men (see chapter 3). The consequences of long-term unemployment and dead-end jobs are generally treated as relatively less serious for young women: their primary allegiance is still expected to lie in family life and the domestic sphere (Hamilton and Powers, 1989; see chapter 6). Where research concentrates on young people of colour (usually male), there is a further emphasis on potential threats to the status quo, the possibility of social conflict, and the link between youth unemployment and subsequent criminal activity (see chapter 4).

By the mid-1980s the effects of Reaganomics and Thatcher's monetarism had begun to bite, and a series of texts appeared on both sides of the Atlantic which testified to the economic, social and psychological damage which was being inflicted on working-class young people and young people of colour (Center on Budget and Policy Priorities, 1986; Gilroy, 1987). Mainstream research met these changes and the growing force and theoretical sophistication of radical critiques with a range of discursive strategies. The key strategy was a project of integration, which attempted to reach a synthesis between the dissenting voices of radical critiques and the mainstream perspective, between apparently contradictory discourses and 'competing models'. But first we need to consider the main messages presented by such radical critiques, and the forms in which these messages were encoded.

Asking Different Questions: Dissenting Voices and Radical Analyses

Radical research on the TSW in Britain and the USA has been shaped by influences which have crossed and recrossed the Atlantic. In the field of education, these developments paved the way for what is usually termed the 'new sociology of education' in Britain, and 'critical pedagogy' in the USA. The NSE/CP perspective developed in opposition to the positivist and supposedly apolitical approach of the academic mainstream, and it has been characterized by a commitment to Marxist, feminist and anti-racist politics (McLaren, 1989). This did not produce one uniform and coherent theoretical framework, but a range of related approaches which set out to transform existing power differentials around class, 'race', age and/or sex/gender in education and in society as a whole. By contrast, what I have termed the mainstream perspective is represented by a range of approaches which are either broadly tolerant of the educational status quo, or adopt a liberal position which advocates relatively minor modifications to the current system.

The mainstream psychological literature on the TSW has focused on the individual school leaver, investing the latter with a degree of 'occupational choice' (e.g. Banks et al., 1991). In mainstream sociological texts the emphasis was on the restrictions which local labour market opportunities placed on such 'choices' (e.g. Lewin-Epstein, 1986). The latter presented local labour market opportunities as overriding structurally determined class differences whilst (neo)-Marxists such as Paul Willis saw class relations as an integral part of the deeper social structure of capitalism within which local labour markets were constructed and reproduced (Willis, 1977). The dissenting voices of the NSE/CP perspective questioned the assertions of dominant educational discourses, challenging the role of mainstream research in its legitimation of the status quo, and usually employing qualitative or ethnographic methods derived from social anthropology and the 'new' North American sociology (McLaren, 1989). Debates about the connection between structure, culture, agency and power pervaded the NSE/CP literature during the 1980s, both around Europe (Hazekamp et al., 1987; Grootings and Adamski, 1986) and Australia (Presdee, 1985; Connell et al., 1982), as well as in Britain and the USA.

Such radical analyses developed in a spirit of dissent and critique, challenging the central concepts and narrative forms employed in mainstream research. Esther Gottlieb analysed texts by radical educationalists Freire (1970), Bowles and Gintis (1976) and Carnoy (1974), arguing that they all transferred key terms and concepts from the 'old' frame of reference to the 'new' radical education discourse, using the language of the old paradigm at first, and developing a set of 'new' metaphors and concepts (Gottlieb, 1989). Gottlieb positioned these texts within the genre of the 'American jeremiad': a 'typical form of self criticism (and self-reassurance), dating back to the political sermons of the New England Puritan preachers' (p. 137).

The use of the sermon genre distinguished radical education theories from the detective story genre which has characterized the functionalist and positivist mainstream. Radical texts were not searching for causes: they professed to know 'whodunit' and to examine the *processes* involved in establishing and maintaining structural inequalities within and through the education system. For Gottlieb such texts were limited by the rhetoric associated with the genre of the sermon. Radical texts such as Bowles and Gintis (1976) retained the vision of 'America', albeit a transformed 'America', such that 'their revolutionary impulse can only end up being channelled into an affirmation of the symbol and myth of America' (Gottlieb, 1989, p. 139). Since the discourses of the radical perspective on education have been constructed in opposition to, and also through, dominant discourses, any 'radical' edge is continually being undermined by the language and narrative forms of the mainstream.

Whilst much of the white academic mainstream was busy searching for the 'causes' of MSF and youth unemployment, radical Black scholars felt they knew the answer. Their concern was to ascertain how the 'culprit' (namely the institutional practices of racially structured patriarchal capitalism) had managed to get away with these crimes for so long. This gave greater space to structural explanations of systematic inequalities around 'race', class and gender. As with other 'dissenting voices', the dilemma here was how to address questions of conspiracy, intentionality and functionalism. Such analyses developed through critiques of the mainstream, often adopting an adversarial language and/or a position of advocacy. Radical literature on the TSW often has an urgency, an anger and a political focus that is notably absent from the more oblique liberal contributions of the mainstream (compare Connolly and Torkington, 1990, with Banks et al., 1991).

In the 1987/8 special issue of the US Civil Rights campaigning journal *Urban League Review* on 'Black Education: A Quest for Equity and Excellence', Antoine Garibaldi and Melinda Bartley addressed the question of 'school dropout' (Garibaldi and Bartley, 1987). Unlike Alpert and Dunham, they did not skirt around the high incidence of Black or 'minority' students who 'drop out' (or are pushed): indeed this was their main focus. Garibaldi and Bartley argued that two critical issues have continued to affect young African-Americans to a disproportionate extent since the second wave of US educational reforms during the 1970s: the increased numbers of students who 'dropout', and those who are 'pushed out' through suspensions and expulsions, all without a high school diploma (Rumberger, 1987). The two cannot be separated since 'disciplinary problems [what Alpert and Dunham would term "school misbehavior"] are strongly related to a student's probability of being expelled and/or their subsequent propensity to drop out' (Garibaldi and Bartley, 1987, p. 228; my insertion). Garibaldi and Bartley argued that suspension and expulsion are more often used as disciplinary methods against young people of colour, advocating the use of less severe alternatives to these practices. As such, potential solutions lay in the hands of teachers and education policy-makers rather than changes to the behaviour and attitudes of individual school students.

Despite a common emphasis on the role of 'race' and racism, such radical analyses of the TSW for young people of colour exhibit considerable diversity. All dissenting voices do not necessarily operate in perfect harmony, and the prevailing climate is one of debate and argument couched within the terms of the radical perspective. Much of the debate in radical youth research centres around the discourse of resistance, ways of understanding 'difference' between young people, and the relationship between structure, culture and agency.

Bruce Hare for example, had little time for resistance theory, which identifies youth cultural forms as a potentially creative use of oppositional strategies, or as cultural negotiations within a limited set of material conditions (Hare, 1987). Hare saw African-American peer youth culture as 'a long-term failure arena', because despite the creation of alternative models for Black achievement (e.g. music, sport) 'it offers little hope of long-term legitimate success' (p. 109). For Hare, the negative elements of this youth culture come from the school and not from African-American culture in general. Hare's text constructed young African-Americans as relatively passive and in need of help and guidance from their adult mentors, reinforcing the presumed 'immaturity' of young people.

The emergence of radical structural/materialist analyses of sex/gender relations has had a different political history compared to similar work around 'race' and/or class, although all three are closely interconnected (Brah, 1988b). Young women, and particularly young working-class women and young women of colour, have usually been ignored in research on the TSW. Apart from those many texts which have little or nothing to say about young women or gender relations, there is also a considerable body of literature which has indicated the extent of differences in the TSW for young (white) women and men (e.g. Wallace, 1987; Coffield et al., 1986). Despite this literature, many studies have continued to focus on the experiences of young (white) *men* in developing *general* theories of the TSW (e.g. Halsey et al., 1980).

Feminist critiques of youth research gathered pace during the 1970s, and this had an impact on both the radical and mainstream perspectives. Most mainstream studies were still engaged in the search for 'sex differences', representing young women as different from the white male norm, and often concentrating on connections between the TSW and young women's future marital and domestic lives.[5] J. A. Clausen for example, used information from the Berkeley Longitudinal Studies to examine the extent to which young women's personal attributes might influence their 'life choices' in order to predict the stability of subsequent marriages and careers (J. A. Clausen, 1986). The ideal here was to have those personal attributes which would result in 'realistic and rewarding choices' in education, occupations and marriage. Any young women who did not fit within the pattern of stable heterosexual relationships, unbroken careers and 'realistic choices' which Clausen constructed as 'normal' were represented as psychologically 'deficient' individuals.

Some mainstream analyses addressed young women's experiences of the TSW via an examination of sex roles rather than a search for sex differences. Bush for example, used longitudinal and cross-sectional survey data to examine how gendered socialization at home and at school might interact to produce traditional and non-traditional occupational aspirations and family expectations for adolescent girls (Bush, 1987). Whilst Clausen's study located the individual subject as the source of future 'life choices', Bush represented equality of opportunity and an end to sex discrimination as its goal. Such texts tend to focus on 'sex differences' or 'sex discrimination' in relative isolation, with minimal consideration of inequalities around class, disability, ethnicity or sexuality.

Studies using the sex roles framework are frequently informed by feminist critiques of 'malestream' research, and this sometimes produces a contradictory combination of discourses drawn from radical and mainstream perspectives. Raymond Calabrese and Clement Seldin for example, argued that the 'male-oriented learning environment' of US secondary schools created a response of 'adolescent alienation' amongst female students (1986). Measuring 'alienation' by means of a quantitative attitude scale, Calabrese and Seldin advocated a series of interventions which would not look out of place in a feminist programme.[6] These included an

increase in the percentage of female teachers, education programmes for male teachers, and strategies to empower female
students. Calabrese and Seldin concluded that such changes should
'eventually result in an environment where females will feel free
to achieve without sacrificing their identity or femininity' (p. 125).
Feminist analyses would argue that it is precisely this hegemonic
notion of femininity which *should* be sacrificed and deconstructed,
since it rests on pressures to attract and keep a man, often at the
expense of academic work or 'career aspirations' (Griffin, 1985a).

We can illustrate the distinctiveness of a feminist analysis by
considering an article by Helen Bright, a teacher in a mixed
London comprehensive school who examined the processes at
work in a British 'male-oriented learning environment' (1987). For
Helen Bright, female students were being silenced and literally as
well as ideologically confined to the edges of the classroom by the
relative numbers of young men, their sexist attitudes and practices,
those of their teachers and parents, and by gender-based divisions
in the curriculum (see Stanworth, 1983). Some of Helen Bright's
recommendations are similar to those of Calabrese and Seldin, but
unlike the latter, she did not argue that physiological changes at
menarche might account in part for the marginal position of
female students. For Bright, mixed classrooms provided evidence
of patriarchal power relations at work.

It is not solely the content of research texts which distinguishes
between radical and mainstream perspectives: the discursive frameworks through which these texts are constructed define which
arguments can be made and which voices must remain silenced.
Feminist research on the TSW has drawn on the genre of the
sermon identified by Esther Gottlieb and the narrative form of
the autobiography mentioned by Corinne Squire in her analysis
of the construction of gender in western feminist social psychology
(Squire, 1988). The use of the autobiographical genre owes a debt
to the feminist principle 'the personal is the political', which
stresses the value of women's experiences as a starting point for
political analysis. So a number of feminist texts on the TSW for
young women have interspersed reports of research studies with
autobiographical pieces from women teachers and school students
(e.g. Weiner and Arnot, 1988; Holly, 1989). The focus on women's
experiences led to a powerful argument that male-specific analyses
were seldom relevant to the TSW for young women, and that
studies about young men's *and* young women's lives which did not
examine the relations of gender, sexuality and 'race' as well as

class were incomplete (Mirza, 1992). The development of feminist work through critiques of the academic mainstream has sometimes led to the uncritical construction of women's experiences as based on a uniformity which obscures differences around 'race', class, sexuality, disability and age. Debates between the dissenting voices of the radical perspective have seldom had a major impact on mainstream research, although radical analyses have not been completely ignored by mainstream researches. The most sophisticated strategy in mainstream research on the TSW during the 1980s involved attempts to forge a synthesis between radical and mainstream perspectives.

The Strategy of Integration: Forging a Synthesis between Competing Models

The challenges posed by rising youth unemployment, the worsening position of white and Black working-class young people, and the dissenting voices of radical analyses had a profound and varied impact on mainstream research on the 'TSW' during the 1980s. Radical youth cultural studies brought debates over collective cultural practices, resistance and structural inequalities into the academic repertoire during the 1970s, along with discussions of the power relation between the researcher and the researched, and a shift towards 'qualitative' or 'naturalistic' methods (Trueba, 1990). Mainstream research adopted a number of strategies to deal with the challenges posed by these changes, including calls for a return to the 'traditional' approach as epitomized by the biological determinism of the psychology of adolescence (see chapter 3). Another strategy involved attempts to forge a synthesis between radical and mainstream models which had been constructed in opposition, such that any synthesis would be grounded in the terms of the mainstream perspective.

British sociologists Ken Roberts and Glennys Parsell described contemporary research on the TSW as characterized by 'new situations and old arguments' (1988, p. 2). By 'old arguments', they were referring to the two main models which defined entry to waged work as determined primarily by choice or by opportunity: that is, humanist and structuralist analyses respectively. Research on the TSW during the 1970s was characterized by a reinforcement of antagonisms between these opposing analyses, often via dualistic comparisons between different theories. A joint article in a special issue of *Society* entitled 'Controversies: Social Mobility' exemplifies this constructed clash of opposites (Featherman and Willhelm, 1979).

The 'problem' of social mobility is concerned with changes in job *status* as reflected in upward or downward occupational mobility over time. David Featherman used data from national US surveys to argue that the apparent improvement in Black men's job status during this period was due to improvements in the US education system. Sidney Willhelm argued that whilst African-Americans made slight educational gains during the 1970s, Featherman had ignored qualitative differences between Black and white educational systems, and both articles considered only men's experiences of social mobility. These two competing analyses actually constructed the 'problem' of social mobility in quite different ways: in discursive terms the two pieces were talking different languages.

During the 1980s, constructed oppositions between competing explanations such as the Featherman versus Willhelm debate declined somewhat in favour of attempts to forge a synthesis between competing models. In the USA, some mainstream reactions to John Ogbu's work advocated a synthesis between various radical analyses and mainstream explanations (e.g. Erickson, 1987; Moll and Diaz, 1987). Ogbu's work criticized the individualized perspective of mainstream studies, emphasizing the importance of structural inequalities in the US education system and job markets, whilst providing a meeting point for mainstream and radical perspectives. Frederick Erickson attempted to continue this project of amalgamation, combining the sociolinguistic explanations of the cultural difference model with Ogbu's theory. Erickson wanted to forge this synthesis within the framework of 'resistance theory', and whilst one sentence defining this approach used the language of radical analyses, the rest of Erickson's text reverted to the narrative form of the detective story in a more traditional search for the causes of 'school underachievement' (Erickson, 1987).

Attempts at synthesis have not been confined to the US literature. British social psychologist Terry Honess advocated the use of an 'integrative framework' in the study of school leavers which emphasized 'the blocking or exercise of personal powers and the succumbing to, or overcoming of, personal liabilities' (1989, p. 30). The individual subject is here imbued with 'personal enabling conditions', including sets of 'powers' and 'liabilities'. These are examined in relation to specific 'social/external enabling conditions', including 'circumstances', 'interpersonal network' and 'subculture'. Local unemployment conditions appear not as structural aspects of the local labour market, but as a subcultural element of 'social/external enabling conditions'. Honess also aimed to integrate quantitative and qualitative methodologies in an attempt to bridge the divide between psychological and sociological research (Honess, 1989).

Such attempts at synthesis stemmed in part from the impact of cuts in social science funding during the 1980s. Collaborative projects and 'relevant' research became the order of the day as academics competed for increasingly scarce resources. Those texts which drew on some features of radical analyses without upsetting the discursive framework or the political agenda of the mainstream were relatively acceptable to research funding agencies. The dissenting voices of radical research might have moved the ideological ground of mainstream youth research to some extent, but the victim-blaming thesis and the search for the causes of constructed 'social problems' retained their positions of discursive dominance. Many studies began referring to 'gender relations' rather than 'sex differences' for example, borrowing their terminology from feminist research whilst omitting any analysis of patriarchal dominance or women's oppression (e.g. Honess, 1989). Most of the calls for a synthesis between 'competing models' have been notably reluctant to adopt or even acknowledge the ideological and political ground occupied by the various dissenting voices of the radical perspective. The potential for *transformation* contained in the 'sermons' of radical analyses have either been ignored or incorporated within the dominant discursive framework of mainstream research on the TSW. Some radical texts did persevere in attempts to produce another form of synthesis, but on their own terms and beyond the domain of these 'competing models'.

From Synthesis to Nonsynchrony: Dealing with 'Difference' from a Radical Perspective

The texts which are usually presented as the core of the radical perspective are those which place class at the centre of their theoretical framework (e.g. Gottlieb, 1989). Those which focus on 'race' and racism, disability, sexuality, gender or their intersections with class are generally confined to the margins of an already marginalized set of radical analyses. Black and feminist scholars (and some neo-Marxists) have questioned the value of classical Marxist analysis and Anglocentric forms of feminism for understanding the relationship between sex/gender, 'race' and class in the education system and the job market (e.g. Brah, 1988a; McCarthy, 1989). So the 1980s were a period of reassessment in the field of radical as well as mainstream research.

With the growth of feminism during the late 1970s and early 1980s, the analysis of intersections between gender, class and generation in the TSW became more common in radical research. Yet studies by white feminists, like neo-Marxist work, have often ignored or marginalized the role of 'race' and racism. In a review of two British edited texts from Open University courses on 'gender and schooling', Avtar Brah noted the continuing tradition of ethnocentrism and racism in white feminist research (Brah, 1988a). 'Token' articles calling for major reassessments of key concepts at the heart of feminist theory (e.g. patriarchy, the family and reproduction; Carby, 1982) were placed within a mass of chapters which ignored the role of 'race' and racism in relation to sex/gender and class. As Avtar Brah put it, after welcoming the inclusion of *some* discussion of 'race' in these texts: 'the anti-racist project demands much more than the juxtaposition of seven articles which address Black experience and questions of racism as against forty essays which are overwhelmingly silent on the subject' (1988a, p. 118).[7]

On the other side of the Atlantic, Cameron McCarthy looked at the US literature on curriculum theory and the sociology of education, arguing that the analysis of 'race' and racism has been marginalized within mainstream educational research and in the work of radical neo-Marxists, all of whom tend to 'subordinat[e] . . . racial inequality in education to working class exploitation' (1989, p. 2). McCarthy also noted the prevalence in mainstream literature of the construction of one key 'problem' for research investigation: the educability of 'minority youth'. This focus produced a mass of studies which compared various characteristics or attitudes of white students with those of young people of colour, frequently presenting pathological explanations for the supposed inadequacies of the latter group (see Phoenix, 1990).

Radical scholars like McCarthy and Brah were not advocating another form of synthesis between competing explanations of MSF or 'school dropout', but a series of theoretical and political coalitions through which to understand the operation of power relations around sex/gender, age, 'race', class and dis/ability. Their emphasis was not on synthesis, but on understanding the complex and contradictory associations between, and the relative autonomy of, these various sets of power relations. In Britain as in the USA, most attempts to deal with 'difference' and 'diversity' of working-class young people emerged from the radical perspective (or cultural structuralism) of cultural studies.[8] In the USA, similar developments in radical research were informed by the work of Michael Apple, Lois Weis and others at the University of Wisconsin in Madison (Apple, 1982; Weis, 1988). In Britain and the USA, these arguments were also influenced by the growth of Black feminist theory and practice within and outside research on the TSW (e.g. Bryan et al., 1985).

Such attempts to deal with 'difference' and 'diversity' rest on the notion that we cannot understand the TSW for *any* young people if we do not appreciate the experiences of *all* young people. This meant finding ways of doing radical research which did not examine gender relations in isolation from 'race', ethnicity, class, age or sexuality, or as if *all* young people (or all young men) shared an identical experience of the move from school to the job market. It meant examining the ways in which the education system and the youth labour market are, as Avtar Brah put it when referring to social relations in schools, 'inscribed within the discursive practices constituted around "race", class and gender' (1988b, p. 121).

Cameron McCarthy referred to this approach as 'nonsynchronous', distinguishing 'nonsynchrony' from the 'parallelism' which characterized so many of the cultural analyses within Marxist/feminist research. What McCarthy termed the parallelist position 'directly challenges the primacy of class in an understanding of institutional and social relations' (1989, p. 17). No longer were racial and sex/gender dynamics reducible to the operation of class relations and economic forces alone. The main model used in the parallelist position is an additive one, in which researchers speak of 'double' and 'triple' oppressions (e.g. Sarup, 1986). This framework leaves little space for possible contradictions, discontinuities and tensions between the operation of class, 'race' and/or sex/gender relations. One is trapped in a conceptual hierarchy of oppressions, arguing about which group is 'more oppressed' (see Mirza, 1992, for critique).

According to McCarthy's concept of 'nonsynchrony', individuals and groups do not automatically share identical consciousness or interests at any one moment. Schooling (and the job market, family life and so on) 'constitutes a site for the production of the politics of *difference*' (1989, p. 19, my emphasis). McCarthy viewed the politics of difference or nonsynchrony as expressions of culturally sanctioned, rational responses to struggles over scarce (or unequal) resources. The important question here is not whether 'differences' have a basis in material reality, nor whether they produce divisions between people, since the priority is to understand how 'differences' are constructed in practice, and how they can shape, limit and restrict our lives (Luttrell, 1989; Omi and Winant, 1986).

By the end of the 1980s, many radical analyses were considering the intersections of 'race', sex/gender, age, class and (less frequently) dis/ability, rather than the overwhelming focus on class relations which had characterized the radical texts of the 1970s. This produced various empirical attempts to deal with 'difference' in the move from school to the job market from a radical perspective which also addressed the debate over the relation between culture, structure and agency. Analyses which drew on post-structuralist approaches also addressed 'difference', but through the deconstruction of the concept of the unitary individual self. This produced debates about multiple consciousness and multiple identities (or rather subjectivities), leading to some profound reassessments of the liberal humanist notion of individual choice and of the relation between structure and agency.

Culture, Structure and Agency: 'Difference' and Deconstruction

Debates over the relationship between structure, culture and agency characterized much of the radical research of the 1980s. The rise of the New Right precipitated a crisis for radical structuralist theories in social research as well as for the political Left. Cultural reproduction and resistance theories were criticized from within the radical perspective for their inadequate treatment of differences among young people and the construction of 'oppressed youth' as either passive victims or heroic cultural warriors (Furlong, 1991). The economic determinism of structural Marxism was seen to represent working-class young people as passive victims with no space for resistance and struggle, and to have considerable problems in appreciating the role of gender, ethnicity and generation in the TSW, to say nothing of sexuality and dis/ability. The resistance theories of youth subcultural studies were also criticized for romanticizing working-class (mainly white, heterosexual, able-bodied and male) youth cultures, the capacity for transformatory political action amongst this group, and (once again) for the relative lack of awareness of power relations around sex/gender, 'race' and ethnicity (e.g. J. C. Walker, 1986a; McRobbie, 1980).

One way through these dilemmas was to draw on the various post-structuralist approaches which had been influencing literary criticism, cultural studies and media studies in the USA and Europe (Cole, 1988; Weedon, 1987). This strategy entailed a critical reassessment of the conceptual basis of resistance theory, which rested on a relatively straightforward distinction between oppressive social conditions and oppressed individual subjects with their collective cultural practices of resistance (Lather, 1990). By the end of the 1980s, several texts had adopted this form of radical cultural analysis informed by post-structuralist and feminist perspectives (e.g. Willis et al., 1990; Roman et al., 1988).

Lois Weis edited a text entitled *Class, Race and Gender in American Education* which reflected some of these debates over 'difference', deconstruction, the discourse of resistance and the relationship between culture, structure and agency (Weis, 1988). This book pulls together critical research on 'academic under-achievement' amongst young people of colour, girls and young women, and working-class white students. It is divided into two parts, with a series of chapters in the first section written from a structuralist perspective, and the second section devoted to contributions from a culturalist perspective. Most contributors to the Weis text presented oppositional cultural forms as means of reproducing young people's low achievements and subordinated positions. The organization of the text reflected the dualism between the (class-focused) structuralism of Marxist analyses and cultural reproduction theories which emphasized the scope for (mainly white, male) working-class opposition to exploitative conditions. As with the Open University texts considered earlier by Avtar Brah, the theoretical perspective advocated by the editors of such texts was not necessarily reflected in all of the chapters. Some contributions to the Weis text focused on class and/or gender *only* and ignored 'race' and racism, whilst others seemed to reproduce racist assumptions about young African-Americans (see Okazawa-Rey, 1989, for review).

Considerable attention has been paid in the radical literature to researchers' interpretations of specific cultural formations, especially as reflections of 'resistance' or 'collusion' (Aggleton and

Whitty, 1985). Researchers have constructed specific youth cultural practices as overwhelmingly negative (e.g. Hare, 1987); potentially creative (e.g. Willis, 1977); as negotiations or strategies defined and limited by material and ideological boundaries (e.g. Griffin, 1985a); as forms of political resistance or accommodation (e.g. Mac an Ghaill, 1988); and as examples of collusion with conditions of oppression (e.g. Wolpe, 1988). There is no one 'correct' or privileged interpretation here: they all reflect a combination of researchers' theoretical and political perspectives, and the context in which the research was conducted. The various strands of radical youth research struggled with this debate over the status of researchers' readings throughout the 1980s (Roman and Christian-Smith, 1988).

In an influential examination of white working-class feminine cultures, Angela McRobbie identified some young white working-class women's assertions of female heterosexuality as rejections of the idealized notion of the (white middle-class) 'nice girl' in patriarchal culture and ideology (McRobbie, 1978). Such strategies could equally be read as reinforcing the demands of heterosexual relations. What might operate as opposition in one context or with reference to one set of power relations could be constituted as conformist in another. Whilst young people themselves may assess the implications of the various cultural strategies available to them, it is researchers and educationalists who have most influence on the naming of those practices in TSW research and educational practice. It is they (or rather we) who speak in a privileged voice.

Academic achievement is usually associated with conformity and collusion with the status quo: with femininity for males (e.g. Willis, 1977; Wolpe, 1988); with 'acting white' for young people of colour (e.g. Ogbu, 1987; Iadicola, 1983). These observations have been given different connotations by different researchers, in some cases taken as evidence of 'resistance', in others of 'collusion'. For Paul Willis and many others, the presumed effeminacy of white working-class pro-school masculine cultures reflects the flip side of assertions of working-class male competence, anti-intellectualism and macho prowess amongst 'the lads'. For Ann-Marie Wolpe, such phenomena can be used to question young men's 'masculinity' (that is their *hetero*sexual masculinity), despite the presence of girlfriends. For Ogbu, the oppositional strategies of some students served to block or even police the achievements and aspirations of their peers. This is not to imply that some researchers are correct and others mistaken, nor do these varying interpretations reflect the limitations of using qualitative ethnographic research methods. If anything, such diversity indicates that cultural practices operate at a deeper level of contradiction and complexity than most researchers might have considered.

The position of young women, and especially young women of colour, throws the identification of specific cultural practices as simply 'conformist', 'cynical' or forms of 'resistance' into confusion, casting doubt on some of the basic assumptions of radical research on the TSW (Mac an Ghaill, 1988; Chigwada, 1987). Many young Afro-Caribbean women in Britain, for example, are anti-school but pro-academic work, striving to gain qualifications and a 'good job', and viewing themselves as potential breadwinners (Mirza, 1992).

These debates deconstruct the concepts of 'resistance' and 'collusion' from a radical political perspective, reassessing our understandings of the cultural processes involved in the TSW, and the nature of 'differences' between young people around gender, class, 'race' and sexuality. Such debates over the intersections between culture, structure and agency can also be identified in the arena of youth training, in which the rapid expansion of government-sponsored youth training programmes in Britain and the USA attempted to 'bridge the gap' between school and the job market, and to obscure rising rates of youth unemployment (Finn, 1987).

Robert Hollands's study of youth training schemes in the English West Midlands during the 1980s avoided the tendency in some radical texts to represent Thatcherite youth training provision as a monolithic force for oppression (1990; see Cockburn, 1987). Whilst Hollands's main interest was in the reproduction and regeneration of *class* cultures and identities, he did acknowledge the different experiences of white working-class young people and young people of colour, both young women and young men, and the roles of racism and sexism in shaping their positions in youth training, family life, leisure and the job market. Politically, Hollands criticized the British Labour movement for its failure to address the changing interests and positions of unemployed working-class young people and the rise of 'new vocationalism' during the 1980s (see Bates et al., 1984).

Empirical examples of attempts to deal with 'difference' between young people are more common in studies of education and training than those focusing on entry to the job market, mainly since schools, colleges and training schemes provide relatively easier access for researchers than the employment sector (e.g.

Borman and Riesman, 1986). Other studies from within the radical perspective questioned the distinctions between education and employment, and between (waged) work and leisure. Kathryn Borman for example, looked at 'playing on the job' in young people's workplaces (1988). Using cultural analysis tied to a social anthropological methodology, she argued that 'playing on the job' provided an important source of tension release, an opportunity to create solidarity between young workers and a means of escape from boring routine work.

Differences in working conditions and ideological expectations for young women and men limited the former's opportunities to engage in workplace play. More than this, playful behaviour often created solidarity between male workers whilst marginalizing and demeaning young women. Borman set her four case studies in cultural and institutional context, arguing that 'adolescent humour' can take a variety of forms, from slapstick humour to practical jokes and funny stories. Since young women are more likely than their male peers to work in relative isolation from their co-workers, they have fewer chances to engage in such play, or to develop the degree of solidarity found amongst many groups of young men. This can then reinforce a common assumption that women lack a sense of humour.

Other studies have taken a critical look at the dynamics of cultural interaction around 'race', class, gender and sexuality. Michael Moffatt's anthropological study of race, friendship and 'culture' among US college students traced one year (1978–9) in the life of a dormitory in Rutgers College at which Moffatt was teaching (1986). This followed an attempt at 'integration' in which a Black 'special interest' section was formed in half of the dormitory, the remainder of which was predominantly white students. Gender was crosscut with 'race' in this respect, since the college had become co-educational by alternating rooms at the same time as the 'racial integration' during the late 1960s. Moffatt's analysis concerned the ways in which the notions of 'culture' and 'community', and the discourse of 'race' were negotiated by different groups of students in the dorm. In Moffatt's terms, 'the simple folk sociology of friendship that dominate[d] the students' categories' could not handle 'the historical legacy of fear and perceived difference' left by American racism, and 'students' egalitarian constructs ha[d] no place for legitimate "difference" ' (p. 174–5; my insertions).

When Black students in the 'special interest' dorm refused what white (and some Black) students defined as participation in the process of integration, all groups drew on a discourse of 'culture' to explain this, and a means of avoiding the less 'acceptable' biological form of racism. Just as white students denied the possibility of their having any racist prejudices, white males denied any sexist inclinations with even greater vigour. As Moffatt argued, this version of events was not shared by all Black and female students, and whilst the 'biological' form of racist discourse had apparently been superseded by cultural explanations, biological determinism remained an important element in the construction of sex and gender relations. These took on a material form with sex-segregated bathrooms and bedrooms. The lack of any means for understanding 'difference' within the dominant discourse of liberal relativism served to undermine the position and the demands of Black students in the 'special interest' section, who were frequently perceived as 'unfriendly' by other (predominantly white) students. Moffatt argued that by 1984 the more visible gay community (he did not specify whether this term included lesbians) at the college posed a more profound threat to the ideological liberalism of the dominant college culture than the politicized Black students, since 'gender and sexuality became unhooked in profoundly disturbing . . . ways' (p. 176).

In Moffatt's text the dynamics of power relations around 'race', gender and sexuality (and to a lesser extent class) were not assumed to be equivalent or simply additive. He emphasized the ways in which the dominant discourses set the parameters within which *all* students experienced social relations in the dorm, even those who were striving to transform those relations: it was not simply a matter of identifying those individual subjects or cultural practices which were 'resistant' or 'colluding'. Even in 1984, when the dorm seemed to be functioning more smoothly than in 1978/9, the dominant discourse remained unchanged. Set in the individualized rhetoric of liberal relativism, it led students to protest, 'Why shouldn't we all get on? We're all just people' (1986).

Attempts to deal with 'difference' in radical cultural research around the TSW have as yet been relatively uneven. Various combinations of 'race', class, gender and age relations have been considered, but radical studies which take a critical perspective on heterosexuality and address the experiences of young lesbians and gay men are few and far between (exceptions include Halston, 1989; Trenchard and Warren, 1987). Radical perspectives on dis/ability and the TSW are almost totally absent, as are the voices of young people with disabilities (Oliver, 1988; Shearer, 1981). This issue tends to be confined to a clinically oriented perspective within mainstream research on education and training. Few studies have taken a critical look at the lives of the most privileged groups of young people: white upper- and middle-class heterosexual males, most of whom do not move directly from school to the job market, but from university to a professional career.

It remains relatively unusual, even within radical research, to examine the implications of sex/gender, 'race', disability or class for dominant groups of young people: one exception in the New Zealand context is Alison Jones's study of Pacific Island and Pakeha girls (1991; see also Canaan, 1990). Radical research retained its focus on subordinated groups into the 1980s, setting out to challenge the representation of such groups as 'deviant' or 'deprived' in the mainstream literature, and to allow their voices to be heard within the terms of radical perspectives on the TSW. Other important absences in radical cultural research around the TSW include the voices of more diverse groups of 'minority' young people such as Native Americans, Chicano/as, Asian-Americans, young British people of Greek and Turkish descent, young Jewish people, and more sophisticated understandings of contemporary forms of racism, anti-Semitism and ethnocentrism (exceptions here include Factor and Stenson, 1989; Rodriguez, 1986; Gilchrist et al., 1987).

The radical perspective locates the problem of the TSW not within the presumed cultural deficiencies of working-class and Black students, but in the ideological, economic and political structures of racially structured patriarchal capitalism (e.g. Bhavnani, 1991). Working-class young people are assumed to stand little chance unless the education system and the job market undergo some profound structural changes. The youth job market did undergo some profound structural changes during the 1980s, but not in the direction advocated by radical researchers. The main changes involved an increase in youth unemployment levels, which along with the rise of the New Right, precipitated a set of crises for mainstream and radical perspectives in youth research.

Notes

1 For example, a 1981 issue of the prestigious journal *Science* was devoted to genetic and hormonal explanations of sex differences in anatomy and behaviour (*Science*, March 1981).

2 See Bullivant (1987) for an example of an Australian study in this area.
3 The influence of Ogbu's work in the US literature is demonstrated by the 1987 special issue of the journal *Anthropology and Education Quarterly*, in which most contributions addressed Ogbu's arguments.
4 See Ogbu (1989) for a modification of his initial notion of 'castelike status', in which he distinguished between 'voluntary' and 'involuntary' minorities, depending on the processes through which different groups were brought into US society.
5 As a starting point here I have used the four-stage model suggested by Margrit Eichler to comprehend the development of anglophone feminist sociology (Eichler, 1985).
6 Calabrese and Seldin's analysis can be contrasted with that of Ann Foreman, who combined Marxist, feminist and psychoanalytic frameworks to argue that patriarchal ideologies of femininity produced a specific state of alienation (Foreman, 1977).
7 A reprint of an article I had written in 1981 was included as one of these 'overwhelmingly silent' essays, so my work is also implicated in Avtar Brah's critique (Griffin, 1985b).
8 See Bhabha (1990) for a discussion of the political and conceptual implications of 'difference' and 'diversity'.

3
Constructing the Crisis: The Impact of Youth Unemployment

It may well be that in the next ten, fifteen or twenty years we will have a new philosophy towards unemployment. We may have to move away from the Protestant Work Ethic. (James Prior, Conservative MP, speaking in Opposition, *Guardian*, 22 March 1979).

At 16 unemployment should not be an option. (Margaret Thatcher, 1989 Conservative Party conference) — Birch

Apart from the potential anti-social behavior of youth unable to obtain jobs, a larger issue is whether society is justified in denying young people the opportunity to partake in adult society. (Bresnick, 1984, p. 10).

The above extract from Margaret Thatcher's speech at the 1989 Tory Party conference appears to reflect some commitment to ending the spectre of unemployment which had haunted so many young people in Britain during the 1980s, perhaps heralding the 'new philosophy towards unemployment' mentioned by her fellow Conservative James Prior ten years before. The 1989 speech actually referred to the withdrawal of social security benefits from British school leavers aged between sixteen and seventeen, who would enter the 1990s compelled to take a place in full-time education, on a government training scheme, or a job. It was not *unemployment* which ceased to be an 'option' for sixteen-year-olds in the Britain of the 1990s, but the right to claim welfare benefits and appear on the official register of those who were 'unemployed and seeking work' (Finn and Ball, 1991). Those school leavers in areas with no local jobs or training places available were then unable to claim unemployment benefit and register as unemployed: they entered a limbo of invisible dependence on their families and friends – or homelessness and destitution.

Researchers on both sides of the Atlantic devoted considerable attention to the possible causes, remedies and implications of youth unemployment during the 1980s. David Bresnick's words

reflect the contradictory reaction of mainstream research to these
issues. Older ideological panics over the potential 'social problem'
posed by certain groups of unemployed young people are combined with a liberal concern about individual rights and opportunities. Any block placed in the path of entry to full-time (waged)
work is taken as a potential source of disruption in the transition
to adult status, a theme which has been equally prevalent in radical
analyses, albeit with very different political and social connotations. (e.g. Willis, 1984). Mainstream research has focused on the
possible causes of youth unemployment; its psychological, social,
cultural and economic consequences; and policy developments
designed to deal with 'disaffected youth' and reduce the spiralling
unemployment statistics. Such official concern over youth unemployment is not specific to the 1980s: it can be traced throughout
the post-Second World War period alongside various ideological
and structural changes in the organization of 'work', 'leisure' and
notions of 'youth'.

The Perennial Problem: Panics over Youth
Unemployment in Historical Context

Concern over youth unemployment levels has not been confined
to periods of recognized economic crisis in western industrialized
societies. Once 'wandering people' such as vagrants and beggars,
along with peasants and waged labourers, became forged into the
European working class, the modern concept of unemployment
began to emerge, moving into and across the 'New World' with
the colonizing forces of early European settlers. With the development of capitalist production, paid work and productive effort
became synonymous, and unemployment was used to describe a
social situation (i.e. being outside paid work) rather than a personal condition. As Raymond Williams has pointed out, 'there has
been a steady ideological resistance to this necessary distinction'
(1976, p. 326), and representations of youth unemployment in
1980s research provide continuing evidence of such 'ideological
resistance'.

Although workers were being thrown out of waged work
throughout the nineteenth century, official concern over unemployment emerged only in the early twentieth century.[1] In pre-industrial
societies, the aristocracy and their representatives tended to view
the work of labourers as primarily determined by seasonal vari-

ations. With the increasing pace of industrialization, sharper distinctions began to emerge between waged work and 'recreation', or that time spent outside of waged labour which came to be defined as non-work (Thompson, 1967). Unwaged domestic work and childcare are frequently constructed outside the boundaries of 'real work' and productive effort altogether, with profound implications for women's position in family life and the labour market (Griffin et al., 1982).

By the 1890s, unemployment began to be constructed as a *social* problem, a product of market forces over which individuals had minimal control (Ashton, 1986). This was mainly a response to the growing organization of the industrial working class on both sides of the Atlantic, but it did not altogether displace the older notion of the feckless and idle unemployed (Golding and Middleton, 1983). The contradictory construction of unemployed people as a class of irresponsible individuals who refuse to find a job, and the notion of unemployment as a condition beyond the control of unfortunate job-seekers can be traced to the late nineteenth century. Such contradictions are still reflected in contemporary employment policies, welfare provision and academic research, as represented in continuing debates about what should be done *to* the unemployed alongside suggestions as to what should be done *for* them (Kelvin and Jarrett, 1985).

The 1920s brought a period of economic depression to Britain which hit working-class employees in the manufacturing industries of Northern England, Scotland and Wales to a disproportionate extent. The following decade saw a world-wide slump which had particularly disastrous effects in the USA and Germany between 1929 and 1933. By this time the recession had been felt by both working-class male manual workers and middle-class female teachers. In Britain the National Unemployed Workers' Movement (NUWM) played an important role in organizing and supporting unemployed people, and there was also 'mass activity' around unemployment and poverty in North America and Germany during the early 1930s which came under increasing attack from the authorities, and in Germany from the expanding Nazi Party.

The 1940s saw a series of government interventions in the economy, from Roosevelt's 'New Deal' to Britain's policy of low interest rates, import controls and the eventual mass mobilization for the Second World War. The 'reconstruction' period which followed brought low unemployment rates, and a growing ideological sense that unemployment (like class divisions) was 'a thing of the past'. Keynesian economics represented the 'cure' for unemployment in state intervention, as both British and US governments pursued policies of full employment. As in the First World War, mobilization brought a demand for female labour, and the postwar period coincided with a renewal of dominant ideologies of domestic femininity, with calls for women to 'return to the home' (Summerfield, 1984). During the 1950s, Britain began a series of recruitment campaigns in the Caribbean and the Indian subcontinent to boost the workforce in its expanding public sector with the cheap labour of Black workers (Sivanandan, 1982). The legacy of slavery and the use of workers from Central and South American countries provided the USA with its own pool of cheap labour. The 'oil crisis' of 1973 and 1974 is usually presented as the event which signified the end of this period of economic growth, heralding a steady increase in unemployment levels and a series of moral panics over young people and youth unemployment.

Whilst official concern over youth unemployment has been more prevalent during periods of economic recession and high official unemployment such as the 1920s and 1930s, it has not been completely absent even during periods of relative prosperity (Griffin, 1987). Youth unemployment provided a less central focus for adult concern during much of the 1960s, but as the 1970s progressed, it began to figure in an increasing proportion of academic texts, often presented as a looming threat which could disrupt an already fragmented post-war 'consensus' (Hall et al., 1977).

Mainstream research on youth unemployment has been engaged in a search for the causes and the consequences of unemployment, and for means of alleviating or reducing its worst effects. As in studies of 'minority school failure' or 'delinquency', we find a series of debates which locate the primary cause(s) of unemployment in the personal characteristics of unemployed individuals (see chapter 2). Whilst psychological and sociological positivist approaches emphasized the search for causes, the social democratic perspective focused on the deleterious effects of, and potential remedies for, unemployment. Texts operating from Marxist, feminist and anti-racist perspectives have tended to ask different questions. Most radical texts would not engage in a search for the causes of youth unemployment: they are more interested in the processes through which youth unemployment is reproduced, challenged and negotiated in specific relations of domination and subordination. Various radical analyses have represented unemployment not as an autonomous expression of capitalism, but as an essential structural feature of racially structured capitalist patriarchies (Bhavnani, 1991). Other contemporary Marxist accounts have examined the role of ideology in the construction of unemployment as a transitory phase necessary for 'weeding out the weak' (S. Hall, 1988).

Mainstream texts have also attributed youth unemployment to the relative number of young people in a given population (e.g. Moynihan, 1977). For other researchers, the 'problem' is not simply one of numbers. As Ray Marshall argued, 'even though the number of unemployed youth might diminish in the 1980s for demographic reasons *the social tensions produced by this problem would not*' (1984, p. 119 emphasis added). Whether young people are represented as the instigators of rising youth unemployment and general social unrest due to an increase in their numbers or as a consequence of an earlier 'bulge' which had now passed, these arguments used the victim-blaming thesis to construct unemployed young people as the primary cause of their own and other people's 'problems'.

Academic representations of youth unemployment in the 1980s were characterized by explicit concern over the 'crisis' facing young people in Britain and the USA during the decade of the 'New Right' under Thatcher and Reagan respectively. This 'crisis' of youth reflected a series of crises within youth research itself at the level of theory and of finance. Finally, the late 1970s and the 1980s brought a crisis for young people themselves, especially if they were unemployed, homeless or otherwise relegated to the margins of British and US societies.

Research on Youth Unemployment during the 1980s: Constructing the Crisis

Academic representations of youth unemployment in the 1980s were marked by a combination of moral panic and paternalistic concern, and constructed mainly through the language of crisis. This reached a crescendo in the middle of the decade, especially in Britain. Much of the debate centred around rising official unemployment levels and speculations about whether youth unemployment represented a cause or a symptom of this 'crisis'. Some radical researchers cast their ideological nets wider, arguing that the 'crisis' was for and about young people and youth research, with implications for the future of western industrial societies: specifically the capitalist system (P. Cohen, 1988).

Some mainstream analyses represented high youth unemployment as producing a crisis in the relationship between 'work' and 'leisure'. Others contrasted the dire situation in Britain during the 1980s with US society and the 'American jobs miracle'. Whilst US adult and youth unemployment levels were relatively lower than in most western European countries during the 1980s, certain sections of US society, most notably young African-Americans and other young people of colour experienced a far from prosperous decade. The rhetoric of crisis was not simply a reflection of high official unemployment levels, it was also a product of profound ideological and political changes wrought by the rise of the New Right in Britain and the USA (Hall and Jacques, 1983).

Varying constructions of this 'crisis' can be found in mainstream and radical texts. From the former group, British sociologist David Marsland saw the negative consequences of mass youth unemployment as a key element in this crisis 'of' rather than 'for' youth. For Marsland, the problem with 'structural youth unemployment on the current scale' was that it 'seems likely to escalate disaffection and alienation, and conceivably to pose a real threat to democratic institutions' (1986, p. 1). Marsland went on to detail the failure of government measures to meet this 'challenge', including the apparent failure of British schools 'to inculcate minimum levels of civility, or to socialize young people adequately to society's basic values' (pp. 1–2).

Marsland was concerned about a crisis of *control* over youth, especially the control operated by 'responsible adults' over 'the hedonistic principles of youth culture' (p. 2). The 'crisis' was one of adult *authority*, since for Marsland 'the authority – that is the legitimate, effective power to inculcate principles and rules – seems to be generally lacking [since] parents, teachers, police, work supervisors, across the board, find themselves increasingly impotent to handle young people effectively' (p. 2). Those principles and rules which the legitimated representatives of adult authority 'find themselves' unable to impart signal the second dimension of this 'crisis': that of *morality*. 'Society' is represented as 'unclear or divided' about 'our' basic values. The very nature of 'civilized culture' was at stake, and the latter was differentiated from those *un*civilized youth cultures so deplored by Marsland.

Marsland's constructed polarity between 'responsible adults' and 'hedonistic youth' is far from new. What was specific to the 1980s was that this replay of 'old' discursive configurations coincided with a virulent attack on British sociology for 'neglecting the topic of youth', and when it was covered, for 'mishandling the concept and theory of youth' (1986, p. 5). The 'crisis' was presented as a problem in youth *research* which could be solved only by bringing psychological positivism (back) into the arena of sociological analysis. Marsland's text on the 'crisis of youth' is one example of a wider backlash against the radical youth cultural theorists of the mid-1970s.

Mainstream sociology had struggled to reorient itself following the radical critiques of Marxist, feminist and anti-racist youth cultural analyses during the 1970s and 1980s. Within the sociology of youth, Marsland turned the distinction between 'mainstream' and 'radical' around, locating 'the conventional' in the work of Talcott Parsons, and 'the dominant' paradigm in the work of 'the Marxists', as exemplified by Stuart Hall, Sheila Allen and Mike Brake. The latter emerged in a marginal and subordinate relation to the mainstream of youth sociology, but Marsland represented 'the Marxists' as 'the new orthodoxy' which had come to dominate 'the traditionally established sociology of youth' (p. 7). The 'biased' work of 'the Marxists' must then be toppled by a return to the old (and 'apolitical') orthodoxies. This argument allowed Marsland to justify his attack on a radical perspective which had become (according to him) part of the sociological mainstream.

Marsland wanted to reassert the 'bio-psychological' foundations of youth: the old orthodoxy which stressed the universality of adolescence. Unlike those mainstream researchers mentioned in the previous chapter, Marsland's response to radical critiques was not to call for a synthesis between competing models, but a return to the positivist mainstream of 'bio-psychological' theory which obscured diversity amongst young people, and especially the operation of structural power relations around age, 'race', class and sex/gender.

Philip Cohen, one of the perpetrators of the 'new orthodoxy' so reviled by Marsland, was also writing about a 'crisis' in the sociology of youth and its negative impact on youth policies during the same period (1986). Cohen also called for a new look at Parsons, Mannheim and Erikson, but unlike Marsland, Cohen wanted to challenge those hallowed 'bio-psychological founda- tions', which he preferred to identify as 'bio-political'. In addition, Cohen argued that the material conditions of youthfulness in the west had changed so fundamentally as to render many existing theories inadequate: including the Marxist model. Cohen did not constitute this 'crisis' as one of morality or adult control over young people, but of the irrelevance of most academic theories to the lives of most (working-class) young people, exemplified by a lack of political support and guidance from adults. The 'crisis' also reflected the failure of the British Left to prevent and challenge the rise of the New Right, to address the priorities of young people themselves and to recognize their diversity.

Whilst the rhetoric of panic was most common in British youth research, it was also evident in some US texts. Here the 'crisis' was focused more specifically around the unemployment of young African-American men (Osterman, 1980; Bresnick, 1984). The collection of papers edited by Richard Freeman and Harry Holzer for example, examined this 'crisis' from the perspective of mainstream economic analysis (Freeman and Holzer, 1986). The main concern of this text was with African-American male youth unemployment, which was represented as a problem since 'the urban unemployment characteristic of the Third World appears to have taken root among black youths in the United States' (p. 3).

This panic was set in the context of the supposed failure of the equal opportunities and affirmative action policies which were introduced during the 1960s and 1970s. The apparent failure of such legislation was not attributed to inadequacies in the policies themselves (e.g. their failure to challenge institutionalized racism), or the defensive strategies of racist institutions, but to the presumed deficiencies of young African-Americans. Since mainstream analyses such as those in the Freeman and Holzer text assumed that 'racial discrimination' should have been all but overcome as a result of anti-discrimination and affirmative action legislation, the continued existence of disproportionately high unemployment rates amongst young African-American men *did* appear to constitute a crisis, at least for mainstream theories about 'race', youth unemployment and the relative position of African-American and white working-class young people.

By the middle of the 1980s, official US government statistics began to reflect the social and economic damage which Reaganomics had inflicted on working-class Americans, and especially on young African-Americans (Center for Budget and Policy Priorities, 1986). Radical and mainstream scholars were quick to include this information in a debate over the 'new Black underclass' which is covered in greater detail in chapter 7. One of the key elements in the story of youth unemployment in the 1980s on both sides of the Atlantic was the steady rise in official unemployment rates, especially during the first half of the decade. A vital issue here concerns the many and various changes to the methods of calculating the British figures.

The Official Story of Youth Unemployment: Lies, Damned Lies and Statistics

Official youth unemployment figures cannot be interpreted as an accurate reflection of the numbers of young people outside waged work at any given time. In order to be included on official unemployment registers young people have to fulfil a number of criteria, which in Britain varied considerably as the decade wore on. Margaret Thatcher's Conservative government had introduced no fewer than *sixteen* changes to the methods of calculating the official unemployment figures between 1979 and 1986. By the end of the decade, there had been *nineteen* changes in all, only one of which had produced an increase in the unemployment level, and even then this was quickly obscured by a compensatory mechanism. Most of the other eighteen changes reduced the official unemployment level, yet no equivalent upward compensations were in evidence, leading to the unavoidable conclusion that these changes were thinly disguised attempts to 'massage' the figures (Finn and Ball, 1991).

Following the relatively high employment levels of the 1960s, youth unemployment rates in the USA rose during the early 1970s, standing at just under 20 per cent of sixteen- to nineteen-year-olds in 1975. By the start of the 1980s, youth unemployment rates had fallen to around 16 per cent for sixteen- to nineteen-year-olds, and 9 per cent for twenty- to twenty-four-year-olds. The 1980s brought an increase to just over 23 per cent of sixteen- to nineteen-year-olds by 1982, followed by a gradual decline to 15 per cent at the end of the decade for the same group, and 8.6 per cent for twenty- to twenty-four-year-olds.[2]

Perhaps the starkest message of these figures is the massive disparity between unemployment rates amongst young African-Americans and whites, a difference which is also found amongst adults.[3] The official unemployment rate for young African-Americans stood at around twice that of their white peers, with a horrifying peak in 1982 and 1983, when just under 50 per cent of African-American sixteen- to nineteen-year-olds were officially recorded as unemployed. Even in 1977, when youth unemployment accounted for almost 25 per cent of total US unemployment, government training programmes were playing a significant role in lowering (or rather obscuring) unemployment rates amongst young people of colour. By the 1980s, financial cutbacks had reduced this buffer to some extent, and African-American youth unemployment rose to over 40 per cent between 1981 and 1985.

The official British unemployment figures must be treated with even greater caution, and direct comparisons with the USA, or even with earlier British statistics, are extremely difficult. In Britain the overall unemployment rate was below 5 per cent during the 1960s and early 1970s. It began to increase after 1976, showing a sharp upturn in the early 1980s to over 10 per cent. Only the many changes to the methods of calculating the figures during the mid-1980s brought the overall British unemployment rate below 10 per cent again in 1988 – still relatively higher than the US figure. The pattern for youth unemployment rates was broadly similar, although a detailed breakdown by age and sex was available only after 1981. By 1984, just over 22 per cent of sixteen- to nineteen-year-olds and just over 17 per cent of twenty- to twenty-four-year-olds were officially unemployed. These figures began to fall to nearer 15 per cent for the younger and older age groups after 1987, but the official unemployment rate for eighteen- to nineteen-year-olds remained at 20 per cent.

The national UK figures do not provide information on Black and white youth (or adult) unemployment. Local studies indicate that unemployment amongst young Afro-Caribbean men can be well over 50 per cent in some areas, and all Black British young people are affected to a disproportionate extent by unemployment and underemployment compared to their white peers (Cross and Smith, 1987). Young men tend to have somewhat higher unemployment rates compared to their female peers, reflecting in part the impact of young women's relatively greater domestic responsibilities.

The British and American contexts have varied in several respects. As David Ashton has pointed out, 'youth unemployment was a problem in the USA long before it was defined as such in Britain' (1986, p. 105). Ashton attributed this to differences in the education systems and the institutional regulation of the job market in the two countries. There was a relatively faster growth in the US labour force during the post-war period, and working students and high school 'dropouts' are included in the US unemployment figures. Official youth unemployment rates in the USA have been relatively high since the Second World War, unlike Britain where youth unemployment began to appear as a 'problem' only in the late 1960s. During the 1980s rising youth unemployment levels in Britain brought the official situation in the two countries closer together.

The use of official figures is widespread in texts which examined young people's unemployment and their position in the 1980s job market from the mainstream perspective. Such studies are characterized by a search for the causes and effects of youth unemployment, following the narrative form of the detective story. They usually involve a series of comparisons between different groups of young people, notably African-American and white working-class young men in US research studies. One of the consequences of rising youth unemployment rates during the 1980s was to undermine the force of the victim-blaming thesis in mainstream analyses of youth unemployment, shifting the focus of official and academic explanations towards the impact of structural factors.

The Search for Causes, Consequences and Remedies

Once youth unemployment had been set in place as the centrepiece of the 'crisis of youth' in the 1980s, the academic search for causes, consequences and remedies intensified. During the first half of the decade, research concentrated on the main explanations for youth unemployment which had dominated youth studies in the preceding years. Mainstream research focused on the psychological and social consequences of unemployment on individual young people, and the effects on self-esteem, mental health and self-confidence (e.g. Stokes, 1984). Those texts which acknowledged the possible role of structural factors still tended to concentrate on unemployed individuals, their families and cultural backgrounds, rather than government policies or the changing characteristics of local labour markets. Explanations for the cause(s) of unemployment often centred on the supposed 'unemployability' of certain individuals or groups, especially young people of colour or white working-class young people.

The most obvious clue to the use of the victim-blaming thesis is the concept of 'unemployability', a parallel concept to the notion of 'employability' discussed in the previous chapter. In Munene's survey of sixteen- to nineteen-year-old British women, 'unemployability' was defined in terms of 'motivation and realism in career choices . . . as measured by proven difficulties in finding a job, little or no qualifications, or waiting to join a pretraining opportunities scheme' (1983, p. 247). 'Employability' was measured by 'successful work at a clerical job or aspirations for higher secretarial position' (p. 247). In these terms, un/employment status becomes coterminous with un/employability: a social condition is constructed in terms of the psychological characteristics of the individual subject (see Williams, 1976). Structural factors are psychologized here, with the implication that unemploy*ment* is a product of unemploy*ability*.

Two explanations for the causes and consequences of unemployment have emerged from the mainstream perspective: the unemployment/ill-health thesis; and the unemployment/crime thesis. Using complex multivariate statistical models, these approaches have constructed unemployment as either a product of physical and/or mental ill-health or crime, *or* vice versa. One of the most influential figures in US debates over the unemployment/ill-health thesis has been Harvey Brenner, who related the official incidence of overall unemployment to government statistics on health, arguing that unemployment tends to produce ill-health (1978). Stern has turned this thesis around and argued that *ill-health* causes unemployment, but this analysis is equally questionable in relation to increased unemployment levels amongst the young, a section of the population who are generally assumed to be relatively healthy (Stern, 1982; Taylor and Jamieson, 1983).

Demographic explanations located the cause of youth unemployment in the greater proportion of young people in a given population or entering a particular job market, and to high wage levels. In Britain, the early 1980s brought a number of texts which argued that young people had effectively 'priced themselves out of the job market' (e.g. Junankar, 1987). The US equivalent of this theory rested on the supposed effects of minimum wage legislation, but it has since been established that these factors have only a marginal impact on youth unemployment levels (Freeman and Wise, 1982).

In the USA, the search for the causes and consequences of youth unemployment, like the rhetoric of crisis, focused around young African-Americans, especially young men. Freeman and Holzer for example, identified several factors which were found to influence the employment (or rather unemployment) of African-American young men. This list, generated from the results of an extensive social survey, included attributes of individual young African-American men, their family and cultural backgrounds and structural factors, avoiding any explicit mention of racial discrimination. The closest Freeman and Holzer came to acknowledging the potential impact of racism was when they expanded on the 'variable' entitled 'treatment of job seekers' to encompass 'black youths [being] treated *less courteously*, reducing [the] likelihood of hire' (1986, p. 10, added emphasis). Freeman and Holzer did admit that 'despite affirmative action efforts and *the elimination of blatant discrimination* from the job market . . . black youths still face discrimination from employers' (pp. 11–12, added emphasis).

Although segregation is now officially over, and the US has anti-discrimination and civil rights legislation, other research indicates that 'blatant discrimination' on the grounds of sex, 'race', disability, age and educational background continues to be prevalent on both sides of the Atlantic (Freeman and Wise, 1982; Cockburn, 1987). By the end of the 1980s, Reagan had undermined many of the legislative gains of the 1960s, but the denial of 'discrimination' remained an important discursive strategy in mainstream research on youth unemployment.

As youth unemployment levels rose during the 1980s the victim-blaming thesis began to lose much of its force in the face of growing evidence on the importance of structural and economic forces. The mainstream literature re-formed itself around arguments over structural explanations for youth unemployment, although it was notably reluctant to abandon the victim-blaming thesis altogether. Academics with a policy-making background began to express concern over rising youth unemployment levels, searching for the cause(s) of this phenomenon not in young people's supposed 'unemployability', but in social, political and economic conditions.

From the mainstream perspective, Ernest Spaights and Harold Dixon of the University of Wisconsin attempted to combine psychological, social and economic elements in their study of unemployment amongst young African-Americans (Spaights and Dixon, 1986). The responsibility for reducing Black youth unemployment was still seen to rest – at least partially – with young people themselves: 'black youth should learn to code-switch, i.e. use the language of the white culture to minimize discrimination based on cultural differences' (p. 385). Spaights and Dixon also argued that *whites* 'should be made aware of the black situation, and blacks' efforts to solve the unemployment problem' (p. 385). Their text implied that most young African-Americans need 'to develop basic job skills' and are unable to 'code-switch'. Spaights and Dixon were attempting to create a synthesis between competing models which challenged but did not totally reject the victim-blaming thesis.

The economic and political changes of the 1980s also presented a profound challenge for researchers working from the radical perspective, from classical Marxists through to youth cultural researchers. Some Marxists argued that the massive loss of jobs reflected a fundamental transition in the development of the mode of production: not an epiphenomenon, as social democratic researchers would contend (Jordan, 1982). The British recession of the 1980s saw employment levels decreasing in almost all sectors, with a decline in capital accumulation and the rate of profit. For Jordan, this meant that capital had to be exported to other countries with lower wage rates, especially those in the so-called 'Third World'.

British sociologist Pat Ainley considered the impact of rising youth unemployment on 'the traditional working class life cycle', concluding that the latter was 'strained but not broken', since most working class young people 'still pass . . . through its anticipated stages of release from school into a period of moving between similar "dead end" jobs with lengthened periods of unemployment that may begin as an extended holiday from school between them, eventually "settling down" to longer periods of work' (1986, p. 13). 'Working class youth' is treated here as a relatively undifferentiated category, whilst in practice the main focus in this literature has been on young white men. Ainley's argument was constructed around the potential threat which rising youth unemployment posed to working class young people's experiences of the TSW and the transition to adulthood, *and* to the challenge posed to radical youth research by these changes (see Willis, 1984; Wallace, 1987).

The 'crisis' of the 1980s affected the Left and radical analyses as much as traditional liberal humanist approaches. The class-based economic determinism of traditional Marxism had been challenged by the New Left, by feminism and by the radical gay, lesbian and Black politics of the 1960s and 1970s. The retrospective discourse formed an important element in the Left's response to this 'crisis' during the early 1980s, especially in Britain.

The Retrospective Discourse: Looking Back to the 1930s in the 1980s

As the 1980s progressed, the crisis (or crises) deepened, and researchers began to look back to the high unemployment of the

Great Depression for explanations and potential solutions. This retrospective move was as much about attempts to deal with the crisis facing liberal and left politics on both sides of the Atlantic as about a search for explanations of unemployment in the 1980s. A new form of 'historical inevitablism' (Taylor and Jamieson, 1983) sought to find parallels between the situation during the late 1970s and the Depression of the 1920s and '30s. The difficulties in applying theories developed during the 1930s to the situation in the 1980s arose from the various political and historical differences between the two periods, and from inadequacies in some of the 1930s' accounts as explanations for reactions to unemployment *at that time* (Massey and Meegan, 1982).

The recession/depression of the 1920s and 1930s was more serious since the workforce was smaller and the unemployment rate was relatively higher compared to the situation in the 1980s. There were no redundancy payments, and low wages meant that fewer people had any savings; furthermore benefit levels were so much lower that more people faced starvation and poverty almost as soon as unemployment hit. At another level, the situation in the 1980s was seen to be 'far more widely felt and profound' amongst young people, with major ideological and policy shifts in the areas of education, training and employment (Horne, 1986, p. 24).

In the social psychological literature, the early 1980s saw a 'rediscovery' of studies on unemployed men in Marienbad, Austria during the 1930s (e.g. Fryer, 1987); and in Greenwich, London, during the same period (e.g. Kelvin and Jarrett, 1985). Most of these studies had identified various stages in individual reactions to job loss amongst adult men, and many also examined the impact of male unemployment on local communities, including women and children in their analysis. The widespread assumption that unemployment hits women less hard than men and that employment is less socially and financially important for women was prevalent in the 1970s and 1980s, although some male researchers inserted apologetic notes about the relative lack of research on women's experiences in their texts (e.g. Fineman, 1987).

The work of Marie Jahoda and her colleagues in Marienthal tells us a great deal about the different academic and political contexts in which social psychological studies of unemployment operated during the 1930s and the 1980s. The team of Lazarsfeld, Jahoda, Ziesel and others formed part of the politically committed 'action research' tradition in social psychology which is far removed from the supposedly apolitical and 'objective' stance of many contemporary academic psychologists (Jahoda et al., 1972). Subsequent research on the psychological impact of unemployment has been heavily influenced by the *theoretical* aspects of the Marienthal studies, but their *methodological* and *political* implications were generally overlooked when this research enjoyed a revival during the 1980s (Fryer, 1987; one exception is Bhavnani, 1991).

The retrospective discourse has been less prevalent in the USA, although some texts looked to the 1960s rather than the 1930s in their comparisons. Joseph Bensman and Arthur Vidich of New York City University argued that unemployment was used as a means to control the inflation caused by the Vietnam War, a method that was eventually found to be ineffective (Bensman and Vidich, 1976). They represented Nixon's policies as 'a subversion of Keynesian capitalism through its own forms', and attributed the then widespread acceptance of such policies to 'the wish to control blacks and youth' (p. 207). For liberal and radical researchers in the USA, the 1960s rather than the 1930s provided the main reference point for comparisons with life under Reagan.

The retrospective discourse signified the absence of any alternative political means of dealing with the 'crisis' which the 1980s posed for much of the Left and for radical and mainstream perspectives on youth unemployment, especially in Britain. The sense of disorientation and assault on some of the taken-for-granted assumptions of the post-war period contributed to this phenomenon. Despite the growing challenge to the dominance of the victim-blaming thesis, a section of the psychological research literature on youth unemployment continued much as before, employing the discourses of criminality, disaffection, the clinical discourse, and the discourse of education and training to reproduce older arguments about unemployed young people.

The Clinical Discourse: 'Coping Strategies' and the Unemployment/Mental-Health Thesis

The 1980s saw something of a boom in research on the psychological impact of unemployment (e.g. Warr, 1984; Bresnick, 1984). The clinical discourse has continued to pervade most mainstream analyses, and many studies are conducted by medical and clinical practitioners working within hospital settings. Mainstream researchers focused their search for the causes and consequences of youth unemployment on the characteristics and cultures of individual young people, often advocating possible remedies or 'coping strategies' for alleviating the most damaging psychological and social effects of unemployment. Collective strategies for challenging the structural context of unemployment were scarcely on the agenda as the effects of unemployment were psychologized and individualized. Judith Gold from the University of Ottawa for example, presented unemployment as 'a modern-day stressor of concern to psychiatrists both psychotherapeutically and pharmacologically' (1984, p. 138). Psychotherapists are advised to be 'active, frequently confrontative, and immediate in responses' (p. 138) in order to deal with young people's feelings of discontent and anger over their situation.

The clinical discourse revolves around the unemployment/mental-health thesis, or the presumed relationship between youth unemployment and 'psychological well-being' or mental health in a male-specific framework. Andrew Donovan and Michael Oddy for example, examined the 'psychological well-being' of twenty-four employed and twenty-four unemployed British school leavers, both female and male (1982). They argued that unemployed young people showed 'higher levels of depression and anxiety, higher incidence of minor psychiatric morbidity, lower self-esteem, poorer subjective well-being, and worse social adjustment' compared to their employed peers (p. 15). Young women showed 'poorer psychological well-being' than males regardless of employment status, but for Donovan and Oddy, the big question was whether 'poor mental health is a cause or a consequence of unemployment' (p. 15). Their main concern was with *male* unemployment: young women's apparent challenge to their thesis about the negative effects of unemployment was afforded scant attention (see Henwood and Miles, 1987).

Mainstream research on the psychological consequences of unemployment used the clinical discourse and the unemployment/mental-health thesis to locate such debates around the individual subject. Whilst research studies might emphasize the damaging psychological, social and economic consequences of unemployment, and even reject the victim-blaming thesis, the onus usually remained on training or helping unemployed young people *as individuals* to 'cope' with their situation and to change it through their *own* efforts (i.e. by getting a job). Even if young people were not actually blamed for their own unemployment, the immediate solution to their predicament was seen to lie in individual efforts which would have their primary pay-off at the psychological level. Getting a job where few existed became a matter of *individual* perseverance and mental attitude in an uncanny parallel with the ideologies and practices of government-sponsored youth training programmes.

The work of British social psychologist Glynis Breakwell has been relatively sympathetic to the plight of unemployed young people, setting the psychological dimensions of their lives in social and political context (Breakwell et al., 1984). Breakwell argued that unemployed young people tended to internalize the victim-blaming thesis, trying to justify their position using pleas of helplessness, and often failing to develop any argument in self-defence (Breakwell, 1985). Breakwell suggested that unemployed young people could be 'taught coping strategies' which involve 'a reconceptualization of the causes of unemployment and a reevaluation of the moral standing of those who offer abuse' (p. 56). Such 'coping strategies' would involve the attribution of unemployment to 'the system', or market forces, rather than to the inadequacies of individual young people. This was a significant shift away from the concept of 'unemployability' which had played such an important role in mainstream psychological research on youth unemployment.

In Britain, a major set of studies on the psychological impact of unemployment during the 1980s was carried out at the Social and Applied Psychology Unit (SAPU) of Sheffield University, most of which involved traditional quantitative research methods, usually funded by central government departments and research councils. In the early 1980s, this group interviewed two cohorts of over 2,000 sixteen-year-old young people five times in the years after they had left school. Using standardized questionnaire measures of psychological distress and self-esteem such as the GHQ, they hypothesized that 'lower psychological well-being accompanies longer unemployment' (Warr et al., 1982, p. 207). In one group of young women, longer unemployment was associated with *lower* levels of psychological distress, and this was seen to be connected with their withdrawal from the job market due to pregnancy and childcare commitments (Warr et al., 1982).

Later studies suggested that there were significant gender and ethnic variations in the psychological effects of youth unemployment. Warr, Banks and Ullah reported that unemployed Afro-Caribbean young people showed 'significantly lower levels of distress and depression than did whites', although no differences in anxiety,

financial strain or concern over being unemployed (Warr et al.,
1985, p. 75). They also challenged the assumption that unemployed
Black young people (especially Afro-Caribbean males) were engaged in a mass withdrawal from the job market which would
explain their higher unemployment rates (Ullah, 1985).

By the latter half of the 1980s, some of the researchers who had
worked at SAPU and in other mainstream contexts were beginning
to ask more searching questions about the founding assumptions
of most mainstream studies about the psychological impact of
youth unemployment. Such critical re-evaluations reflected the
responses of the psychological mainstream to the challenges posed
by Thatcherism, the radical analyses of Marxist, feminist and
Black scholars, and the crisis in social science research and teaching, all focused around the implications of rising youth unemployment. In Britain, this response was most explicit in the
introduction to an edited text by David Fryer and Phillip Ullah
(1987). They questioned many of the assumptions which were
fundamental to the unemployment/mental-health thesis. Fryer and
Ullah made a careful distinction between notions of work, employment and unemployment; pointing out that unemployment is
a dynamic condition and not a static social position; and that for
many people, waged work may have damaging psychological,
social and physical consequences. Fryer and Ullah also highlighted
the tendency to refer to unemployed people as 'the unemployed'
in many academic texts, as a sort of uniform and undifferentiated
mass (e.g. Hayes and Nutman, 1981). They pointed to the massive
focus on the lives of unemployed *men* in this literature, with far
less attention paid to women's experiences of waged work or
unemployment, arguing that experiences of unemployment (as well
as waged work) can vary with class, gender, 'race' and region.

The main argument of the Fryer and Ullah text is reminiscent
of the strategy used in mainstream research on the TSW which
attempted to forge a synthesis between competing models, incorporating some of the theoretical and methodological critiques from
radical research into mainstream social psychology, and making
explicit efforts to avoid the tentacles of the victim-blaming thesis
(see chapter 2).

In a parallel text set in the US context, Phillip Bowman used
the theory of learned helplessness to advocate a discouragement-
centred approach to Black youth unemployment (1984). In a
survey of nineteen- to twenty-eight-year-old unemployed African-
Americans, Bowman asked about respondents' labour market

experiences between the ages of sixteen and twenty-four. He found that most remembered being active job-seekers, and non-job-seekers gave reasons other than discouragement for their withdrawal from the job market. Those who *did* mention discouragement cited labour market barriers, reflecting 'the reality of low job availability for Black youth' (p. 68). Bowman called for intervention programmes which recognized the psychological implications of looking for employment in a job market with few opportunities for young African-Americans, one of a growing number of mainstream researchers to challenge the individual focus of the clinical discourse, the unemployment/mental-health thesis and the prevailing emphasis on individual 'coping strategies'. For Bowman and others, the chief solution to youth unemployment does not lie in therapy but with structural interventions in the youth labour market.

In the research literature on youth unemployment, jobless (especially working-class) young people have been constructed through the clinical discourse either in the passive mode as relatively 'deprived', discouraged and/or psychologically damaged, or as underqualified and 'unemployable'. Unemployed young people have also been represented in a more active form as discouraged, 'disaffected' and 'alienated'. Such psychologized states are presumed to provide the basis for a rejection of dominant educational values or the disciplines demanded in waged work (Bhavnani, 1987). Where unemployed young people (especially young white working-class and Black men) are presented as actively defiant, this has usually been situated within the discourse of criminality, and couched in terms of the unemployment/crime thesis.

The Discourse of Criminality: 'Riots' and the Unemployment/Crime Thesis

The discourse of criminality constructs youth unemployment (especially amongst young working-class men) as a potential source of 'social problems' or 'anti-social behaviour' (e.g. Conger, 1979). Debates about the relationship between unemployment and crime form an important element of this discourse, just as debates over the connection between unemployment and mental health played a vital part in the operation of the clinical discourse. The impetus behind the unemployment/crime thesis arises partly from explanations for, and constructions of, criminality amongst working-class young men, and partly from the search for the causes and consequences of youth unemployment. Another version views boredom and the need for excitement as the prime motivating force behind young people's involvement in crime, operating through the leisure/boredom thesis (see chapter 4).

The unemployment/crime thesis implies that official unemployment levels should correlate with official crime rates in a causal and functional relationship, although there are complex arguments about the direction and nature of this interaction and about the validity of official statistics (Box and Hale, 1982). One version of this argument revolves around the unemployment/prison thesis, in which fluctuations in capitalist economies are assumed to require a supply of cheap and relatively unskilled labour which would form a labour surplus in times of slump. This rather mechanistic analysis implies that prisons serve to 'mop up' any labour surplus during periods of recession, searching for correlations between unemployment levels and penal policies to support this thesis. The relationship can appear to be impressively close, at least for young white and African-American working class men in some US contexts, although other researchers have identified periods in which US prison populations have *increased* during periods of economic boom (Box and Hale, 1982).

The central tenet of the unemployment/crime thesis is that the condition of unemployment (especially for those groups with fewest social responsibilites and least financial support) tends to increase the likelihood that unemployed people will become involved in various criminal activities. Being unemployed, especially for long periods, is seen to put people 'at risk' of involvement in criminal activities or with criminal subcultures. Becker's economic incentive theory is frequently allied to the criminal subculture thesis or the 'mixing with a bad crowd' argument (Cloward and Ohlin, 1960). This phenomenon is assumed to occur because unemployed young people are psychologically discouraged or depressed; angry and defiant; mix with a criminal subculture; need the money; or a combination of the above (Gold, 1984). Debates then focus on whether youth unemployment leads to crime or vice versa, as in the relationship between the clinical discourse and the unemployment/mental-health thesis. Young people are presumed to be inherently vulnerable to 'outside influences', so they are able to fit easily within the thesis that youthful criminal activity is often a consequence of involvement in a criminal subculture.

Critiques of the unemployment/crime thesis in US research around youth unemployment predated the 'crisis' of the 1980s.

The presumed link between youth unemployment and crime has been cited as a prime reason for governments' desire to reduce official rates of youth unemployment to within 'acceptable levels' (Taylor et al., 1973). 'Disaffected' unemployed working-class young men are represented in mainstream analyses as a dangerous potential threat to 'law and order' through the discourse of criminality. The radical perspective turned this argument around using the discourse of resistance to propose that 'disaffected' unemployed working-class young men *could* pose a potential threat to the 'status quo' which could be identified as a form of collective cultural resistance, and that governments used various ideological and political methods of 'social control' to defuse that potential threat (Hall and Jefferson, 1975). So mainstream and radical analyses have drawn on the unemployment/crime thesis in very different ways.

A specific series of events brought the unemployment/crime thesis and the discourse of criminality to the forefront of academic and press concern during the 1980s, especially in Britain. This involved the uprisings or 'riots' which took place in various cities throughout the early 1980s. Many academic and 'popular' media representations of the 'riots' identified youth unemployment and 'race' as central elements in these events (Gilroy, 1982). Conversely, much of the British research literature on youth unemployment represented Black youth unemployment (specifically amongst young Afro-Caribbean men) in the context of the urban 'riots' of early 1980s, often making connections with the US situation during the 1960s.

Even the relatively sympathetic approach of some radical researchers is restricted within the terms of the unemployment/crime thesis, since it is assumed that high youth unemployment exacerbates 'criminal behaviour' in the form of 'rioting', even if the latter is understood in relatively positive terms through the discourse of resistance rather than that of criminality (e.g. Kettle and Hodges, 1982). Such an approach, however sympathetic, feeds into a dominant representation of young Black people (especially young British Afro-Caribbean men) as potentially disruptive and criminal (e.g. Cashmore and Troyna, 1982). What is usually absent from these texts is any sustained examination of the role of policing strategies or insiders' accounts (Gilroy, 1982). Studies based on interviews with people who were actually involved in some of these incidents indicate that local people often united against the police; that police actions focused on Black communities usually instigated

such 'riots'; and that insiders' accounts include far more references
to the positive, even carnival atmosphere than do the accounts of
outsiders (Reicher and Potter, 1985).

Another far smaller section of British research has made connections between white working-class (predominantly male) young
people, crime and violence in the North of Ireland. Unemployment
appeared in these texts as a potential cause and/or effect of
working-class young people's subordinated position and relative
powerlessness. For Peter McLachlan, youth unemployment acted
as a potential 'trigger' for violence in the North of Ireland, along
with 'politicians, environmental conditions . . . the media and the
NI security forces' (1981, p. 285). McLachlan argued that 'violence
has become a normal means of communication and a mode of
play' in the North, particularly for young men (see Jenkins, 1983;
chapter 5 below). This analysis operates through the discourses of
resistance and survival rather than those of criminality and disaffection. The discourse of criminality represents youth unemployment as a source of potential danger due to the supposed upsurge
in criminal activity amongst 'disaffected' unemployed working-
class young people. The discourse of disaffection represents the
latter group as potentially dangerous as a consequence of boredom
and the lack of 'responsible' adult guidance on how to spend their
'unstructured free time'.

The Discourse of Disaffection: Youth Unemployment and
the Leisure/Boredom Thesis

The discourse of disaffection is closely related to the discourse of
criminality and the unemployment/crime thesis. Both sets of discursive configurations construct unemployed working-class young
people (especially young men of colour) as a potential problem.
Whilst the discourse of criminality and the unemployment/crime
thesis are specifically concerned with young people's presumed
involvement in criminal activities, the discourse of disaffection
concentrates on the leisure/boredom thesis and especially the threat
posed by the 'unstructured free time' which unemployment brings
(see chapter 5). The leisure/boredom thesis proposes that youthful
'delinquency' and 'deviance' is encouraged when working-class
young people have 'nothing to occupy their time', and especially
when they are out of adult control and surveillance (Clarke and
Critcher, 1985). In this context, leisure becomes a synonym for

unemployment and vice versa, such that the 'problem' of unemployed young people is cast in terms of their capacity for 'disaffection' (see Bhavnani, 1987).

The discourse of disaffection provides an important element in the official texts of government training programmes, especially through courses on 'social and life skills' and 'learning for leisure' (Griffin, forthcoming). From the radical perspective, prolonged youth unemployment is seen to break the transition from school to (waged) work, thereby preventing young people from attaining the adult status (and the adult wage) represented by full-time employment (Willis, 1984). The discourse of disaffection scarcely figures in radical analyses, since unemployed working class young people are more frequently represented through the discourse of resistance as rejecting the exploitative social conditions of the youth job market.

From the mainstream perspective, British sociologist Ken Roberts of Liverpool University has produced a wealth of texts dealing with education, leisure and waged work for young people, and especially the impact of rising youth unemployment (e.g. 1984). Roberts presented working-class young people in a relatively positive light, seldom resorting to the victim-blaming thesis. As Roberts argued, 'it says more about the distribution of ideological power than the real sources of young people's difficulties that unemployment has led to education and school-leavers being questioned more strenuously than the economy' (p. 5).

Roberts's work during the 1980s was marked by frequent calls for the 'reappraisal' of key concepts such as 'work' and 'leisure', and the 'rethinking' of traditional approaches to the TSW, leisure and unemployment for young people. The object was to 'reappraise', but not to *deconstruct* dominant notions of 'work' and 'leisure', especially not along the lines suggested by radical researchers (e.g. Clarke and Critcher, 1985). Roberts's texts still drew on the discourse of disaffection, since 'disadvantaged' working-class young people are represented as being prone to involvement in 'deviant' and 'delinquent' activities, especially if they are unemployed. For Roberts, the solution is not to blame unemployed young people for their 'disaffection' however, but to provide improved leisure facilities and employment opportunities (1986).

The discourse of disaffection constructs unemployed working-class young people, and especially young men, as in need of 'responsible' adult surveillance in order to make 'appropriate' use of their leisure time. The hormonal surges which are assumed to comprise an inevitable component of adolescence, combined with the 'naturally' aggressive energy of working-class masculinity, provide the foundation for this discursive configuration. The discourses of disaffection and criminality are combined in one of the solutions which have been proposed for 'dealing with' working-class male youth unemployment: the (re)introduction of National Service.

The Military Solution: National Service and Working-Class Male Youth Unemployment

Calls for the introduction of voluntary or compulsory National Service amongst white and Black working-class males have recurred at regular intervals since the Second World War.[4] This 'military solution' is presented as a means of reducing youth unemployment levels, instilling a sense of 'discipline' which is perceived to be lacking in working-class young men, and channelling their supposedly 'natural' aggressive energies towards socially acceptable ends. In feminist analyses, the military solution has been presented as a central element of the initiation into hegemonic masculinity (Russell, 1989).

In the USA, the military solution and male youth unemployment are usually discussed in the context of the military draft during the Vietnam War. Eberley for example, attributed rising US youth unemployment during the first half of the 1970s to the ending of the military draft when America pulled out of Vietnam, and to the subsequent drop in male college enrolments as a result of the draft threat. Compulsory National Service was ruled out as unconstitutional, but Eberley advocated a voluntary programme of 'guaranteed service opportunities' (Eberley, 1977). Eberley's arguments were echoed in January 1979 by the Report of the Committee for the Study of National Service entitled 'Youth and the Needs of the Nation' by the Potomac Institute in Washington, DC, and Michael Katz has produced a cogent argument against this report which placed their proposals in social and historical context (1980).

In most texts on youth unemployment the military solution appears as a subsidiary theme. Robert Mare and Christopher Winship from the University of Wisconsin argued that differential unemployment rates formed the most important exception to the relative improvement in the socio-economic status of African-American young men compared to their white peers between 1964 and 1981 (1984). Mare and Winship looked at various explanations for this phenomenon, including 'increased substitution of schooling and military service for employment by young Blacks . . . reduced work experience and disrupted employment for young Blacks at older ages as a result of later average ages leaving school and the armed forces; and . . . 'creaming' from the civilian out-of-school population of young Blacks with above average employment prospects as a result of higher school enrollment and military enlistment rates' (p. 39). For Mare and Winship, the military arena was represented as a potential *cause* of differential youth unemployment rates, rather than as a *solution* to this problem.

There has never been a shortage of wars (declared or unofficial) to which working-class young men could be sent. Britain was at (undeclared) war in the North of Ireland throughout the 1980s, with a short 'official' war in the Malvinas/Falklands in 1982, but these events scarcely impinged on debates within academic youth research. The increasingly interventionist foreign policy of the USA brought battles and invasions in Grenada and Central America during the 1980s, and the early 1990s saw both countries play an active and destructive role in the Gulf War. So the military solution to working-class youth unemployment continues to have a powerful institutional foundation. When allied to the discourse of disaffection, the military solution has had an impact in correctional institutions with the 'short, sharp shock' regimes for dealing with 'juvenile crime' in Britain. Arguments about the need to inculcate the necessary disciplines of waged work into young people through education and training have also operated alongside the discursive framework of the military solution. This alternative, and apparently more benign solution to the 'problem' posed by 'disaffected youth' is located at the level of educational and training provision.

Discourses of Education, Training and Enterprise: The Informal Economy and Youth Unemployment

The notion that young people's 'unstructured free time' is a breeding ground for 'social problems', especially amongst young working-class people and/or young people of colour, lies at the heart of the discourse of education and training. Specific groups of young people have been represented as 'deficient' and in need of training in the 'responsible' use of the enforced leisure associated with prolonged unemployment. By the end of the 1980s an additional discourse had entered government texts about youth training, especially in Britain. This centred around the discourse of 'enterprise' and the assumption that training could and should encourage those abilities and aptitudes which were assumed to be associated with 'enterprise'. This discourse marked an important shift in dominant representations of training for unemployed young people as a form of education for employment or 'leisure' (i.e. unemployment), and as a form of therapy or correction for 'troubled adolescents'. The enterprise discourse brought a move towards the representation of training as education for *self*-employment, thereby increasing the onus on unemployed people to survive joblessness and poverty with minimal support from the public or the private sectors. This emphasis on self-employment referred in part to the pressure placed on working-class young people to start their own businesses as a means of avoiding unemployment, and to the assumption that unemployed people should be made increasingly responsible for finding their own jobs (MacDonald and Coffield, 1990).

Both radical and mainstream perspectives have emphasized the role of the informal economy and self-employment in enabling young people to survive prolonged periods of unemployment (Griffin, forthcoming). The governments of Thatcher and Reagan were both at particular pains to subject the so-called 'hidden economy' to increased control and regulation, precisely because it provided a space for economic activity outside government and other institutional supervision. This regulatory strategy rested uneasily with the stress on encouraging 'enterprise' and minimizing state intervention which Margaret Thatcher presented as a prime virtue (Brown and Sparks, 1989).

In the USA, Henry identified 'two opposing perspectives' in the literature on the informal economy which he termed the 'unofficial or communal economy' (1981). The first represented the informal economy as 'an alternative form of work which has the potential to absorb unemployment . . . as a vehicle for entrepreneurial intervention, as the human side of capitalist enterprise, and even as the vanguard for an alternative society' (p. 460). This tendency is exemplified by the work of British sociologist Ray Pahl, in which the loss of paid employment can provide the opportunity for people to engage in 'new mixes of work' (1982, p. 20).

The second perspective views the hidden economy of unemployed labour as a integral part in the development of the capitalist economy, rather than an *alternative* to it. Henry argued that the informal economy has produced 'a market for cheap goods and services constructed outside the formal economy' which has evolved just as 'there exists a pressure towards less fulfilling jobs and unemployment' (1981, p. 461). In contrast with Pahl's relatively optimistic perspective, this approach views unemployment as creating a specific informal and marginal market sector in which poor people struggle over the exchange of cheap and largely inferior goods and services. Far from heralding a new and more egalitarian future, this will have particularly negative consequences for women and young people, who may be unable to 'plug into' such a marginal informal economy.

The discourse of education and training rests on the representation of unemployed working-class young people as 'deficient' and prone to 'disaffection'. Their presumed deficiencies may be seen as a consequence of their unemployed status, their 'deprived' family lives or cultural backgrounds, or their 'inadequate' personality characteristics. This potential for 'disaffection' can also be attributed to their status as unemployed. Education and training are represented as the primary means of preventing such 'disaffection', as well as alleviating the worst effects of these presumed deficiencies.

The discourse of education and training draws on several different models of education. At one level, unemployed working-class young people are to be 'kept busy' and out of trouble, off the official unemployment register and in touch with the vital disciplines of waged work and good citizenship. The chief educational model here is one of control and containment. In addition, the enterprise discourse incorporates a model of innovation and initiative based on the notion of education as a means of encouragement, confidence-building and even empowerment which is more usually found in radical analyses of education.

These two models of education as a means of control and containment, and as a form of encouragement and confidence-building, are united in the discourses of education, training and enterprise through the construction of unemployed working-class young people as 'deficient' and 'disaffected' and by the use of the victim-blaming thesis. Representations of the informal economy exemplified this contradiction, since the informal economy appeared as both a problematic source of illicit earnings for unemployed working-class young people, *and* as the arena in which they were expected to demonstrate their new-found 'enterprise skills' in government-sponsored small business ventures (Hollands, 1990).

The Discourse of Development: Broken Transitions to 'Normal' Heterosexuality and Nuclear Family Life

There has been considerable debate over the impact of youth unemployment on transitions to family life. Some researchers have argued that rising unemployment has broken down traditional and non-traditional (heterosexual) courtship patterns, marital and family structures, and this has been seen as a positive or a negative development, depending on the political perspective of the researcher (e.g. A. Campbell, 1984). Other texts operating from outside the discourse of development have suggested that such changes form part of a more fundamental disruption of the transition to adult life for working-class young people (e.g Willis, 1984). Another argument is that high youth unemployment has increased levels of family conflict (Coffield et al., 1986). Other researchers have emphasized the complexity of experiences of unemployment and family life, questioning the existence of any universal or straightforward relationship between the two spheres (e.g. Fryer and Ullah, 1987).

Where the discourse of development has shaped these debates, the transition to monogamous heterosexuality and a nuclear family is constructed as 'normal' and part of a 'natural' development towards mature adulthood. The power of this discourse lies in this recourse to biological determinism and to theories of 'natural' development which locate alternatives to heterosexual monogamy in individual subjects who are constructed as 'deviant' or at best as 'different' (see chapter 6). Academic concern about the impact of prolonged unemployment for young men has focused around disruption to their entry to full-time waged work, whilst anxiety over the move to 'normal' heterosexuality and nuclear family life has been mainly confined to the effects of unemployment on young women, with only a few exceptions (e.g. Wallace, 1987; Coffield et al., 1986).

The main focus of this concern is that prolonged unemployment might undermine social, ideological and economic pressures which ease young people into 'normal' (hetero) sexuality and family life. This is especially relevant for young women, since sexuality and family life are central to dominant constructions of adult femininity. This concern has been especially acute over the position of young working-class and Black women, since their family patterns are assumed to deviate from the nuclear family form which is constructed as normal (Phoenix, 1988).

For mainstream researchers, any disruption of the path to 'normal' heterosexuality and family life is viewed with moral concern and even distaste. In radical texts, and especially feminist analyses, what counts as 'normal' in this respect (genital hetero-sexuality and the nuclear family) is represented as a consequence of oppressive (hetero) patriarchal institutions, particularly for women. Feminist analyses have argued since the late 1970s that unemployment and employment (indeed the whole transition from school to the job market) has quite different implications for young working-class women compared to their male peers (e.g. McRobbie, 1978; Griffin, 1987). Feminist analyses deconstructed and profoundly disrupted the discourse of development as it related to sexuality and family life, questioning the representation of specific forms of sexuality, family life and femininity (and masculinity) as normal and ideal. The relative 'success' of feminist analyses in terms of their impact on the 'malestream' research literature also produced something of a backlash which has taken a variety of forms. Attempts to avoid the implications of feminist analyses have included a marked reluctance to examine the opera-tion of power relations around sex/gender (or class, age or 'race') and a determined adherence to descriptive studies of sex differences, sex roles or gender stereotyping. Another strategy is to question the existence of structural power differentials around gender and sexuality, as in Susan Hutson and Richard Jenkins's study on the impact of youth unemployment on family life and the transition to adulthood in South Wales (Hutson and Jenkins, 1989).

Hutson and Jenkins did not deny the validity of British feminist analyses altogether. They described such researchers as having different 'predilections and interests' to their own. From their own study, Hutson and Jenkins argued that 'female sexuality can be respectably and openly acknowledged within the context of an established relationship' (1989, p. 81). They found no evidence of the 'atmosphere of sexual threat, harassment and tension manifest in the work of Griffin, Lees and McRobbie' (1989, p. 81). Hutson and Jenkins admitted that this apparent discrepancy could have been explained by the different age groups and research issues covered in these two different sets of studies, but they also omitted to mention some important points. These 'established relationships' in which female sexuality can be so 'openly expressed' must presumably be heterosexual: lesbian, gay and bisexual relationships were not discussed by Hutson and Jenkins (see chapter 6 below). Hutson and Jenkins did acknowledge that 'the apparent equality of young women within the family can . . . only be understood in the context of a wider, generational pattern of gender inequalities' (p. 155). That is, young people's mothers did most of the domestic work in the household. However, they concluded that 'the transition to adulthood was, in some respects, surprisingly unstructured by gender. The major formal and informal criteria of adult status are not gender dependent' (p. 155). This misrecognizes the crux of feminist arguments, which rest on examinations of (and challenges to) the ways in which gender and sexuality are constructed *through* difference; how certain sets of social relations have come to be sexualized, racialized, and/or imbued with class or age-specific connotations; and the ways in which masculinity (or rather specific masculinities) and sometimes actual men come to be associated with power, dominance, superiority as epitomizing what is considered to be 'normal' (Bhavnani and Coulson, 1986).

The Hutson and Jenkins study is mentioned in detail here because it represents, in a relatively subtle form, the backlash against feminist and other radical analyses in some sections of British sociology during the 1980s. Their strategy did not involve an outright rejection of feminist analyses, but a careful presentation of 'different findings', a reasoned and apparently 'unbiased' approach, and several key absences, such as the existence of young lesbians, bisexuals and gay men for example.

Other analyses turned the relationship between youth unemployment and family life around, suggesting that becoming a parent (especially for young women) could increase the likelihood of unemployment for young women and young men. Several studies during the late 1980s examined the effects of unemployment on young *men*'s involvement in domestic work and family life (e.g. Lewis and O'Brien, 1987). Unlike the earlier research with adult men, these studies were informed (at least to some extent) by feminist analyses. Simon Lalonde, in a social psychological analysis which drew on Marie Jahoda's stage model of unemployment, suggested that 'entering fatherhood so early is one factor that impels many men into premature or permanent unemployment' (Lalonde, 1987, p. 16). British sociologist Joan Payne argued that marriage and 'the birth of one or two children raises the probability of unemployment among young men' (1989, p. 187), but admitted that this is a complex area to research, given the relatively greater invisibility of young fathers. These studies are relatively unusual, since the use of the discourse of development in debates over the relationship between unemployment, sexuality and family life has involved a predominant focus on young women's lives.

Radical Analyses and the Discourse of Resistance

If mainstream analyses of the TSW were thrown into crisis by rising youth unemployment, radical analyses also fell into some disarray during the mid-1980s. The focus on intersections between class and age in the youth cultures and subcultures research of the 1970s had tended to emphasize the capacity for resistance in white working-class masculine cultural practices (Brake, 1984). Heavily influenced by neo-Marxist theory, these structural analyses posed a challenge to the victim-blaming thesis which was so central to the mainstream perspective. They also tended to focus on young white working-class men, and to romanticize their activities as positive cultural resistances (see J. C. Walker, 1986a, and McRobbie, 1980, for critiques).

By the mid-1980s, this radical project was under considerable pressure to acknowledge the racism and sexism of white working-class masculine cultures; to include the experiences of young women, young people of colour and the operation of sex/gender, 'race' and racism as well as class and age relations (Brah, 1988a; McCarthy, 1989). The notion of cultural resistance was brought under critical scrutiny by the growing influence of post-modernism and post-structuralist approaches, as attention shifted from the analysis of lived experiences and cultural forms to include the role of textual signs and discursive practices (Willis et al., 1990; Roman et al., 1988). Yet the influence of subcultural analysis and the discourse of resistance remained, as indicated by the continuing search for subcultures of unemployment and for pockets of resistance to the harsh effects of Thatcher's monetarism and Reaganomics (e.g. Ullah, 1985).

Whilst no specific subcultures of unemployment were identified, apart perhaps from punk during the late 1970s, many researchers argued that the high youth unemployment of the 1980s had a significant impact on youth cultural practices, albeit as one of several intersecting forces (McRobbie, 1988). By the late 1980s,

some radical texts were arguing that the enforced leisure of prolonged unemployment brought financial constraints which undermined the development of visible youth cultural forms (Willis,
1984). There was a move away from the discourse of resistance,
since it was seen as too simplistic to deal with the complexity and
diversity of young people's cultural, ideological and material circumstances (e.g. Hollands, 1990), although some radical researchers continued to use it (e.g. Baron, 1989, and J. C. Walker,
1986b).

For youth researchers operating from a radical perspective in
the USA, the 1980s brought another form of backlash in the
debate over the so-called 'Black underclass', in which unemployment amongst young African-Americans and the embattled position of young African-American men and the 'Black family' played
a central role. This literature was organized aound discourses of
suffering and survival rather than the discourse of resistance (see
chapter 7).

The discourses of suffering and survival played a central role in
the work of radical Black scholars in the USA and Britain. These
texts are not engaged in telling origin stories about specific 'social
problems' such as youth unemployment, 'delinquency' or illegal
drug use. They are asking different questions about the social
context of such 'problems'; about the ideological, political and
cultural dimensions of agency in young people's lives; and about
the urgency of survival and the extent of suffering for young
people of colour. The pessimistic strand in the discourse of suffering is interwoven with more optimistic stories of surviving
against overwhelming odds with analyses of the considerable diversity within and between young people of colour (Bhavnani, 1991;
Cohen and Bains, 1988). Young men have provided the focus for
many of these texts, but young women of colour have not been
rendered so completely invisible as they are in much of the radical
literature on white working-class youth cultures (Mirza, 1992).

Absent Voices in the Research Literature on Youth Unemployment

There are many absent voices in the radical and mainstream
literatures on youth unemployment, including any major analyses
of the role of the sex industry as a potential source of waged work
for young women and for some young men (see DelaCoste and

Alexander, 1987). Another absence here is any radical analysis of the use of young people with disabilities as a cheap unskilled labour force in the various government-sponsored youth training programmes (Oliver, 1988). Perhaps the most striking absence in most youth research texts is the voices of young people themselves. The dominant discourses are mainly shaped and argued over by adults on their own terms, even in many radical analyses. Few academic texts are published or written with a youth audience as even a minority of potential readers.

Whilst the radical literature on youth unemployment and its effects on young African-Americans and on Afro-Caribbean and Asian young people in Britain is relatively developed, only a few texts have addressed the particular histories and positions of Native American, Chicana/o and Asian-American young people in the USA, that of young Greek/Cypriots in Britain, or of young Jewish people in either country, especially the experiences of young women. Other absences include the experiences of young lesbians, bisexuals and gay men, young people with disabilities, and a more critical analysis of power relations around dis/ability, 'race' and ethnicity, sexuality, gender and class as they are structured in dominance for those young people who are (or who are identified as) white, able-bodied, male, middle-class and/or heterosexual.

Relatively few studies have looked at young people's understandings and assumptions about unemployment, as opposed to the larger body of research on young people's experiences of unemployment (one exception is Breakwell et al., 1984). Only a minority of youth researchers in the area of social policy-making have dealt with the possible involvement of young people in decision-making processes. However sympathetic or radical, most analyses speak of adult groups: employers, government agencies, training programme supervisors, welfare, probation, youth and community workers, educators and parents (e.g. Fleming and Lavercombe, 1982). The notion that young people themselves might or even should participate in some of the key decisions affecting their lives has seldom been expressed. This indicates the degree to which the dominant model of irresponsible adolescence has permeated even the most apparently radical analyses. There *have* been exceptions, however, usually in policy-oriented youth work initiatives or policy-making programmes instigated at local level, rather than academic research studies or national surveys (e.g. Willis, 1985; Coffield et al., 1986; see chapter 7 below).

During the 1980s the Wolverhampton Youth Review Team of Birmingham, England, was funded by a Labour-controlled local council to develop an analysis of the long-term effects of unemployment on working-class young people in this West Midlands area which had been hard hit by the recession of the 1980s (Willis, 1985). Paul Willis and his colleagues in the Youth Review Team argued that lack of access to a full-time wage had an impact far beyond the immediately obvious financial concerns. The transition to adult status for unemployed young people is partially blocked, with profound implications for marriage, family life and leisure patterns, providing the basis for a 'broken *cultural* apprenticeship'. National youth training programmes were seen to offer only temporary relief from unemployment for most young working-class people.

The Wolverhampton study was based on a 1 per cent sample survey of all sixteen- to twenty-four-year-olds in the West Midlands city. Willis and his colleagues argued that 'the reality of long-term mass youth unemployment has produced a new social condition for many young people . . . which shifts the grounds on which theoretical debates have stood and renews the questioning of certain fundamentals . . . also replaces on the agenda just what is supposed to be the working class interest in state education' (pp. 155–6). Willis and his colleagues argued that the levels of unemployment amongst white and Black working-class young people in certain regions demanded a fundamental rethink of existing models. This entailed a transformation in the meanings associated with 'work', 'employment', leisure and family life, and posed a profound challenge to *all* theories in youth research. Secondly, Willis was one of the few (male) youth researchers to take on board (at least to some extent) feminist criticisms of the prevailing 'gang of lads' model (Griffin, 1988; see also Hollands, 1990).

Finally, Willis and his colleagues did not consider the impact of mass youth unemployment on working-class young people's position only in the 'public' spheres of education, leisure and the job market; they also examined (at least to some extent) the implications for the 'private' spheres of family life and sexuality. This study was relatively unusual in the extent to which the position of young people, and especially unemployed working-class young people, shaped the key arguments of the text and the associated policy recommendations, in direct contrast to the representations of the latter group as deficient, deviant or delinquent in most mainstream analyses.

Notes

1 Governments in Britain and the USA only began to collect statistics on unemployment on a systematic basis in the 1920s and 1940s respectively.
2 Official US government unemployment figures are taken from the *Monthly Labor review*, published by the Bureau of Labor Statistics, and the British figures are from the *Employment Gazette*, which is published by the Department of Employment.
3 Official figures for 'Hispanics' were only included in the US Bureau of Labor statistics after 1981, with no breakdown by age or sex. There is still no separate information available on unemployment rates amongst Native American, Asian-Americans and many other significant 'minority' groups in the USA. Unemployment figures for Vietnam veterans appeared fleetingly during the 1970s.
4 Both Britain and the USA have had compulsory National Service for certain sections of the male population at intervals during the post-Second World War period.

4
Bad Boys and Invisible Girls: Youth, Crime and 'Delinquency'

There has even been some renewed interest in some of the 'stigmata' of criminality described by Lombroso. Such minor abnormalities of development as asymmetrical ears, absent ear lobes, unusual head circumference and furrowed tongue, which occur with moderate frequency among normal people, are reportedly found with particular frequency among children who are impulsive and restless and likely to develop behaviour problems . . . If these minor anomalies are associated with corresponding developmental deficiencies in the brain this might account for the link with troublesome, hyperactive behaviour. (West, 1982, p. 120)

I wish to do for this form of delinquency [the so-called non-rational and non-professional] what anthropology has always done for other cultures: to make human what seems inhuman; to make comprehensible what seems beyond understanding; to decipher the meanings in acts and attitudes that seem meaningless; and to uncover the rationality and purpose in what seems to be the product of disordered minds bent upon lunatic acts. (Leyton, 1979, p. 14)

The two quotes above are taken from British (West) and North American (Leyton) academic texts which presented overviews of research on 'delinquency' at the end of the 1970s, drawing on empirical studies in which the authors had participated. Both texts in their different ways were attempting to make sense out of the enormous and contradictory mass of explanations for 'delinquency'. As one of the key mainstream sociologists of delinquency in Britain, West was highly critical of subculture theory, which for him epitomized the very worst of the radical perspective. He had far more time for the sort of biological determinism indicated in the above quote, in which 'delinquency' and its putative causes are defined in primarily genetic, physiological or endocrinological terms.

  Although he was more sympathetic to the radical perspective, Leyton also constructed 'delinquent youth' as Other (i.e. different from 'normal' young people), although not in the biological terms used by West. For Leyton, 'delinquent youth' were strange, irrational and exotic. Their mores could best be interpreted for 'rational' society through the voyeuristic gaze of the youth researcher cast as an anthropologist. The Otherness of 'delinquent youth' was seen to lie in their 'different' individual characteristics, family forms or cultural practices rather than their physiognomies. Leyton also managed to combine this voyeuristic gaze with the representation of 'delinquent youth' as basically similar to 'normal' young people, as akin to another tribe rather than another species of being.

These two texts do not represent all of the discursive configurations within academic stories about 'delinquency', but they do provide examples of the manner in which this concept has formed a central discursive construct for academic understandings and representations of young people and criminality. This use of 'delinquency' is not specific to the 1980s: it has been prevalent throughout the period since the Second World War in western academic texts. Attempts like those by West and Leyton to produce overviews of current research on 'delinquency' continued into the 1980s, striving to impose a coherent order onto sets of origin stories about delinquency, partly in response to the radical critiques of the 1960s and 1970s. These review texts defined 'delinquent youth' in relation to their 'normal' or apparently non-delinquent peers through a complex range of discursive strategies.

Telling Origin Stories: Theories of 'Youth' and 'Delinquency'

The academic literature on 'delinquent youth' arises in part from official concern over young people's activities outside direct adult supervision by parents, teachers or employers. During the late nineteenth century, such anxieties were reflected in moral panics over urban street gangs of (mainly male) working-class young people (Kett, 1977; Gillis, 1974). The official literature of the time viewed such young people from the perspective of an outraged but respectable bourgeoisie, and crime became increasingly associated with the activities of urban working-class young people, especially young men. The latter were represented as in need of 'protection' from themselves, each other, unscrupulous adults and the various 'temptations' of urban life. Young working-class women were constructed as one source of such 'temptations', as well as being seen as particularly (if not even more) 'at risk' of involvement in criminal activities, and therefore as *also* in need of 'protection'.

'Delinquency' is generally represented as a youthful rejection of 'normal' 'civilized' behaviours and values which were constructed as universally desirable. 'Delinquents' were an affront to the sentimental Victorian picture of childhood innocence which was presented as a universal phenomenon, although it was largely applicable to the affluent homes and schoolrooms of the well-heeled (and well-serviced) upper and middle classes (Walvin, 1982). 'Innocent' children would not last long on the mean streets of North America and western Europe. One of the central tenets of official concern over 'delinquency' was a forceful critique of urban working-class family forms, child-rearing methods and cultural practices as distinctly inferior to the 'civilized' bourgeois norm. Within such discourses the presumed superiority of Anglo-European middle-class cultures was reinforced through repeated comparisons with the numerous supposedly negative dimensions of 'Other' cultural forms. This theme is still prevalent over a hundred years later, although the 'normal' family has now narrowed to the structure of the nuclear unit (see chapter 6).

These panics over the 'dangerous classes' of 'delinquent' young people operating outside adult control combined with pressures from social reformers to transform the judicial systems in western societies, and specifically *juvenile* systems of reform, justice and correction began to emerge (Burchell, 1979). As John Muncie has noted: 'the birth of the concept of "juvenile delinquency" did not so much engender a greater humanitarian attitude toward young offenders, as justify an increased surveillance and regulation of both themselves and their working class families' (1984, p. 40). The emergence of this concept of 'juvenile delinquency' operated alongside the 'discovery' of adolescence discussed in chapter 1. The second important moment for the emerging ideology of de-linquency occurred in the 1920s and 1930s during another period of crisis for western societies. This time the crisis was one of recession rather than expansion, and moral panics over 'delinquent youth' focused on the activities of upper- and middle-class young women as well as their less affluent male peers, although adult anxieties were still concentrated on urban working-class young people (e.g. Kett, 1977).

From the 1970s and into the early 1980s, several attempts were made to 'integrate' the various origin stories about delinquency into one coherent theory. Most of these texts were based within the mainstream perspective, often with a distinctly ambivalent, if not overtly hostile view of radical analyses of 'delinquency' and 'deviance'. What follows is a brief attempt to set out the key origin stories about delinquency in the context of attempts to organize such stories into some form of coherence within the terms of the mainstream perspective. In presenting another attempt to 'make sense' of the numerous origin stories about 'delinquency', I have not set out to search for and establish the *true* causes of 'delinquency'. I am more interested in the discourses which are reproduced and juxtaposed within such origin stories as the relation between young people and 'delinquency' was re-articulated during the 1980s, and in the various responses to the radical analyses of the 1970s which emerged from both the mainstream and radical perspectives.

Biological Determinism

Psychological research on 'juvenile delinquency' owes a powerful debt to biological determinism, just as sociological research has its roots in an approach which constructed 'minority' and working-class cultures as socially 'deprived' and inferior to the Anglo-European middle-class norm (Muncie, 1984). The growing influence of the Chicago School and the fading force of the genetic definition of class has not eliminated the role of biological origin stories about 'delinquency' altogether, but the emphasis of such debates has shifted towards a focus on 'race', crime and 'delinquency'.

An article by Lee Ellis from the University of North Dakota in the US journal *Deviant Behavior* exemplifies a sociobiological or gene-based evolutionary approach to explanations of the supposed relationship between 'race', class, young people and crime (Ellis, 1987).[1] For Ellis, criminal behaviour stemmed 'fundamentally' from genetic factors, although social factors could also play a part, especially in relation to 'race' and social class. Ellis rested his thesis on a version of sociobiologist E. O. Wilson's 'gene-based evolutionary theory' of r/K selection (1987). Ellis produced seven *'universal demographic correlates of criminal behavior'* which were associated with 'serious victimful criminal behaviour' (i.e. 'violent and property offenses') from his own highly selective literature review of almost 500 studies. These comprised 'number of siblings, intactness of parent's marital bond, race, socioeconomic status, urban–rural residency, sex and age' (p. 155, original emphasis). For Ellis, all of these factors are also related to the r/K selection continuum, such that individuals from large families, whose parents were no longer cohabiting, aged between twelve and thirty, Black[2] and male, are assumed to be most likely to commit 'serious victimful crimes' and to be the most r-selected.

Ellis admitted that his theory could be seen as racist, if one defines racism as 'a belief that genetic and neurological factors contribute to racial variations and the display of many basic behavior patterns' (p. 164). For him the second and 'truer' meaning of racism 'refers to negative or supremacist attitudes towards members of racial/ethnic groups other than one's own' (p. 164). So Ellis argued that he could not be accused of racism since he presented 'orientals' as the least criminal and r-selected group, behind 'whites' and 'blacks', and since he did not hold supremacist views. Ellis's definition ignores the centrality of the biologized category of 'race' for racist ideologies (Zuckerman, 1990).

Ellis's ideas may appear anachronistic to those unfamiliar with the sociobiological literature, but his elision of statistical correlations with causal relationships between demographic characteristics and criminal behaviour is common throughout mainstream research on 'delinquent youth'. The evolutionary aspect of his thesis is more specific to sociobiology, and the latter has provided academic credibility for a range of racist and sexist arguments during the period since the Second World War (Sayers, 1982). Ellis's text is scarcely in the mainstream of the research literature on 'delinquent youth', but he cited Rushton's work which was published in respectable psychology journals during the 1980s, although not without considerable critical opposition (Rushton, 1985).

Biological determinism certainly retained its influence on mainstream approaches to 'delinquency' during the 1980s, and some former critics of biological determinist arguments had shifted their positions in its favour by the early 1980s (West, 1982). As West pointed out, biological (or in his terms 'bio-social') explanations for 'delinquency' have included a mixed and diverse set of arguments, from Lombroso's speculations on the physiological 'stigmata' of criminality to recent research on the lateralization of left and right hemispheres of the brain. Other examples include studies on the relationship between 'delinquency' and hormone levels in young men. There are clear resonances with biologically based theories of disability and the perfectibility of the human body in these origin stories about 'delinquency'. Whilst biological theories of 'delinquency' have come under concerted critical scrutiny in the mainstream criminological literature, they are frequently reviewed out of political context (e.g. Hollin, 1989). The right-wing connections and sympathies of some of these academics, and the uses to which their arguments have been put therefore appear as irrelevant to the 'objective' business of theoretical and empirical work.

The Delinquent Personality: The Psychological Dimension

There is no clear-cut break between biological determinism and models of social, cultural or psychological 'deprivation' and 'deficiency'. Constructions of the biological, the psychological and the social were intermingled in Cyril Burt's influential study of *The Young Delinquent*, which combined the discourses of the late nineteenth and early twentieth centuries.[3] Burt used the now discredited techniques of phrenology to argue from photographs of young men's faces that such physiognomies were typical of young criminals (Burt, 1925). Burt's allegiance to the recapitulation theories of social Darwinism were clear when he argued in phrases which might almost have come from G. S. Hall: 'the delinquent is to be approached more as an animal than as a hedonist . . . he [*sic*] is liable always to be spurred fatally onward by some natural force – a force which closely resembles those vital springs that animate the humbler brutes' (p. 495, my insertion). Whilst Burt's work might appear to be located within the realm of biological origin stories, he constructed 'delinquency' as a problem of personalities which might have an underlying biological origin, but which was exacerbated by 'inadequate' parental discipline.

Some origin stories which emphasized the importance of the psychological dimension followed Burt in attributing 'delinquency' to physiological or genetic deficiencies which produced 'delinquent personalities'. Others presented 'delinquent youth' as a product of 'deprived' families or cultural backgrounds, situating 'delinquent personality' not in the biological realm but in the social or cultural domain (see Rutter and Giller, 1983; Iso-Ahola and Crowley, 1991). In this sense, the psychological dimension operated at the interface between biological and social/cultural origin stories about 'delinquency', and the victim-blaming thesis played a central role in such accounts.

Psychological origin stories about 'delinquency' have also drawn on versions of psychoanalytic theory, and the psychological dimension frequently formed a bridge between genetic predispositions and environmental influences. Integral to these theories was the view of 'delinquency' as resulting from a *failure* of psychological development and socialization, in which 'delinquency' came to epitomize the antithesis of the social in the sense of an opposition to 'normal', 'rational' values and behaviours. In these terms, constructions of 'the criminal' and 'delinquent youth' within the psychoanalytic perspective are similar to those of working-class family forms and cultures through notions such as sublimation and the reality principle. On the borders of psychoanalytic theory are Reckless's work linking 'delinquency' and (low) self-esteem (Reckless and Dinitz, 1967), and John Bowlby's speculations on connections between 'maternal deprivation' and juvenile crime (1968). This latter work generated a boom in studies on working-class family life, which implicated 'working mothers' in the development of 'delinquency' and 'deprivation', incorporating psychological, social and cultural (but not structural) themes into the ubiquitous 'broken home' thesis.

More Stories of Deprivation: The Social/Cultural Dimension and the 'Broken Home' Thesis

The key argument in deprivation theory is that young people turn to 'delinquency' as a consequence of a variety of social, cultural, economic and psychological influences, all of which are constructed as negative. The latter can be defined in primarily economic terms (i.e. poverty); in domestic terms (e.g. the 'broken home' thesis); in psychological terms (e.g. the 'delinquent personality'); or in cultural terms (e.g. 'poor socialization'). Deprivation theory received a major boost in Britain during the 1970s when Sir Keith Joseph as Minister for Health brought the notion of a cycle of 'transmitted deprivation' out of the academic sphere into the popular domain (Rutter, 1972). 'Deprivation' was synonymous in this context with working-class (or non-white middle-class) culture. The cause(s) of 'delinquency', most forms of criminal activity, and a whole range of 'social problems' could be attributed to such 'deprivation', which was then transmitted from generation to generation through 'inadequate' family forms and cultural practices. Structural explanations and the impact of poverty were obscured behind the predominantly social and cultural dimensions of deprivation theory, and 'delinquency' could then be attributed to working-class and Black family forms, child-rearing practices and cultural values (Hollin, 1989).

Bowlby's work on 'maternal deprivation' fed into these theories which constructed 'transmitted deprivation' as a primary cause of juvenile crime. Bowlby's theory has passed into 'popular' and academic common sense as a means of attributing 'delinquency' (and all manner of other 'anti-social behaviours') to married women's employment outside the home (Bowlby, 1968). This did not coincide with Bowlby's original thesis, since he was a progressive whose main concern was child welfare (Hollin, 1989). 'Broken homes' and maternal employment still form crucial elements in lay and academic explanations for 'delinquency', despite the many empirical studies which have questioned such connections (Wells and Rankin, 1986). Family life plays a central role in those definitions of 'deprivation' which are used in origin stories about 'delinquency' (e.g. West, 1982, p. 117).

Stories of 'deprivation' and 'delinquency' emphasized the influence of early childhood experiences, (anti)-social values and cultural forms through the 'broken home' thesis. The key argument here is that once this link between family forms and child-rearing practices and 'delinquency' has been established, a causal relationship can be imputed which is akin to the operation of the unemployment/crime thesis (see chapter 3), although the 'broken home' thesis has not been without its critics (Rutter and Giller, 1983). Edward Wells and Joseph Rankin argued that the much-touted causal relationship between 'broken homes' and 'delinquency' 'remains unresolved and ambiguous' (1986, p. 68). They pointed to the lack of a coherent conceptual definition of the 'broken home' in the research literature, since the considerable diversity of household formations cannot be reduced to a simple 'broken' versus 'intact' dichotomy, and attempts to measure 'delinquency' have proved equally problematic.

Origin stories about 'delinquency' have set out to search for the cause(s) of a socially constructed phenomenon which is situated within the 'deviant' individual (who is usually working-class, Black and/or male), their 'deficient' cultural practices and/or family forms. This operates through the victim-blaming thesis, in which 'delinquent youth' can occupy the position of both victim and perpetrator. Such origin stories seldom construct 'delinquency' as a product of poverty, racism or other structural forces. Those analyses which have looked to social structures and, however partially, deconstructed the notion of 'delinquency', have

been relegated to the margins of the academic and political mainstream.

Challenges to the Victim-Blaming Thesis: Learning to be Delinquent: The Influence of the Chicago School

The impact of the Chicago School was belatedly felt in the
burgeoning literature on the sociology of delinquency which developed after the Second World War, especially in the USA. Social,
cultural and structural elements began to appear in origin stories
about 'delinquency' through a series of challenges to the victim-
blaming thesis (Brake, 1984). These theories did not form a unitary
whole, and the mainstream literature usually makes distinctions
between strain theory, control theory, differential association theory and cultural deviance theory (e.g. Kornhauser, 1978). According to strain theory, the 'delinquent' is assumed to be pressurized
into criminality in order to satisfy 'legitimate desires' which are
encouraged in capitalist consumer societies. If social and economic
circumstances prevent the fulfilment of such desires through conformity, individuals will turn to 'deviant' and illegitimate means.
Strain theory has a psychological core, since 'delinquency' is
attributed to a discrepancy between aspirations and expectations
which is presumed to constitute strain (see Hirschi, 1969, for a
critique of strain theory).

Control theories (a variant, like strain theory, of what Kornhauser termed social disorganization theory) drew on the various
studies of urban working-class (and primarily male) US street
gangs during the 1920s (Kornhauser, 1978). Control theories construct all individuals as having fulfilled wants, presenting 'delinquency' as a product not of frustrated desires, but of calculations
about its perceived costs compared to its perceived benefits. So
the strengths of internal and external controls are crucial determinants of young people's (especially young men's) involvement in
'delinquent activities'. Research informed by control theories has
concentrated on young people's principal social bonds in family
life, community and especially peer groups, since these are presumed to affect the main social controls on 'delinquency'.

Such origin stories are less likely to construct 'delinquent youth'
as Other, taking the form of social learning theories which located
the origins of 'delinquency' in social structures, the operation of
the judicio-legal system and young people's peer groups, whilst

also *de*constructing academic 'common-sense' notions about 'delinquency' which rested on the victim-blaming thesis. The work of the Chicago School laid the groundwork for the focus on delinquent cultures and subcultures which characterized the 'radical criminology' of the 1960s and '70s (Brake, 1984). The narratives of the Chicago School still represented 'delinquency' as a predominantly urban, working-class and masculine phenomenon, and as a rational response by individual subjects to harsh material, social and ideological conditions. A more celebratory tone entered the texts of radical (Marxist) criminologists through cultural deviance theory, which constructed white working-class male 'delinquency' as a form of creative cultural resistance to oppressive economic and social conditions, turning the tables on mainstream arguments through the discourse of resistance (see Hall and Jefferson, 1975). 'Delinquent youth' were not defined as Other in genetic, physiological or psychological terms, but as culturally different in a positive way which was represented as having distinctive political implications.

Radical Criminology and the Deconstruction of Delinquency: Tales of Culture, Structure and Resistance

The telling of origin stories about 'delinquency' has been most pervasive in the mainstream literature, but this has also shaped radical analyses, even in their reactions *against* the pressure to establish the cause(s) of 'delinquency'. The new criminology, also known as radical criminology, subculture theory or new deviancy theory, emerged in the 1940s and 1950s with various studies of urban (male) street gangs (e.g. A. K. Cohen, 1955; Whyte, 1943; see Cloward and Ohlin, 1960). The overwhelmingly negative stance of researchers operating within the mainstream perspective was rejected in favour of an examination of the positive or supportive functions such cultures might serve for 'delinquent youth'. 'Delinquency' was re-constructed in collective rather than individual terms, and a series of debates ensued over the relationship of (working-class masculine) delinquent subcultures to the dominant adult and white middle-class cultures (Brake, 1984).

By the 1960s, delinquency theory had shifted away from theories of anomie and strain, to interactionism and a (re-)examination of the relation between 'delinquent' individuals, their peers and society as a whole (Muncie, 1984). In a series of observational or ethnographic studies Becker and others questioned the distinction between 'delinquent youth' and their supposedly 'non-delinquent' peers, examining the construction of delinquent youth as Other (H. Becker, 1963). In his study of marijuana users Becker argued that 'delinquency' was not simply a product of inadequate or different socialization, but followed an identical pattern to that of non-criminal behaviour. Young people who engaged in 'delinquent activities' were represented as conforming to the values of relatively powerless and autonomous subcultural groups which would not label such activities as criminal or wrong: quite the reverse, since in some cases 'delinquency' was valued and condoned (Muncie, 1984).

The cultural conflict theories or youth subcultural analyses of the mid-1970s made more concerted efforts at deconstructing 'delinquency' from a (neo-)Marxist perspective. Labelling theory, which is usually (some would say inappropriately) attributed to Lemert (1967), formed an important influence on radical analyses within the new criminology of the 1970s, along with cultural conflict (i.e. Marxist or neo-Marxist) theories. Labelling theory stressed the influence of social and political reactions to 'deviance', coming closest to deconstructing the category of 'delinquency', and posing an overt challenge to the criminalization of 'delinquent youth' (Taylor et al., 1973).

So-called 'conflict theories' were forged by the political changes of the 1950s, 1960s and 1970s in western societies: the radical youth movement, Civil Rights and Black Power movements, campaigns against the Vietnam war, radical lesbian and gay movements, the Women's Liberation movement and the rise of the New Left. Debates about the relationship between structure, culture and agency rather than arguments over origin stories began to take centre stage in discussions on the active or passive orientation of 'delinquent youth' (Muncie, 1984). The focus was not on origin stories but historical analysis: how and why did certain young people, youth groups, and youth cultural practices come to be seen and treated as 'deviant' and/or 'delinquent' at particular historical moments? The answers were generally couched in terms of the ideological, political and economic role played by 'youth', and especially (white, heterosexual, male) working-class young people in a given historical context (Hall and Jefferson, 1975).

With only a few exceptions, delinquency research and most youth subcultural studies have been based on a 'gang of lads' model or involved a male-specific perspective (Griffin, 1988).

Ironically, the chance to move beyond this blinkered and gender-specific vision was made more difficult by the primary emphasis placed on class and the lives of young white working-class men in Marxist subcultural theory. Feminists' attempts to argue that gender and sexuality were at least as important as class relations, particularly for young women, were sometimes met with disdain (e.g. McRobbie and Garber, 1975; Powell and Clarke, 1975). But feminists did move beyond this boys'-own stranglehold to debate the possibility of feminist criminology, or a criminology transformed by feminism (e.g. Cain, 1989).

Another 'problem' for the reliance on Marxist analyses during the 1970s and 1980s lay in debates over intersections between 'race' and class (Race and Politics Group, 1982). This 'crisis' for Marxist accounts emerged most clearly in relation to the unemployment/crime thesis. A whole issue of the *Review of Black Political Economy* for example, was devoted to an examination of the degree to which economistic Marxist analyses could account (or not) for the position of young African-American men (Phillips and Votey, 1987; McGahey, 1987). Generally invisible in both sets of discussions, the experiences of young women of colour were lost in debates which concentrated on young white women and young white and Black men respectively (see Carby, 1982, for critique). Only with the growing body of research by Black feminist scholars during the 1970s and 1980s did this radical literature begin to address the intersection of sex/gender, age, 'race' and class (e.g. Ladner, 1971; Amos and Parmar, 1981). As in the literature on the TSW and youth unemployment, the 1970s and 1980s saw a series of attempts to 'make sense' of the apparent divergence between mainstream and radical perspectives on 'youth' and 'delinquency'. Such strategies generally took the form of calls for an integration between competing origin stories about 'delinquency' which attempted to forge a synthesis between divergent and competing models.

Making Sense of Origin Stories: Attempts at Integration between Competing Models

The extensive research literature on 'juvenile delinquency' comprises a diverse mass of origin stories which faced each other in overt competition during the 1970s, with an apparent stand-off between mainstream and radical analyses. Unlike explanations for youth unemployment, the victim-blaming thesis in mainstream research about 'delinquency' was not placed under such severe pressure during the 1980s as a result of economic or political changes, but it had been seriously undermined by the arguments of radical criminology, and especially by the deconstructivist tendency in labelling theory and by the discourse of resistance. Attempts at integration between competing models of 'delinquency' did not take quite the same form as the synthesis between competing models strategy used in the literatures on the TSW and youth unemployment, but the strategies of integration and synthesis both operated from the mainstream perspective (see chapters 2 and 3). Such attempts at integration subjected radical analyses to concerted critique, marginalized them or attempted to knock them off the map altogether.

Many attempts to impose some sort of 'order' on the diverse profusion of origin stories about 'delinquency' presented the task as almost impossible, before launching into just such an 'impossible' enterprise (e.g. West, 1982). Yet despite such difficulties, attempts to forge a 'new' integration between competing models continued throughout the 1980s. D. J. West's text on the longitudinal 'Cambridge study' he directed is an excellent example of this discursive strategy of integration in practice.[4] West admitted that the Cambridge study was atheoretical and primarily empirical: the aim was to collect a set of 'data' and to search for statistical correlations in order to identify the cause(s) of 'delinquency'. Decisions over which 'factors' and 'samples' (the latter all male, working-class and mainly white) to investigate were not made in an apolitical and atheoretical vacuum however, since West gave considerable credence to what he termed 'bio-social' theories rather than to what he called 'subculture theory'.

West attributed the 'state of flux and confusion' in social policies on 'youthful delinquency' to a clash between two 'exaggerated and contradictory stereotypes' which arose from varying perspectives on the potential causes of 'delinquency' (1982, p. 2). West referred to these as 'stereotypes', rather than theories or explanations, since he differentiated between the two as different representations of 'delinquency'. These two 'stereotypes' constructed delinquent young people as 'normal' and like all other ('normal') young people (e.g. labelling theory), *or* as different from 'normal youth' in various ways (e.g. biological determinism, deprivation theory). This concern with the *construction* of 'delinquency' is relatively unusual in such a mainstream text.

West dismissed subculture theory due to a lack of supporting empirical evidence and the former's status as 'an ideological weapon in the war with the Establishment', and he was only slightly more polite about strain theory (p. 123, quoting Kornhauser, 1978, p. 218). West preferred an 'eclectic approach' as most in keeping with his own findings. Yet after over fifteen years of the Cambridge study, West admitted that his 'origin story' about (male, mainly white, working-class) delinquency was still 'based more on guesswork than science' (p. 130).

Attempts at forging an integration between competing models of 'delinquency' have not always been couched in the terms of the mainstream perspective. Writing from a radical perspective, Kevin Minor advocated a critical Marxist analysis in order to produce an 'integrated theory' which could be used to guide implementation of comprehensive control policies (Minor, 1987). He argued that current theories of 'youth crime' explore 'etiological' and 'definitional' dimensions separately, and that each of these dimensions comprises three levels: structural, systems or institutional, and individual. Minor suggested that all three levels of both dimensions should be addressed in order to develop a comprehensive proactive (preventive) rather than a reactive (intervention) approach to the 'problem' of delinquency. Minor retained the origin story narrative of the mainstream perspective, and he did not question the construction of 'juvenile delinquency' in moral panics over young people, crime and leisure in contemporary western societies, unlike those radical analyses which drew on the 'new wave' of British youth subculture theory during the 1970s (see chapter 5).

Not all attempts at integration emerged from the dominant male-specific focus of delinquency research: the 1980s saw a series of non-feminist analyses of gender and 'delinquency'. Most of these texts were responding (at least implicitly) to feminist critiques of malestream youth research, and to feminist analyses of 'delinquency' and 'deviance' (Cain, 1989). Whilst feminist studies have seldom been concerned to produce any 'integration' with the patriarchal models of the malestream, non-feminist analyses of gender and 'delinquency' have generally operated on the theoretical and methodological terrain of patriarchal positivism. Such texts usually presented empirical comparisons of two (or more) malestream theories in terms of their efficacy as explanations for the relationship between gender and 'delinquency' (e.g. Raskin White and LaGrange, 1987); gender, 'race' and 'delinquency' (e.g.

Matsueda and Heimer, 1987); or gender, age and 'delinquency'
(e.g. Seydlitz, 1990).

Raskin White and LaGrange set out to compare social control
and differential association theories of 'delinquency' in order to
ascertain which of the two models could provide the most satisfactory explanation for gender differences in self-reported delinquency as reflected in a US telephone survey (1987). Gender
differences in self-reported delinquency were minimal, except that
young men were almost five times as likely to report engaging in
'acts of interpersonal violence' compared to females, and between
four and twelve times more likely to report more serious offenses
such as receiving stolen property, aggravated assault, vandalism
and grand theft (p. 202). Positive correlations were taken as
indicative of causal relationships, such that 'for all three delinquency scales, delinquent associates appears to be the most salient
predictor of delinquent behavior' (p. 203). Raskin White and
LaGrange's approach was couched more in terms of an empirical
'shoot-out' between competing malestream models than a strategy
of integration between malestream and feminist perspectives. Their
text was presented in the narrative form of the detective story
through which the true cause(s) of gender differences in 'delinquency' could be determined through empirical investigation. They
argued that gender differences in self-reported delinquency remained even after the control theory 'variables' were removed, and
that differential association theory appeared to provide a stronger
explanation for lower rates of self-reported delinquency amongst
young women.

Despite their interest in the difficulties of applying male-specific
models of 'delinquency' to the position of young women, Raskin
White and LaGrange's text scarcely mentioned feminist work,
citing the work of James and Thornton (1980) as well as Hagan
and colleagues (1985). Feminist analyses were marginalized in a
speculative final paragraph, which scarcely represented their contributions to the understanding of gender and 'delinquency' (e.g.
Cain, 1989). Raskin White and LaGrange managed to conclude
where most feminist analyses *started*, suggesting that 'perhaps the
gender–delinquency relationship is rooted in basic masculine and
feminine gender role orientations' (1987, p. 209), although earlier
in the text they appeared to refute this suggestion.

Raskin White and LaGrange's discursive strategy rested on a
distinction between 'political' (i.e. feminist) arguments and 'real'
(i.e. positivist malestream) academic theories. Unlike most feminist

analyses, they scarcely mentioned the impact of structural relations, ideological representations of 'delinquency', and/or the judicio-
legal institutions of juvenile crime (e.g. Horowitz and Pottieger,
1991). All attempts to forge an integration between competing
models were couched in the theoretical, ideological and epistemo-
logical terms of the academic malestream. The following analysis
of the key discourses in 1980s texts on 'youth' and 'delinquency'
should be understood in the context of such strategies of integration.

Discourses in Research on 'Youth' and 'Delinquency' in the 1980s

'Troubled Youth': The Clinical Discourse

The clinical discourse constructs 'delinquent youth' as distinct
from their supposedly non-delinquent peers and as psychologically
'troubled' individuals. This 'psychological disturbance' is generally
attributed to 'poor socialization', since 'troubled youth' are not
necessarily blamed for their 'delinquency': they are frequently
represented as passively subject to conditions of 'deprivation'. A
'cure' is seen to be theoretically possible, mainly via various
therapeutic interventions (e.g. Leone, 1990). The clinical discourse
overlaps with the related discourse of consumption here, since
'delinquency' is likened to a disease which can manifest itself in
various disorders of consumption such as drug abuse, eating
disorders, suicide, and so on. This is somewhat different from the
clinical discourse, with its more amorphous and psychologized
view of 'troubled youth' as 'ego-impaired' or 'disturbed' (Rutter
and Giller, 1983). In order to be dealt with in a clinical and
psychological framework, 'delinquent youth' must be accommod-
ated within the diagnostic criteria of the mental-health professions. The controversy over these criteria is reflected in debates
over the terminology used to describe various categories of 'troubled
youth'.[5]

The medicalization of adolescence has produced a whole range
of constructs which differentiate between specific groups of 'deviant youth' and their supposedly normal peers. David Spinner
and Gary Pfeifer of Brookline Community Mental Health Center
in Massachusetts for example, studied a group of 'ego-impaired'
young men, defining them as 'lack[ing] the ability to organize their
internal experience', advocating the 'process of culture building in

groups' as a means of developing relevant skills for 'structuring and ordering the internal and external worlds' (1986, p. 427). If 'an adequate holding environment' is created, then 'children learn to create cultural structures (ie. therapeutic group culture)' (p. 427). This was represented as preferable to the usual situation in which the therapist functions as an auxiliary ego. This text is relatively unusual since the 'treatment' of 'delinquent youth' within the terms of the clinical discourse is pitched at the cultural rather than the individual level.

Not all treatment programmes for 'troubled youth' are constructed in an uncritical relation to the clinical discourse and the medical model of adolescence, and most critical or progressive interventions have tended to emerge from sociological or social work contexts rather than from clinical psychology or psychiatry. Leonard Brown from the School of Social Work at Rutgers University for example, argued that 'social agencies often create barriers to troubled adolescents through their administrative structure and emphasis on pathology' (1986, p. 107). He preferred to operate from a 'wellness perspective' as a means of countering 'the low self-image of many adolescents who are experiencing social, educational and emotional problems' rather than the pathologizing tendencies inherent in the medical model (p. 107). Brown described an outreach programme centred on young people's leisure activities and based on collaboration between a family service agency and a public recreation department, which aimed to involve young people and their parents. This programme operated outside the psychiatric institutions in the field of social work and recreation, and whilst these young men were not constructed as 'deviant' in pathological terms, they *were* seen as psychologically troubled and in need (along with their parents) of 'professional help'. Once again, the focus was on young working-class men (and their parents) in a text which seemed unconcerned by the implications of this gender-specific focus. Brown's text transplanted the clinical discourse from the hospital and the clinic into the spheres of family life and leisure (see chapter 5).

'Deficient Youth': The Discourse of Education and Training

The clinical discourse and the discourse of education and training operate through the medical and developmental models of adolescence respectively. In the former case, 'delinquent youth' are to be cured; in the latter they are to be rehabilitated. 'Treatment' forms the conceptual and material link between these two discursive configurations, whether in training schemes, correctional institutions, community, youth or social work programmes, or via therapeutic interventions. The effects of various 'treatment programmes' are reported in academic journals produced by clinical psychologists, welfare workers, probation officers and full-time academic researchers, but discourses concerning education, training, the clinical sphere and criminality do not necessarily fit neatly within distinct institutional or disciplinary boundaries.

The discourse of education and training is most prevalent in texts which report on specific schemes aimed at 'delinquent youth'. Young people themselves may not always be the sole focus of such training, since the origin of their supposed 'deprivation' is frequently seen to lie in supposedly 'inadequate' or 'deprived' peer groups or family backgrounds. Snyder, Dishion and Patterson of Oregon Social Learning Center for example, investigated the relevance of differential association theory for young men's 'antisocial behaviour' (Snyder et al., 1986). They interviewed 210 Oregon families with boys in the fourth, seventh and tenth grades, examining 'family supervision', child behaviour and attitudes, and association with 'deviant peers'. Snyder and colleagues concluded that 'both parents' poor supervision and the child's association with deviant peers influence antisocial behavior, with the weight of influence shifting as the child grows up' (p. 29). Although the study itself was male-specific, the analysis is represented as having a universal relevance. Such 'anti-social behaviours' could be unlearned if these links with 'deviant peers' were broken, and parents (especially mothers) could be taught to improve their child-rearing practices in the direction of greater supervision, management and surveillance. A liberal democratic regime is the model here, in which parents control through being 'reasonable', whilst retaining the trappings of parental authority.

Donald Weber and William Burke presented an 'alternative approach to treating delinquent youth', in which the focus for change was 'delinquent youth' and their families of origin (1986). Weber and Burke adopted a 'teaching-family treatment model', which concentrated on 'recogniz[ing] the individual skill deficits of [delinquent] youths . . . and changing problem behaviors, [since] skills incompatible with a delinquent's inappropriate repertoire of behaviors' need to be identified (p. 65). Such 'inappropriate' behaviours are to be identified and changed within the context of a young person's family, following the formalized procedures of behaviourism, and despite the paucity of evidence supporting the presumed association between 'delinquency' and a lack of social skills (e.g. Renwick and Emler, 1991). Weber and Burke's report on their treatment programme is one example of the complex intersections between those discourses which are associated with deprivation theory. In this instance, the discourse of education and training coincided with the clinical discourse such that 'delinquent youth' and their families are represented both as 'deficient' and 'psychologically troubled', and as in need of the appropriate therapy and/or training (see Serna et al., 1986).

The clinical discourse, along with the discourse of education and training, stresses the need for the care and protection of 'troubled' and 'deficient' youth respectively. The discourse of disaffection tells more ominous stories about the threat which is assumed to be posed by 'delinquent youth'. White and Black working-class young people, especially young men, remain the primary focus of such stories, with correctional institutions playing more central roles in academic texts about 'delinquency'. The clinical discourse distinguishes between the psychological turmoil which is seen as 'normal' in young people, and that which marks specific (groups of) young people out as 'troubled and troubling youth'. The discourse of disaffection marks the boundary between that rebelliousness which is seen to be a 'normal' (even inevitable) aspect of adolescence (especially for young men), and that which could pose a threat to 'society'.

'Rebellious Youth': The Discourse of Disaffection

One of the most important discourses in the literature on 'delinquent youth' revolves around criminality and disaffection, such that (certain) young people are constructed as 'delinquent' or 'deviant' in more threatening and criminalized terms. This discourse incorporates several elements which are central to most origin stories about 'delinquency': the influence of peer groups, family forms, social 'deprivation' and psychological 'alienation' (e.g. Snyder et al., 1986). The concept of 'delinquency' is based on an association between young people and criminality, but the notion of youthful 'disaffection' has also been heavily criminalized (see chapter 3). That 'rebellion' which is assumed to play an inevitable part in youth and adolescence is seen to provide the primary connection with young people's involvement in 'delin-quent' activities and subcultures (e.g. Coleman and Hendry, 1990). The notion of youthful rebellion, especially for working-class young men, straddles the categories of 'normality' and 'deviance'. Owing a debt to the Durkheimian concept of anomie and that of alienation with its origins in Marxist analysis, the study of youthful rebellion within the mainstream perspective has revolved around the psychological dimension. Radical analyses have presented ali-enation and anomie as consequences of the social, economic and political organization of racially structured capitalist patriarchies, and such experiences would be constructed as 'normal' responses to these conditions (Foreman, 1977).

The discourse of disaffection deals with the central dilemma of research on 'delinquent youth'. That is, how to categorize certain young people (mainly young working-class men) as 'deviant', whilst they are living in a society which locates crucial elements of that 'deviance' within the boundaries of a glorified hyper-masculinity, and where conformity is feminized (Connell, 1989). In certain forms, 'rebellion' is both encouraged and sanctioned amongst young men. 'Rebellion' is represented as a personality variable which has connotations of clinical abnormality and crim-inal delinquency within the mainstream perspective, although few specific 'treatments' or 'correctives' are proposed in empirical studies (e.g. M. McDermott, 1986; see chapter 5 below). Within the literature on young people and sport, however, youthful (es-pecially male) 'rebellion' is dealt with in relation to the 'problem' of channelling masculine energies into more 'appropriate' activ-ities. In this context, it is assumed that 'rebellious (i.e. working-class male) youth' can be *trained* to channel their potentially disruptive energies into the relatively acceptable forum of compet-itive sport.

The Discourse of Muscular Competition: Sport, 'Delinquency' and Youthful Masculinity

The discursive connections between competitive sport, crime and masculinity have pervaded contemporary research on 'delinquent youth'. This association can be traced to the emergence of mus-cular Christian masculinity and the growing role of competitive sport in (young men's) education since the late nineteenth century (Springhall, 1986; Messner, 1990; see chapter 1 above). The masculine body is constructed through the ideologies and practices of competitive sport, confining 'fragile' feminity – quite literally – to the sidelines (Dyhouse, 1981). The ideal masculine body is also racialized, as reflected in debates over the putative 'causes' of athletic prowess in Black athletes such as Jesse Owens and Tommie Smith (Wiggins, 1989). Apart from 'exceptions' such as Fatima Whitbread, women are most acceptable as competitors in feminized sports such as gymnastics, tennis and the new Olympic sport (for women only) of synchronized swimming (Blue, 1988).

The discourse of muscular competition unites 'youth', sport, leisure, 'delinquency' and masculinity in a particular configuration. This operates in part through the theory of catharsis, in which participation in competitive sport, even as spectators, can serve to drain or channel off all that aggressive (and therefore masculine) energy which is assumed to course through the male body (e.g. Udry, 1989). This energy is seen as particularly likely to be expressed in 'delinquent' activities amongst those less 'controlled' groups and individuals who do not operate within Anglo-European middle-class cultural mores. The emphasis on appropriate forms of *control* over the youthful individual's psychological world, family life and social interactions which is found in the discourse of disaffection is equally prevalent in the discourse of muscular competition. The impulsive energy of youthful masculinity is represented as a normal by-product of the hormonal turmoil of adolescence which can readily be channelled into 'inappropriate' activities.

There is considerable research on the physiological aspects of various sporting activities, and the psychological correlates of competing, winning and losing for individual participants. Much of this work has a biological, biochemical or physiological focus, although some texts adopt a more sociological or psychological emphasis. Much of this literature has concentrated on sports which are traditionally male preserves, and which have maintained this position via the systematic exclusion of girls and women (e.g. Fine, 1987). Only radical analyses informed by a feminist perspective have taken a critical look at the discourse of muscular competition and the importance of competitive sport for masculine youth cultures and for the reproduction of (hetero)patriarchal power relations (e.g. Wimbush and Talbot, 1989; Curry, 1991).

The discourse of muscular competition is shaped by issues of 'race' as well as sex/gender, characterized by a focus on Black (especially African-American and British Afro-Caribbean) young men (e.g. Westwood, 1989). This is set in the context of the considerable official and academic attention which is devoted to origin stories about young Black men's involvement in crime, and the apparent threat which this group are presumed to pose to the status quo. The discourse of muscular competition presents competitive sport as a potential solution to the 'threat' which is supposedly posed by 'rebellious' or 'alienated' young Black men (e.g. Cashmore and Troyna, 1982). From the mainstream perspective, the apparent threat posed by young Black (and white) working-class men is to be contained through the therapeutic use of competitive sport. The radical perspective has tended to represent involvement in competitive sport as a potential form of collective resistance and a means of escape for young working-class men which could also trap them within a macho culture of athletic prowess (e.g. Messner, 1990; Gaston, 1986).

The use of competitive sport as therapy for 'rebellious' working-class young men rests on a distinctly western approach to competition and the use and control of the (masculine) body in sport. Michael Trulson adopted a critical view of this construction in a study which followed the progress of thirty-four 13- to 17-year-old male 'juvenile delinquents' through a therapeutic programme which involved martial arts practices (Trulson, 1986). One group received training over six months in the traditional Korean martial art of Tae Kwan Do; another in a modern form of the martial art which did not emphasize the psychological and philosophical aspects of the 'sport'; and the third served as a control group for contact with the instructor and physical activities. Trulson used quantitative measures of psychological self-esteem, anxiety, aggression and personality characteristics, arguing that the first group showed decreased anxiety, aggression, higher self-esteem, social adroitness and 'value orthodoxy', and the second group showed 'a greater tendency toward delinquency' (p. 1131). Trulson's text was critical of the presumed benefits of competition, since he operated with a reconstructed notion of sport which drew on eastern traditions rather than the western concept of sport as a conflict between muscular Christian masculinities. However, Trulson did retain the notion of sport as a form of corrective therapy and training for 'delinquent youth'.

The discourse of muscular competition presumed that masculine aggressive energies could be channelled into socially acceptable behaviours, bringing 'delinquent youth' back into the fold of 'normal' adolescence. Arguments about youthful criminality, 'deprived' cultures and family backgrounds and psychologically 'deficient' individuals also figured strongly in the various discourses of consumption which distinguished between 'normal' patterns of consumption and those 'diseased' young people who fell prey to multiplying forms of 'substance abuse' through various disorders of consumption.

'Diseased Youth' and Disorders of Consumption

'Delinquency' has been used to cover a vast range of activities, from truancy to arson. High on the list of delinquent behaviours has always been 'drug ab/use', or the use of illegal (and legal) narcotic substances. This literature was transformed during the 1980s into the field of 'substance ab/use' as researchers began to include solvents and food within their remit, and the panic over HIV and AIDS also shaped research on substance ab/use (e.g. Greif and Porembski, 1987). Whilst this literature is strongly male-oriented, the inclusion of eating disorders as a 'new' form of substance abuse has brought more young women within the category of 'deviant' consumers (e.g. McLorg and Taub, 1987). Young people of colour and white working-class young people have been of particular interest to researchers on 'substance abuse' (e.g. Wright and Watts, 1988). We learn little in these studies about the use of cocaine and alcohol amongst the white middle-class 'yuppies' of the 1980s for example.

Notions of lifestyle have been used to construct 'normal' young people as passive consumers of available goods and services, and/or as actively involved in 'choosing' specific lifestyles as (relatively) 'free' individuals (see chapter 5). In a parallel but separate literature, discourses of consumption have been used in connection with various forms of 'substance abuse' to construct categories of 'deviant' and 'diseased' young people as beyond the limits of normality (Iso-Ahola and Crowley, 1991). The mainstream literature about disorders of consumption relies heavily on the discourse of disaffection, that of education and training, and the clinical discourse, frequently operating through the leisure/boredom thesis. According to the latter, individual young people who are not constructed as unsatisfied (or as unable to be satisfied) by their leisure activities are represented as especially prone to delinquency, rebellion, disaffection and involvement in criminal activities and substance abuse (see chapter 5). 'Deviant youth' must first be defined before they can be 'treated', and it is therefore important to be able to predict just *which* individuals are likely to cross the boundary into 'deviance' and *why* (e.g. Bailey, 1989; Kozicki, 1986). The line of explanation in this literature directs us towards the 'deviant' or 'diseased' individual subject, their families and/or cultures, rather than towards structural factors such as poverty, unemployment or racism.

John Hundleby of Ontario, Canada, for example, interviewed 150 young male 'delinquents' on entry to a training school, and tested 196 public school boys on 'a battery of personality and ability measures' (1986, p. 129). Most of the former group were interviewed again three years later at the age of sixteen. Hundleby argued that 'extraversion, fluid intelligence, lack of acculturation, and independence proved to be significant predictors of drug use and alienation' (p. 129). Hundleby's text, and the many others like it, rest on the assumption that the use of illegal substances or 'disorders' in the consumption of legal substances such as food or alcohol denote deviance, disease and/or alienation. Lack of self-control and familiarity with the 'normal' cultural forms of the Anglo-European middle classes are constructed as key indicators of such 'deviance' (Gilbert and Alcocer, 1988; Watts and Lewis, 1988).

Once again, this literature has been overwhelmingly concerned with young men, and their sisters, mothers and girlfriends play the occasional supporting roles (Dorn and South, 1989). Some mainstream studies have reflected a greater awareness of young women's existence and gender differences, although they would not examine the operation of patriarchal power relations. Denise Kandel, Ora Simcha-Fagan and Mark Davies of the College of Physicians and Surgeons at Columbia University for example, interviewed 1,004 young people in grades ten and eleven of New York public high schools about their involvement in 'delinquent activities' and illicit drug use (IDU) during 1971 and again in 1981 (Kandel et al., 1986). They argued that 'persistence of illicit drug use is higher than persistence of delinquency, and is greater among males than females', and that 'delinquency among males and illicit drug use among females appear to have similar *etiologies* and to play similar roles in their lives' (p. 67, my emphasis).

Kandel and her colleagues also suggested that 'failure to enter conventional adult roles, ie. marriage and continuous employment, are important predictors of continued illicit drug use, but not of delinquency' (1986, p. 67). Both 'delinquency' and IDU. are constructed through the metaphor of disease, and 'deviance' is represented in terms of individual *failure* to attain 'normal' positions in the spheres of sexuality, family life and the job market. In the mainstream literature, such 'deviance' is represented in predominantly negative terms as socially and psychologically pathological: but not all youth research texts have adopted this perspective. Some texts have examined substance ab/use from a critical perspective, pointing to the damaging consequences of the link between manliness and alcohol use (e.g. Lemle and Mishkind, 1989), or presenting feminist analyses of the substance ab/use literature (e.g. Ettore, 1989).

'Perverted Youth': The Discourse of Sexual Deviance

Young women enter the research literature on youth, crime and delinquency in particular ways, and since representations of female 'deviance' and 'conformity' are highly sexualized, this operates mainly through the discourse of sexual deviance, especially in studies of prostitution. Another area in which the discourse of sexual deviance plays a key role is in research around 'adolescent homosexuality', which has a predominantly male focus. In the relatively separate literatures on 'deviant' sexualities which include prostitution and 'adolescent homosexuality', researchers frequently express a mixture of moral outrage and (more often) a voyeuristic fascination with 'perverted youth' (see chapter 6).

Academic researchers and liberal social reformers in western societies have long represented prostitution as a form of deviant sexuality amongst young women *and* young men in the context of female heterosexuality and male 'homosexuality' respectively (e.g. Cowie, Cowie and Slater, 1968). Throughout the twentieth century official concern over youthful urban crime has tended to (hetero) sexualize young women, identifying prostitution as the source of their position as potential 'temptresses' of febrile masculine heterosexual impulses, and emphasizing young women's status as potentially 'at risk' of being led or forced into various 'deviant' criminal activities (see Marchant and Smith, 1977). In many respects, prostitution remains the epitome of female heterosexual deviance in the contemporary literature on young people, 'delinquency' and sexuality.

Whilst those who work as prostitutes are criminalized and represented as deviant, male clients have largely escaped the attentions of academics, police and social workers (Lowman, 1989; one exception here is McLeod, 1982). Few publications have presented the experiences of sex industry workers outside the criminal/victim model which is constructed by the discourse of sexual deviance (see N. Roberts, 1986, and Delacoste and Alexander, 1987 for exceptions). In the mainstream literature, the discourse of sexual deviance has operated to define prostitute women and other sex industry workers as sexually precocious, criminal and/or as innocent, passive victims, depending on their class, ethnicity and cultural backgrounds. Radical analyses, including feminist texts, have challenged the discourse of (sexual) deviance, and although some have retained the concept of prostitute as victim, this approach has been rejected by some sex industry workers (see Carlen, 1985, and N. Roberts, 1986).

The literature on young people, 'delinquency' and prostitution tends to consider female and male sex industry workers separately. Texts have usually represented 'rent boys' as exemplars of 'adolescent male homosexuality'. Debbra Boyer's dissertation on male prostitution for example, was subtitled 'A Cultural Expression of Male Homosexuality', and she argued that 'prostitution, as a social fact in the life of adolescent gay males, is understood by them to be linked with their homosexual identity' (1986, p. 151). Once again, the clients and pimps of these young men have escaped the grasp of the discourse of sexual deviance (Lowman, 1989). The latter operates differentially to construct young female sex industry workers as exemplars of *deviant* female *hetero*sexuality, and their male peers as typical of 'adolescent *homo*sexuality', which is represented as inherently deviant from the heterosexual norm (see chapter 6).

Discourses of Resistance and Survival

Youth Subcultural Studies and Radical Analyses

In radical subculture theory, the dominant discourse has constructed 'delinquency' as a reflection of resistance to dominant social values, cultural practices, ideological and material conditions. The discursive configurations of the mainstream perspective on 'delinquency' turn the ideological spotlight onto 'deviant' (mainly white and Black working-class male) young people. In the radical perspective, discourses of resistance and survival challenged that negative definition of youthful deviance, and as Mike Brake has argued, they reinforced the notion that 'subcultures call into question the adequacy of the dominant cultural ideology' (1984, p. 21).

The work of many radical Black scholars has represented young African-Americans (especially, but not only young men) as in danger for their lives in contemporary US society. Survival is the key issue here, and survival can signify a form of resistance in a genocidal racist culture. This is in marked contrast to the work of many radical (and mainstream) white researchers, which has tended to represent young people of colour (especially young African-American or British Afro-Caribbean men) as exotic, super-cool and/or potentially dangerous (e.g. Cashmore and Troyna, 1982). In the former texts, Black researchers cast themselves as parents, guardians or counsellors, rather than voyeuristic observers or as 'one of the lads', which are the dominant positions of radical white male researchers. Young people are definitely not con-structed as 'problems' in this context: dominant social and eco-nomic forces are seen to pose the main threat to young people of colour, rather than vice versa. The sense of impending doom intensified in the radical US literature as Reagan's welfare cuts hit home amongst America's poor and Black communities (Duster, 1988; see chapter 7 below).

'Hustling Youth': Crime as Work

Young men of colour, especially African-Americans and British Afro-Caribbeans, are over-represented in the official crime figures and in correctional institutions. The mainstream literature has focused on the supposedly 'deviant' or 'deficient' characteristics of individual young men, their family structures and/or cultural back-grounds. The radical literature has taken a closer look at the role of policing strategies, the judicial system and the welfare services (e.g. M. A. Walker, 1988; Gilroy, 1987). One example of the pervasive link between the view of crime as a form of 'work' for young African-American men is the 1987 issue of the *Review of Black Political Economy* on 'race and crime'. The journal included a number of landmark analyses and contemporary 'frontier ar-ticles' which addressed themselves to the question of 'precisely what it is about . . . labor markets that would lead to the nearly tripling of the black incarcerated population between 1970 and '86?' (Myers, 1987, p. 15).[6]

As Myers pointed out in the introduction to this special issue, 'there are now more unanswered questions than previous writers . . . believed there were were to be asked' (p. 15). David Good and Maureen Pirog-Good for example, presented a complex micro-economic model of crime and employment which reinforced Du-Bois's original proposition that 'criminal involvement among blacks is intimately linked to labor market outcomes' (1987, p. 14). Good and Pirog-Good used number of arrests as their indicator of crime participation, although the latter is in itself subject to variation according to 'race' (M. A. Walker, 1988). By contrast Phillips and Votey examined the involvement of young people in crime within a wider framework which included the effects of deterrence measures, economic opportunities or their lack, investment in education, and various factors intended to reflect moral compliance with the law (Phillips and Votey, 1987). These articles employed the quantitative techniques and model building methods derived from the mathematical format of economic theory.

Involvement in criminal activities has been represented as a form of work for 'hustling youth' through the discourses of resistance and survival, often located in debates over the role of the hidden or informal economy at a time of high youth unemployment (see chapter 3). Within the mainstream perspective, 'hustling youth' would be represented in predominantly negative terms as a potential threat to the 'real' economy, and as 'delinquent' or 'deficient'. From a radical perspective, involvement in criminal activities such as robbery or handling stolen goods is more likely to be constructed as a matter of resistance and especially survival for oppressed working-class young people.

In contrast to the tendency to romanticize the 'resistances' of young white working-class men amongst radical white scholars, radical analyses by Black scholars have tended to adopt a more sceptical view of the liberatory potential of the macho 'hustler' image. John Gaston for example, argued that popular culture and professional sports had a potentially negative influence on young African-Americans (especially males). The media have fostered a 'cool' role model associated with 'hustler' values, with which young Black men can readily identify. Such images have encouraged an orientation to 'just getting by', fostering 'an unrealistic view of reality' (1986, p. 369). Once young African-American men realize that they have few skills with which to earn money, this leads to 'poor self-esteem'. Media portrayal of professional sports enters the picture at this point, fuelling young men's fantasies of becoming stars.

Gaston suggested that such young men would come to treat high school 'as a step toward the National Basketball Association rather than as a means of obtaining education' (p. 369). He interviewed (or rather 'profiled') 'former athletes who were victims of this myopia', concluding that 'the black community must demand quality education for young black males in order to protect the future of the black family' (p. 369). Gaston did not consider the implications of his analysis for young Black women, whether in sports, in school or in family life, and as in so much youth research literature from both the mainstream and radical perspectives, young women of colour are obscured behind a focus on *either* young Black men *or* young white women (Carby, 1982).

One difficulty with this type of critique of a macho 'hustler' culture among young men of colour is that the latter (or the Black community as a whole) can be represented as at fault for 'failing' to find an adequate response to white racism. The onus is placed on Black communities, and especially young people of colour, to resist and survive existing systems of domination. In addition, such texts usually take a model of 'normal' stable marriage and family life as evidence of a 'satisfactory' cultural response to racism. There is no recognition that 'normal' heterosexual relationships and traditional family life may not be unequivocally beneficial for women of colour, as many Black feminists have argued (e.g. Davis and Davis, 1986). Feminist analyses have challenged the male focus and the male norm found in most mainstream and radical research on 'delinquent youth'.

Invisible Girls: Upsetting the Masculine Applecart

The block on any acknowledgement of the gendered construction of 'delinquency' and 'deviance' in the academic literature had its counterpart in the various agencies and institutions which have been set up to deal with 'delinquent youth'. Social work, the probation and prison services, youth and community work, the education and welfare systems have all taken the 'malestream' approach to 'delinquency' and 'deviance' for granted. Young men were assumed to be actively (and often aggressively) 'deviant' and frequently seen as a threat to the status quo. Young women, however, were usually treated as passively 'at risk' and in need of protection from 'society' *or* as actively 'deviant', usually in sexual terms (e.g. Petrie, 1986). In stories about delinquency, hearth, home, family life and the domestic sphere usually represent the feminine and the social, whilst life on the streets (not shopping, but 'hanging around') comes to signify masculinity and the anti-social (e.g. Baron, 1989). Feminist analyses have presented a profound critique of this model.

From the mid-1970s, feminist researchers and 'practitioners' in various youth-related agencies began to challenge the male focus of most research on 'delinquent youth', and to render the position of girls and young women more visible (Morris, 1987). Young women themselves also organized in schools and youth projects (Hemmings, 1982). For young women (and researchers) of colour, these struggles often took the form of oppositions to racism *and* sexism (e.g. Bryan et al., 1985).

Feminist youth researchers and criminologists had a powerful impact throughout the 1980s, both on the patronizing complacency of traditional 'malestream' youth research, and on the tendency to romanticize the macho sexism and racism of the 'lads' in some Marxist analyses and other radical youth cultural approaches (Cain, 1989). By the 1990s, (some) feminist researchers were con-solidating their arguments, defending gains at a time of right-wing backlash, and moving feminist analyses and practices beyond a narrow focus on age and sex/gender (or sex/gender and class) to examine the dynamics of young people's lives in racially structured capitalist patriarchy (Mirza, 1992; Bhavnani, 1991).

Several tendencies emerge with clarity from the vast and dis-parate literature on 'delinquency'. Firstly, the focus on young white working-class, African-American and/or British Afro-Caribbean *men* is almost overwhelming. This pathologizes these groups and obscures the experiences and often the very existence of young women, their white/WASP middle-class peers, and other less pri-vileged minorities such as British Asian young people (P. Cohen and Bains, 1988); young Native Americans (Watts and Lewis, 1988); and Chicana/o young people (Rodriguez, 1986; Gilbert and Alcocer, 1988). Secondly, there is frequently a constructed social distance between 'deviant youth' and adult youth researchers, whether on the grounds of age, 'race', class, culture, ethnicity or educational background, which is especially common in the main-stream literature. Finally, there is an acute and pervasive tension between representations of 'delinquent [or deviant] youth' con-structed as Other (i.e. exotic, criminal), and as 'normal', or indis-tinguishable from their 'non-delinquent' peers.

Stories of threat are characterized by the construction of (certain) young people as potentially dangerous *and* by a liberal concern to 'protect' the helpless from 'temptation' by unscrupulous others.[7] Such concern to 'protect' helpless young people from themselves, their peers and their own 'deviant' cultural origins runs alongside a more authoritarian thesis about the need to punish wrongdoers (Burchell, 1979). Stories about 'delinquency' juggle the contradictory representations of young people as victims (of other 'delinquent youth', environmental conditions, physiological and/or psychological characteristics), and perpetrators (of 'delinquent activities'). The absences are equally significant here. We seldom read of the need to 'protect' working-class young people or young people of colour from the periodic or sustained use of harsh policing strategies directed at certain groups of young people (one exception is Gilroy, 1987).

The three main influences which have shaped this analysis, feminism, post-structuralism and Gramsci's notion of hegemony, can all be identified in the above critique (see chapter 1). Feminist analyses of the male norm in most research on 'delinquent youth' began to move towards broader arguments about intersections between sex/gender, 'race' and class whilst challenging the dominant 'gang of lads' model. The victim-blaming thesis which is so central to the mainstream perspective locates a certain set of cultural mores and individual attributes as dominant and normal, thereby relegating everything (and everyone) outside the domain of Anglo-European middle-class culture to the status of 'deviant', 'deficient' or totally invisible. Finally, post-structuralism enables us to examine the various discursive configurations through which distinctions between 'delinquent' and 'normal' young people are established and maintained.

Notes

1 This journal is not a strictly sociobiological journal: it usually publishes articles which are more sociological in approach.

2 Presumably Ellis was referring to people of African origin or descent here, although he did not use those terms.

3 This study of young white working-class men was first published in 1925, with a revised edition in 1945.

4 This study was named not after the site of the research (which was carried out in London), but after West's academic base at Cambridge University's Institute of Criminology. Initially supported by funding from the British

government's Home Office, the study involved repeated rounds of inter-views with a cohort of young men aged eight to nine in 1961, through to 1976 when they were aged twenty-three and twenty-four (West, 1982).

5 Most relevant here are debates in the clinical psychology and psychiatric literatures over the definitions of various 'disruptive behaviour disorders' amongst children and adolescents in terms of the official diagnostic criteria used by clinical practitioners, known as DSM-III and III-R (Cantwell and Baker, 1988).

6 These landmark articles included W. E. B. DuBois' examination of crime in Philadelphia (first published in 1899) and an extract from Gunnar Myrdal's influential text on inequality and justice (first published 1944).

7 I have found Donna Haraway's analysis of intersections of gender, 'race' and science in the development of primatology valuable here for its examination of a different set of 'origin stories', stories of danger and constructions of the exotic (Haraway, 1989).

5
The Threat of 'Unstructured Free Time': Young People and Leisure in the 1980s

That's the key to any good gang: the guy who's good at fighting, the guy who's good at talking, the guy who's good at sneaking in under the others and getting someone in the crotch, and the flash one who looks good and pulls the birds. (Martin Kemp, 'Spandau Ballet', *New Musical Express*, 24 January 1987)

The above quote by British pop star-turned actor Martin Kemp exemplifies the overwhelmingly male and heterosexual focus of most research on young people's leisure in the 1970s and 1980s from both the mainstream and radical perspectives. It exemplifies what I have called the 'gang of lads' model, on which much of this work is based (Griffin, 1988). From the mainstream perspective the 'gang of lads' represent the potential threat posed by 'delinquent youth', whilst from the radical perspective the 'good gang' is understood primarily through the discourse of resistance.

There is an extensive research literature which deals with young people's time outside education and waged work. In the 1980s, the predominant theme in this literature was youth unemployment, especially its possible causes and consequences (see chapter 3). The wealth of studies concerned with youth unemployment represented the latter as a form of enforced 'leisure', and young people's relationship to leisure was commonly articulated around the concept of 'delinquency' and 'deviance' (see chapter 4). These various research literatures overlap, and the boundaries between them are often a matter of discursive convenience. Such boundaries reflect 'fault-lines' generated by research funding priorities, government policy initiatives and the segmentation between state departments and research disciplines.[1] For the purposes of this chapter I have concentrated on those texts with a *predominant* focus on young people and leisure, as opposed to a primary concern with youth unemployment or young people and criminality.

Theories of 'Youth' and 'Leisure': A Problem of Definition

Those sites in which young people (especially if they are working-class, Black and male) are outside adult (especially white middle-class male) supervision lie beyond the confines of the schoolroom and the (waged) workplace, so young people's 'leisure' activities have had a special place in academic stories about 'delinquent youth'. I am not arguing that the research literature on 'delinquency' exists solely as a result of panics over what certain groups of young people might get up to outside adult institutional controls: the picture is more complex than the functional slant of this social control thesis would imply.

Panics over young people's uses of leisure and their supposed 'delinquency' or 'deviance' have appeared in different social and political contexts throughout the post-Second world war period. Sometimes the focus is on the activities of specific youth subcultural groups (e.g. Rastafarians, punks, Beastie Boys fans); sometimes on leisure activities which are associated with specific subcultures (e.g. 'drug abuse'; 'Acid House parties'; stealing badges from VW cars). The context is always crucial here: such panics are never entirely random events and they frequently reflect crises or contradictions in wider structural relations (P. Cohen, 1986; see chapter 1 above).

In the 1950s several texts attributed the apparently new and horrifying youth cultural phenomena to the post-war boom which had brought increased prosperity and spending power to white working-class young people, creating a target market of 'teenage consumers' (Abrams, 1959). Research around young people and leisure is characterized by a tension between mainstream and radical perspectives which reached a particularly acute state in the decade of Thatcher and Reagan. This chapter, like others in this book, traces the path of that tension as different elements of mainstream and radical perspectives struggled to come to terms with the political, economic and ideological climate of the 1980s.

The definition of 'leisure' is no more straightforward than that of 'delinquency'. Mainstream approaches to 'delinquent youth' have searched for the causes of this phenomenon and resisted all attempts to deconstruct the concept of 'delinquency'. Mainstream perspectives on 'leisure' have been less reluctant to admit the disputed nature of this concept, and origin stories are not the dominant narrative form in the research literature on young people and leisure. The crisis for research on 'delinquent youth' in the 1970s and 1980s revolved around challenges to the victim-blaming thesis and attempts to deconstruct the concept of 'delinquency'. For the literature on young people and leisure, the crisis centred around the relation between 'work' and 'leisure', concepts which were brought into question during the 1970s by rising unemployment, feminist analyses of women's unpaid domestic work as anything but 'leisure', and changing ideologies of consumerism and patterns of consumption (Deem, 1989; Tomlinson, 1990).

The various social, political and economic changes of the 1970s and 1980s threw leisure studies into some disarray, but both mainstream and radical perspectives had managed to reorientate themselves to some extent by the end of the 1980s. This disarray stemmed as much from feminist and Marxist critiques of traditional notions of 'work' and 'leisure' as from changes in young people's experiences in relation to these disputed and transformed categories. For radical analyses, this was only partly a crisis of control: it was also a conceptual crisis, as young people and rising unemployment exploded traditional notions of 'work', 'leisure' and the basis of political organization (P. Cohen, 1986; Willis et al., 1990). Feminist analyses in particular turned everything upside down, upsetting the masculine applecart, investigating a range of attempts to address feminist critiques from both the mainstream and radical perspectives (e.g. Tomlinson, 1990; Moorhouse, 1989).

Mainstream approaches to leisure prior to the mid-1970s operated according to a distinction between 'work', as epitomized by full-time employment, and 'leisure', defined as time outside that waged labour. In many cases, analyses adopted an explicit focus on adult men in full-time jobs as their normative category: all those outside this pattern posed something of a problem for mainstream leisure studies (Griffin et al., 1982). Definitions of 'work' in the 1980s leisure studies literature distinguished between waged and unwaged work, discussing concepts such as productive effort, activity and labour, although waged labour retained its position as the paradigm case of 'work' experience (Deem, 1988).

Definitions of leisure have also been concerned with notions of time and activity, which took central place amid debates over *whose* definitions were to be used: the researchers' or those of 'laypeople' (Moorhouse, 1989). Debates concerned with quantitative units (time outside waged work or sleeping); meaning (what different groups define as leisure); quality and freedom (from obligations) predominate in these texts. Many leisure studies texts specialize in distinctly verbose statements about leisure as a means of providing space for the expression of individuals' 'true selves'. The predominant discourse of freedom in leisure studies reflects the construction of leisure in capitalist economies, reproducing the myth of individual choice (Rojek, 1989). Science fiction narratives and speculations about 'the future' form an equally common theme in the leisure studies literature, as do discourses of consumption and 'choice', education and training (Tomlinson, 1990).

Stories of threat and voyeurism pervaded research on young people's leisure during the 1980s, as did origin stories about 'alienation' and 'rebellion'. Discourses of consumption and freedom appeared in mainstream texts, whilst radical analyses incorporated debates about the relation between culture, structure and agency, and discourses of defence and survival moved in alongside resistance theory. Some mainstream texts rediscovered the concepts of lifestyle and lifespace in attempts to replace class and social structure as key conceptual terms. What follows is an analysis of the main discourses in the related research literatures on 'youth' and 'leisure' of the 1980s.

Discourses in 1980s Research on Young People and Leisure

'Deficient Youth': The Discourse of Education and Training

The notion that young people's unstructured free time is a breeding ground for 'social problems' and that they need to be taught to use this time in 'constructive' ways lies at the heart of the discourse of education and training. The disciplines of waged work and good citizenship must be instilled into unemployed working-class young people in case they should forget such vital 'skills' whilst out of direct contact with the institutions of adult authority (see chapter 3). One of the discursive consequences of the stories about deprivation which have dominated the research literature on young people and leisure is the construction of (certain) young people as particularly 'deprived' and/or 'deficient', whether as individuals or in terms of their cultural/social backgrounds, and especially with respect to their family lives. If this 'deficiency' is assumed to be an innate or immutable characteristic, such young people are to be contained, disarmed, and removed from 'normal' society as beyond 'help' and control. If, as is more common, such 'deprivations' are presented as external in origin, these young people can be redeemed: educated back to a 'normality' which reflects Anglo-European middle-class cultural mores.

The discourse of education and training constructs such 'deficient youth' as individual subjects who can only be brought to their full efficiency and potential through rehabilitation. If 'delinquent youth' can be removed from 'deviant' subcultures, taught to unlearn their 'anti-social' ways, and trained in more 'appropriate' skills, values and cultural practices, they can be saved from the psychological and social damnation of delinquent careers. The sympathetic voice of the nineteenth-century liberal child-saving reformer obscures the harsher undercurrent of this discourse, in which cultures other than those of the Anglo-European middle classes are defined as inadequate by default (see chapter 1).

The discourse of education and training can also be found in texts focusing on youth unemployment (see chapter 3); sexuality and family life (see chapter 6); and schooling and the TSW (see chapter 2). The spheres of clinical treatment, educational learning and rehabilitative training overlap most clearly in the extensive social skills literature which expanded during the 1980s with the increase in government-sponsored youth training programmes (Hollands, 1990). What Philip Cohen has referred to as 'lifeskilling ideology' is central to the discourse of education and training (1982). In this discursive context, working-class young people must be *taught* how to live, so that 'middle class codes of vocation and career' are applied to young women's 'apprenticeships' in unpaid domestic work, for example (p. 46).

These codes are also applied to parenthood and to leisure. Leisure may well be constructed as 'free time', but it must be used in ways which are judged to be 'appropriate' for the individual's physical, social and psychological (if not economic) betterment. The biological model which constructs adolescence as determined by hormonal surges means that young people are assumed to be especially prone to 'sensation-seeking', an instrumental rather than expressive orientation to leisure, and 'a lack of personal leisure skills' (Iso-Ahola and Crowley, 1991, p. 261).

Young people are therefore a fruitful focus for lifeskilling ideology, since their 'natural' urges must be directed into appropriate
channels.

In Britain, these discursive connections are most explicit in the
various official texts of the Manpower Services Commission
(MSC), the agency charged with the administration of government-
sponsored training programmes for much of the 1980s (Finn, 1987;
Griffin, forthcoming). In the USA, there is a parallel literature
associated with similar youth training programmes (Snedeker,
1982). Schemes for unemployed (and predominantly working-class)
young people included taught components in what was usually
termed 'social and life skills', in which the emphasis was on
'learning for leisure', a delicate euphemism for the 'enforced idle-
ness' of prolonged unemployment.

'Rebellious Youth': The Discourse of Disaffection

Unemployed working-class young people are represented as particularly 'deficient' and potentially 'rebellious' in their supposed
inability to organize this 'unstructured free time', and this constitutes a primary focus for lifeskilling ideology which operates
through the discourse of education and training and the discourse
of disaffection. One example of the construction of 'rebellious
youth' through the discourse of disaffection in the mainstream
perspective is provided by the work of British social psychologist
Mark McDermott. In a study which analysed data from the USA,
McDermott used information about 132 US high school students
to construct a questionnaire measure of 'rebelliousness' (1986). He
argued that scores on this measure correlated positively with
truancy rates and the number of disciplinary referrals in school,
and negatively with academic achievement. Truancy rates and
disciplinary problems at school (along with criminal records) are
commonly taken as indices of 'delinquency', and this psychological
state of 'rebelliousness' is assumed to affect all areas of young
people's lives (see Snyder et al., 1986). Replicating the study with
136 British young people, McDermott found that 'rebelliousness'
scores correlated with a number of quantitative measures of psychological state, including 'individualism, locus of control, psychological well-being, creativity, irritability and telic dominance [all
of which] illustrate the significance of rebelliousness to clinically-
relevant constructs' (p. 1).

McDermott identified 'rebelliousness' as a 'conspicuous youth culture', which was 'implicated in a variety of psychological phenomena' (p. 2). Radical youth cultural researchers constructed the arena of collective cultural practice in terms of interplay of ideological, political and material power relations. McDermott's text reworked this into a collection of individualized psychological states. McDermott's five-part definition of rebelliousness involved: 'mastery negativism', or gaining and maintaining control and dominance as well as a sense of autonomy and independence; 'sympathy negativism', a reaction of resentment and disappointment in response to not being sympathetic with, or being made to sympathize with others; 'telic negativism' which arises in relation to goal-seeking or a reaction of anger to frustration in the progress of goal-seeking; and 'paratelic negativism' which concerns excitement and stimulation, arousal-seeking and provocation. Finally, 'negativism for its own sake' is 'about rebellion, awkwardness and opposition for its own sake . . . for the pleasure of negativism itself' (p. 5).

From these five elements of rebelliousness McDermott constructed a thirty-six-item scale, with six items for each type of rebelliousness. Following a factor analysis from the survey of British young people, McDermott changed the 'sympathy' and 'paratelic' forms of negativism to 'reactive' and 'proactive' respectively. He defined 'reactive rebelliousness' as 'a behavioural and/or an emotional reaction to an interpersonal disappointment, re-buff or frustration . . . characterised by retaliatory, vindictive, vengefulness' (p. 15). Conversely, 'proactive rebelliousness' is 'essentially gratuitous, indulged in for its own sake and is allied to sensation-seeking behaviours . . . [It] is actively pursued by the participant, unlike in the reactive form' (p. 15). The ways in which respondents selected questionnaire items was assumed to reflect their potentially 'proactive' or 'reactive' behavioural tendencies.

McDermott noted that males scored higher on reactive rebelliousness than young women, but he did not discuss the gendered elements embedded within his questionnaire measures. The connections between the idealized elements of hegemonic western masculinity and the nature of 'reactive rebelliousness' were not to be considered. McDermott did admit that 'rebelliousness of both kinds may not be as phenomenologically relevant for females as males given fewer significant associations between rebelliousness and other variables for the former group' (p. 17).

McDermott's text represented youthful 'disaffection' as both normal and potentially dangerous through the careful distinction between 'rebellious youth' and their 'non-rebellious' peers. Certain groups of young people are seen as more likely to become bored, frustrated or alienated, and individualized psychological states are presented as seed-beds for the truancy, poor academic performance and school 'dropout' which are taken as indicators of youthful 'rebellion'. The psychological dimension in which the discourse of disaffection is embedded serves to obscure any consideration of social, economic or structural forces which might lead certain groups of young people (namely white working-class young people and/or young people of colour) to be more likely to 'drop out' of school or obtain fewer academic qualifications than their more affluent white middle-class peers (see chapter 2).

Whilst McDermott's study concentrated on the impact of 'rebelliousness' in the educational sphere, his analysis connects with a wider research literature in which youthful 'disaffection' is represented as a major social problem in other areas (Bhavnani, 1987). The leisure/boredom thesis, which argues that 'delinquency' arises from young people's presumed inability to use their leisure time in 'constructive' ways plays an important role in linking the discourse of disaffection to the realm of leisure and youthful criminality (see chapter 4). The discourse of education and training enters the picture once again here, since 'inadequate' individual young people must be *taught* how to use their leisure time in positive ways and how to curb their 'rebellious' impulses.

Discourses of Consumption and Freedom

Lifestyle and 'Choice'

Following the series of moral panics over youth cultures which characterized the post-Second World War period, the construction of teenagers as consumers came to play a central role in youth research narratives (A. K. Cohen, 1955). Young people have been cast as consumers in several interconnected discourses, since they are represented as having a youthful 'fling' whilst making up the vital youth market for a whole range of goods from records and clothing through to illegal substances. Whether as the consumers of T-shirts, records, magazines or crack, young people are represented as a particularly malleable and vulnerable group *and* as an unusually defiant, knowing and fickle audience. Outside what has come to be called the 'substance abuse' literature, in which young people are generally pathologized as diseased and/or deviant (see chapter 4), the consumption of 'normal' young people is generally understood in the mainstream literature through notions of 'lifestyle', 'choice' and the discourse of freedom. Part of the process of transition to adulthood for 'normal' young people involves learning to make 'appropriate lifestyle choices', whilst needing 'protection' from the rigours of unfettered consumer capitalism.

In the mainstream sociology of leisure, surveys of young people's leisure activities and consumption patterns have laid out the boundaries of 'normality' in societies which rely on young people's consumption of various goods and services (e.g. Department of Education and Science, 1983). During the 1970s, radical analyses had pointed to the importance of class, 'race' and sex/gender as relations of domination and subordination which structured both target youth markets *and* young people's use and re-use of such products (Clarke and Critcher, 1985). These analyses presented a profound challenge to the model of 'free choice' which lay at the heart of the mainstream perspective in the literature on young people and leisure. In the 1980s some researchers 'rediscovered' theories of lifestyle and life course analysis as a means of dealing with the critiques of youth cultural studies (e.g. Moorhouse, 1989).

Discourses of 'normal' consumption which deployed the notion of lifestyle did incorporate the arguments of radical youth cultural research, but only within the terms of the mainstream perspective. This could produce some confused and confusing arguments, since the discourse of freedom and individual choice which is central to the concept of lifestyle has been subjected to considerable critical scrutiny (e.g. Tomlinson, 1990). Advocates of a 'return' to the concepts of lifestyle and status in leisure studies, whether in the sense of individual choice or within the context of the 'power relations of consumer culture' (Moorhouse, 1989, p. 35), have generally operated in opposition to radical analyses, although not all of these texts have operated from a mainstream perspective. The chief focus of this opposition has lain in objections to 'a neo-Marxist concern with class relations' (Moorhouse, 1989, p. 32), and/or to feminist analyses which have unsettled the dominant 'gang of lads' model by questioning fundamental concepts such as 'work' and 'leisure' (e.g. Rojek, 1989).

Some texts used the notion of lifestyle as a synonym for youth subculture, sometimes making links with 'leisure' and un/employment status. Psychologists John Marks and Edward Glaser for example, interviewed 160 eighteen- to thirty-year-old men from four different groups who were all 'pursuing lifestyles without sustained employment' (1980, p. 173). Marks and Glaser followed the usual male focus associated with the gang of lads model, interviewing young men who were identified as 'hippies, bikers, surfers and criminals'. These were compared with demographically matched groups of young men who were preparing for waged work or were already in employment. Marks and Glaser emphasized the importance of class differences in these young men's 'lifestyles', with fathers' influence the most important of the 'family variables' measured; friends' influence was the most important in school; and employment experiences were less likely to differentiate between the two groups. Marks and Glaser used the concept of lifestyles in a text which equated youthful deviance (at least for young men) with a *rejection* of waged work and education through '*chosen* joblessness' (Marks and Glaser, 1980, p. 173, my emphasis). Here lifestyles were not represented in terms of specific consumption patterns but as forms of 'deviance' and 'rebellion'. This text owed much to the radical arguments of youth cultural analyses, yet it eschewed the notion of culture (with its collective and political connotations) in favour of the more individualized concept of lifestyle.

Richard Jenkins also preferred the concept of 'lifestyles' over youth cultures or subcultures in his study of entry to the Belfast job market (Jenkins, 1983). Jenkins identified three white working-class 'lifestyles' based on interviews with young women and men in the Northern Ireland city: those of 'lads, citizens and ordinary kids'. This was essentially a distinction between masculine 'life-styles', in which 'lads' were defined as defiant and anti-school, whilst 'citizens' were pro-school and conformist. Although Jenkins did interview young women, and he recognized the importance of domestic responsibilities and family life in a descriptive empirical sense, young women were presented as an adjunct to the 'ordinary kids' category. Jenkins all but managed to ignore the political context in which these young people were living in Belfast, and 'lifestyle' replaced youth culture in an explicit rejection of the radical implications of the latter concept for relations of domination and subordination.

Within the radical perspective, as in the mainstream, youthful consumerism has been regarded with a degree of distaste, albeit for different reasons. In mainstream analyses, this distaste stems from the construction of young people as supposedly gullible innocents at the mercy of social and economic pressures from the advertising industry which provides evidence of their need for adult 'protection' (e.g. Abrams, 1959). From the radical perspective, the growth of the 'youth market' is seen as a potential means of undermining young people's revolutionary (socialist) potential and the cultural basis for political resistance (Brake, 1984). Both versions of these theories were shifting their ground throughout the 1980s. Radical analyses began to argue increasingly that young people were capable of transforming the politics of consumption for their own ends, and discourses of pleasure, danger and desire became the focus for radical analyses, especially in Britain (e.g. Willis et al., 1990; McRobbie, 1988).

'Promiscuous Youth': The Discourse of Sexual Deviance

Most stories of threat and danger in mainstream studies about young people and leisure concentrated on the activities of young working-class men. Young women figured in this literature only through panics over 'premarital adolescent [hetero]sexuality'. The discourse of sexual deviance constructs (certain) young women as 'promiscuous', frequently representing them both as passive victims of unscrupulous men *and* as actively 'deviant' in heterosexual terms (e.g. Marchant and Smith, 1977). This discourse also appears in studies on female 'delinquency' (see chapter 4), and in the more clinical literature on family life and sexuality (see chapter 6). In this chapter I concentrate on the leisure studies research literature, in which mainstream analyses construct young women's heterosexual 'deviance' as an 'inappropriate' use of their 'unstructured free time'.

Sexuality is one of the primary sites around which female 'delinquency' is constructed, and the search for the causes of such 'deviance' frequently leads to family life (Cain, 1989). 'Deviant' young women are represented as either being *too* heterosexual (i.e. 'slags'), or as not heterosexual *enough* (i.e. lesbians or frigid: Griffin, 1982a; Cowie and Lees, 1981). There is a considerable body of mainstream research on the moment of 'transition to coitus', with particular regard to the implications of this transition for young women as a potential predictor of 'delinquency' (e.g. Pugh et al., 1990). Whilst monogamous heterosexuality within marriage is institutionalized as inevitable and 'natural', premarital heterosexuality is not encouraged, and this literature has also debated whether 'early adolescent coitus' can be defined as a specific form of 'deviance' or 'delinquency' (e.g. Newcomer and Udry, 1986).

Susan Sprecher, Kathleen McKinney and Terri Orbuch investigated the perseverance of the sexual double standard concerning premarital heterosexuality (1986). This refers to the notion that a woman who is heterosexually active before marriage is a 'slag', whilst a man behaving in the same way would be represented in more positive terms as a 'stud'. Sprecher and her colleagues argued that the sexual double standard was alive and well, with more negative evaluations of female than male heterosexuality. This relatively traditional study undermined the discourse of sexual deviance by focusing on the ideological context in which female heterosexual deviance was constructed.

The discourse of sexual deviance is caught between the older patriarchal form of what Wendy Hollway has called the 'have/hold discourse' which distinguished between 'good' and 'bad' women, and the newer 'permissive' discourse, which advocates a more egalitarian expression of sexuality for women *and* men (1989). These intersecting discourses are reflected in a study by Doreen Walker and Brian Pendleton, which related psychological androgyny to premarital heterosexual activity in young women (1987). Psychological androgyny is associated with a combination of masculine and feminine characteristics, and has been presented as more psychologically healthy than traditionally sex-typed gender identification, especially for women. Walker and Pendleton argued that androgyny was 'positively associated with permissive [hetero]sexual attitudes and behavior, as well as with frequent use of effective contraceptive methods' (p. 1). Androgynous 'permissive' attitudes and behaviour and the use of contraception are both presented here as a positive step forward for young women. There is no mention of how this might contribute to the compulsory nature of institutionalized heterosexuality, in which the permissive discourse operates to pressurize young women into saying 'yes' to male demands for intercourse (Griffin, 1985a).

The core of adult concern over female premarital heterosexuality lies in fears over the incidence of 'teenage pregnancy'. What the mainstream literature refers to as 'unplanned teenage pregnancy', especially amongst young working-class women and young women of colour, represents a crisis of control over 'promiscuous youth', and although much of this work has appeared in the clinical literature on family life and sexuality, I examine it in this chapter since many of the key arguments and discursive moves are so similar to those made in relation to young working-class women in the leisure studies literature. The literature on 'teenage pregnancy' has not only been concerned with age and gender relations, or rather age and gender differences: 'race', class and culture have been equally crucial. The discourse of sexual deviance has drawn on stories of deprivation about 'deficient families' and 'disadvantaged cultures' to construct premarital heterosexuality and 'teenage pregnancy' as 'problems' which are located in in young women and as an indicator of 'deviance' *per se* (see chapter 6).

Sandra Hofferth, Joan Kahn and Wendy Baldwin used information from US National Surveys to demonstrate the increasing proportion of 'sexually active' young women since the 1960s, searching for differences on the basis of 'race' and age (Hofferth et al., 1987). 'Sexual activity' refers to penetrative heterosexual intercourse in these texts: all other forms of sexual activity are ignored. Hofferth and her colleagues argued that the 1970s saw 'a major transformation in sexual behavior' in the USA. When Hofferth and colleagues looked at the US National Surveys of Family Growth for 1971, 1976 and 1979, they examined differences between Black (i.e. African-American) and white young people and between young women and young men, using information collected from metropolitan areas amongst fifteen- to nineteen-year-olds. The pattern for these groups was quite different, suggesting that (premarital) 'sexual activity among white [female] teenagers increased during the 1970s, and leveled off between 1979 and '82 [to 43.3 per cent]. Among black [female] teenagers . . . [premarital] sexual activity rose during the early 1970s, leveled off between 1976 and 1979, and declined between 1979 and '82 [to 53.6 per cent] (p. 47).'

Hofferth and her colleagues concluded that the 'sexual revolution' had affected young white women who entered adolescence during the late 1960s and early 1970s to the greatest extent. More of this group were having premarital heterosexual intercourse, and at increasingly younger ages. For young African- American women, rates of premarital sexual activity were higher before the 1970s compared to their white peers, and the 'sexual revolution' had therefore had less of an impact on the latter group. Hofferth and colleagues argued that the two major aspects of the transformation in heterosexual activity wrought by the 'sexual revolution' for white women were that women became 'sexually active' at increasingly younger ages, and fewer teenagers got married. Therefore, 'sexual activity among young women became primarily nonmarital or premarital' (p. 46).

This put an increasing proportion of young women 'at risk' of premarital pregnancy during the 1970s, yet the actual pregnancy *rate* fell at this time, presumably due to the increasing use of contraception (notably the Pill). However, the overall pregnancy rate (i.e. the number of pregnancies per 1,000 young women aged between fifteen and nineteen) increased substantially during the 1970s. Hofferth and her colleagues made explicit links between rates of female heterosexual activity and 'teenage pregnancy', and their interest in demographic social changes reflected the concern of many mainstream US clinicians and policy-makers. The same degree of research attention has not been paid to the sexual behaviour of white, middle- or upper-class heterosexual men, and the question of *why* young women (especially poor working-class women and young women of colour) should have become the focus for so much academic and media concern is not addressed in this literature (see chapter 7).

Much of the literature on heterosexual deviance has focused on young women, since 'heterosexual promiscuity' is seen as a sign of 'deviance' in young women, and an indicator of 'normal' masculine sexuality in young men. It is only if the latter are gay that they are defined as 'deviant' and 'sexually promiscuous' (Gonsiorek, 1988; see chapters 4 above and 6 below). In the mainstream literature on 'adolescent sexuality' the existence of lesbians, gay men, and bisexual people is obscured, (hetero)sexually active single people are pathologized (especially if they are not white and middle-class), and the compulsory nature of heterosexuality, marriage and family life which follows the nuclear norm is never addressed. Indeed the mainstream literature on 'adolescent (hetero)sexuality' had been relatively separate from that on lesbian and gay young people.[2] The mainstream literature has considered the relative influence of biological, psychological, social and cultural factors on 'adolescent (hetero)sexuality', although much of this work paid little attention to feminist analyses around sexuality (e.g. Miller and Moore, 1990). Feminist analyses would present the transition to heterosexuality for young people as a crucial moment for patriarchal control, especially for young women (e.g. Vance and Pollis, 1990; Griffin, 1985a).

Young people, and especially young women, have always figured prominently in mainstream research around sexuality. The discourse of biological determinism would present this as an inevitable consequence of the sexualized hormonal turmoil which is presumed to play such a central role in adolescence (Conger, 1979). From the radical perspective, the link between young people and sexuality is a historical and political connection which rests on the construction of 'youth' as a key transition point in the spheres of leisure, sexuality and family life (Plummer, 1989; Griffin, 1985a). These two perspectives have developed in a climate of polarized opposition, although some writers have seen evidence of a shift in the mainstream/malestream perspective, towards a more sympathetic recognition of feminist analyses (e.g. Berardo, 1990).

The 1980s also saw some unusual uses of feminist analyses in the mainstream literature on young people, leisure and sexuality. Presenting a structural analysis, Beegley and Sellers argued that 'sex' (by which they meant heterosexual intercourse) is more common amongst young single US people due to the growing gap between the age of puberty and marriage; the increased promiscuity of (heterosexual) role models in the media; 'medical advances which have made sex safe', and 'egalitarian sex role norms which have eliminated the double standard' (1986, p. 313). Beegley and Sellers represented these changes as progressive, citing feminist theories to argue that (hetero)sexual equality had been reached, a point which most feminists would probably dispute (e.g. A. Campbell, 1984; see also Sprecher et al., 1986). The proposition that '[hetero]sex need no longer be withheld during courtship' (p. 313) is taken to represent a moment of sexual liberation for young men *and* women.

Some feminist and other radical writers have argued that panics over female sexuality frequently coincide with moments of crisis in patriarchal or sex/gender systems (Rubin, 1975). Feminist analyses have rejected the discourse of sexual deviance, preferring to construct young women as passive victims of male heterosexual demands (e.g. Coveney et al., 1984), and/or as engaged in assertive acts of resistance to the dominant culture of femininity (e.g. McRobbie, 1978). Such texts were closer to the leisure studies literature than to the clinical domain of the mainstream perspective, but the relative separation between young heterosexual, bisexual and lesbian women remained. Radical analyses are often Anglocentric and culturally-specific, but they have questioned the construction of dominant assumptions about female sexuality, adolescence and deviance in a way that mainstream studies have resolutely refused to do.

Discourses of Resistance, Defence and Survival

Radical Analyses and Youth Subcultural Studies

Some of the most unsettling moments for mainstream research on young people's leisure came with the arguments presented in the radical youth cultural analyses of the 1970s (e.g. Hall and Jefferson, 1975). The youth subcultures literature bridged the related domains of 'youth', 'delinquency' and leisure, focusing mainly on the activities of young, white, heterosexual working-class men. The predominance of a cultural Marxist analysis within these texts emphasized the importance of class relations for structuring these young men's lives, limiting their educational and employment horizons, *and* for shaping the forms of their resistances to such conditions (Murdock and McCron, 1975). 'Leisure' was no longer represented simply as time spent outside employment or education, but as a contested space, time for the forging of creative collective cultural resistances.

Influenced by the work on youth subcultures emerging at Birmingham's Centre for Contemporary Cultural Studies (CCCS), this literature also devoted considerable attention to the meanings and roles of musical styles and cultural forms for young people (see Frith, 1983). Through the 1980s and into the 1990s, this moved beyond an interest in which musical forms coincided with specific (predominantly working-class male) subcultures (e.g. Teddy boys and rock 'n' roll; bikers and heavy metal, Rastafarians and reggae), to a concern with young people's consumption, production and reproduction within and of various media (e.g. Willis et al., 1990; Brewer and Miller, 1990); musical forms and styles as a mode of cultural and political expression (e.g. Hebdige, 1987; Gilroy, 1987); and the intersections of sexuality, gender, 'race' and class in cultures of consumption (e.g. McRobbie, 1988; Roman et al., 1988). By the end of the 1980s, the relation between structure, culture and agency formed a central element in these debates as radical researchers questioned the value of resistance theory and their own role in the research process.

Mainstream sociological research about 'youth' and 'leisure' was preoccupied with the arguments of radical analyses throughout the 1980s. This was not a two-sided conversation, but a multi-faceted discussion within and between radical and mainstream perspectives, involving many different voices, although some have had rather more air-time than others. Radical subcultural analyses scarcely dented the boundaries of psychological positivism: the latter's focus has remained predominantly individualistic. The closest which the mainstream psychological perspective has come to considering the arguments of subcultural analyses is in research about peer influence and adolescent status (see Salmon, 1991, for review). The most profound critiques of the discourse of resistance emerged from within the radical perspective during the 1980s.

The discourse of resistance frequently locates the radical researcher on the side of (predominantly white, heterosexual and male) working-class young people, enabling him (*sic*) to speak on behalf of the oppressed.[3] Working-class male youth subcultures are usually portrayed as exciting, somewhat inarticulate and crude,[4] and this is represented as symbolizing their rejection of 'cissy' middle-class modes, their creative cultural potential and their capacity to survive in harsh economic and social conditions (Willis, 1977; Borman and Riesman, 1986). Such cultures have often been romanticized by radical researchers quite as fervently as they would have been criticized from within the mainstream perspective (see J. C. Walker, 1986a, and Hollands, 1990, for critiques).

The events of the late 1970s and early 1980s threw radical youth subcultural research into some disarray, highlighting the disjuncture between the structuralist arguments of cultural Marxism and the growing force of post-modern and post-structuralist ideas, as well as the influence of feminist analyses, and the work of radical Black Marxist/feminist researchers. The parallel emergence (and eventual marketing) of punk and reggae produced more confusion, especially when considered in relation to rising youth unemployment and the 'riots' in British and North American cities during the early 1980s. The fruitless search for a radical subculture of unemployment amongst working-class young people and the difficulties most (white) radical researchers faced in accounting for these 'riots' exemplifies this confusion. The radical arguments of the 1970s were seen to be inadequate for addressing the political and economic conditions of the 1980s (e.g. P. Cohen, 1986; see chapters 3 and 4 above).

Radical youth researchers in this period were beginning to face the difficulties involved in 'speaking for' working-class young people from the position of outsiders. Marxist sociologists Taylor and Jamieson argued that British youth unemployment in the late 1970s and early 1980s 'induced a heavy pessimism amongst youth', citing punk rock culture and the 'riots' in some British cities during the summer of 1981 as the prime influences on this phenomenon (1983, p. 32). Writing from a different discursive framework outside youth cultural research and leisure studies, two radical British social psychologists represented these 'riots' in a different light in a study based on interviews with some of the participants (Reicher and Potter, 1985).

Reicher and Potter argued that for many of the people involved in these 'riots', such events were seen as positive and even celebratory: a triumph over the oppressive forces of 'law and order' which instigated them and were seen to be invading local 'turf'. Reicher and Potter did not represent these young people (or adults) as resisting and struggling to survive in the face of oppressive material conditions, but as marginalized individuals with a different and subordinated perspective on a specific incident of 'crowd behaviour'. For Reicher and Potter, the dominant voices heard in explanations of these 'riots' were those of 'outsiders' such as the police, journalists and local shopkeepers and pub landlords (Reicher and Potter, 1985).

The relation between youth cultural forms and class-based structural conditions no longer appeared to be so clear-cut, especially when some radical researchers pointed to the sexism and racism of white working-class masculine cultures and the importance of understanding structural intersections between sex/gender, age, 'race' and class (Brah, 1988a; McCarthy, 1989). By the late 1980s, most researchers working from the radical perspective became increasingly less confident about assigning specific meanings to particular youth cultural practices as 'resistant' or 'conformist' (e.g. Aggleton and Whitty, 1985). Referring to the punk-influenced culture of slam-dancing in the USA of the late 1980s, Leslie Roman presented an ethnographic and semiotic analysis informed by a materialist feminist approach to popular cultural forms (1988). She argued that the paid work (and unemployment) experiences of middle-and working-class punk young women 'provided them with markedly different symbolic and material resources with which to articulate their feminine sexualities in the dance' (p. 178).

A transformed youth cultural studies became an arena for debating questions about the relationship between structure, culture and agency raised by the political conditions of the 1980s. Angela McRobbie for example, was a key figure in the emergence of a feminist voice within British cultural studies around 'youth' during the 1970s (McRobbie and Garber, 1975). She shifted from the identification of a specifically (white, heterosexual) working-class culture of femininity in the late 1970s (McRobbie, 1978), to analyses of style and dance which were informed by semiology, French structuralism, post-modernism and feminism by the late 1980s (1984, 1988). Her work moved closer to the blurred boundary between academic research and journalism throughout the 1980s, and eventually away from the domain of 'youth research' altogether (1992).

The mid-1970s to early 1980s was also notable for the emergence, international recognition and subsequent rip-off of reggae music and Rastafarianism as sources of a positive spiritual and political movement amongst Afro-Caribbean young people, especially in Britain. The institutional force of racism in the international music industry meant that reggae and earlier Black (i.e. African-American and Afro-Caribbean) musical forms developed their own independent recording and distribution systems outside the major record companies long before punk came along (Gilroy, 1987; Tyler, 1989). Moving beyond the discourse of resistance, many radical analyses argued that punk and reggae provided important musical and cultural bases for forms of political organization amongst young white and Black Britons (e.g. Gilroy and Lawrence, 1988; S. Jones, 1988).

The late 1980s also saw a shift away from the discourse of resistance towards discourses of defence and survival in radical youth research texts. There was a resurgence of a long-standing moral panic over 'football hooliganism' in Britain (Clarke and Critcher, 1985). Some radical researchers took a new look at this most recent 'crisis' from the perspective of the predominantly young, white, working-class male fans, informed by these debates over cultural resistance. At Manchester Polytechnic's Unit for Law and Popular Culture, Steve Redhead and Richard Haynes preferred to operate through discourses of defence and survival rather than that of resistance, representing these football fans as beleaguered by the social and economic conditions in Thatcher's Britain, harsher policing strategies, and a newly dehumanizing treatment by the institutions of professional football, from the Football League to the 'popular' press (Redhead, 1991; Haynes, 1992).

By the mid-1980s, radical youth cultural research had come under considerable critical scrutiny for concentrating on young, white, heterosexual working-class men with minimal analysis of the 'race', gender and/or sexual dimensions of their lives, and for presenting an overly romantic picture of the cultures of these white working-class 'lads' (McCarthy, 1989; McRobbie, 1980). The discourse of resistance began to be used in a more reflexive manner, with a growing reluctance amongst researchers to 'read off' the meanings and political implications of specific youth cultural forms as either 'resistant' or 'conformist'. Peter Aggleton and Geoff Whitty for example, interviewed young white women and men of the 'new middle classes' in a southern English town, operating within a neo-Marxist perspective which informed their interest in the 'radical significance, or otherwise, of student "resistance" to schooling' (1985, P. 60). They defined 'resistance' as 'all forms of behaviour that apparently challenge the routine and structuring of the schooling process' (p. 60).

Aggleton and Whitty made a distinction between 'resistant' intentions and 'resistant' effects, examining the targets of acts of resistance amongst these white middle-class young people. They differentiated between 'acts of challenge directed against power relations operating widely and pervasively throughout the social formation and those directed against localised principles of control' (p. 62). The former were identified as 'resistances' and the latter as 'contestations'. Aggleton and Whitty were careful to acknowledge potential tensions between 'resistant' subjectivity and 'resistant' behaviour, and 'the possibility that 'resistant' behaviours witnessed at one site of practice (say the home) may be the result of "resistant" intentions *displaced* from another site of experience (say the school)' (p. 63, original emphasis).

Once in secondary school, many of these young people adopted a series of challenges towards elements of perceived oppression in everyday pedagogical practice. This might include a refusal to wear school uniform, or persistent absence from school. For Aggleton and Whitty, such reactions signified 'effects arising from the *transportation of practices* . . . from the family site to the school' (p. 65, original emphasis). Aggleton and Whitty noted that the latter typically took personal, individualized and non-collective forms.

The subcultural leisured context of these young people's lives was based around various local clubs, bars, coffee shops and an arts centre, as well as their homes. There was a distinct preference for sites frequented by the town's gay (male) community, and/or people with interests in fine art, literature, cinema and radical politics. Young women stressed the importance of developing a sexual politics in such sites. Young men, however, seemed to retain dominant modes of heterosexual masculine practice, differentiating between relationships which were perceived as offering 'opportunities for long-term personal development and those that were not' (p. 67). Young men did admit to the occasional homosexual experience, usually during a 'drunken evening' on holiday. For some of the young women, feminist commitment had resulted in a deliberate involvement in lesbian relationships as well as committed heterosexual relationships.

Such radical analyses of young people's sexual relationships have been notably absent from the radical youth cultural literature, with the exception of feminist research (see chapter 6). Aggleton and Whitty's text provided a detailed picture of age, gender, class and (hetero)sexual relations in a white middle-class cultural milieu, addressing the implications of a transformed discourse of resistance. The study provided no similarly detailed consideration of the racial or ethnic positioning of these young people, apart from a mention of their use of 'foreign and exotic' styles in clothing, appearance and aesthetic leisure consumption. The Aggleton and Whitty study in one example of a radical analysis which had attempted to incorporate feminist critiques of the 'gang of lads' model which prevailed in most youth research.

Young Women and Leisure: Challenging the 'Gang of Lads' Model

Many radical analyses adopted a similar perspective to that of Martin Kemp quoted at the start of this chapter in their analyses of working-class male-dominated youth cultural groups (see Dorn and South, 1983 for review). Male researchers' relatively uncritical interest in the gendered nature of cultural processes and practices involved in gang life has produced an emphasis on 'bad boys' and the consequent invisibility of young women. Where young women's existence has been acknowledged, their 'deviance' or 'resistance' has been defined either as less severe than that of their male peers, and/or in largely sexualized terms (e.g. Baron, 1989). Other texts presented young women as at the forefront of cultural resistance, rather than as passive partners of 'rebellious' young men. Aggleton and Whitty for example, argued that young women's 'critique of patriarchal relations . . . displayed more potential for becoming an effective resistance than did any of the other contestations mentioned in the[ir] study' (1985, p. 70).

The visibility of young women in feminist studies of the 1970s and early 1980s and the critical analysis of sex/gender relations posed a challenge to the traditional 'gang of lads' model which had pervaded both the radical and the mainstream literatures on 'youth' and 'leisure'. This initially produced a range of studies which sought to put (certain groups of) young women in the spotlight. Some of these texts struggled (often with mixed success) to adapt male-specific theories and practices to young women's lives (e.g. McRobbie and Garber, 1975; see Griffin, 1988). This strategy was gradually abandoned as feminist researchers began to ask different questions, ceasing to relate their analyses to the male-as-norm model. The work of Black feminists indicated that most (white) feminist research presented an Anglocentric picture which did not necessarily apply to young women of colour, arguing that feminist research did not 'only' concern relations of gender and sexuality (e.g. Ladner, 1971; Amos and Parmar, 1981).

Feminist studies have tended to concentrate on young white working-class women, with relatively less attention paid to the experiences of young women of colour. One exception here is Clara Rodriguez's study of 'Menudo', and its implications for the Chicana community in New York, especially for young female working-class Puerto Ricans (1986). Menudo is a Puerto Rican pop group of young teenage men, each of whom is replaced once he reaches the age of around fourteen. Examining 'the production of popular culture within capitalism's global reach', Rodriguez identified 'an amazing amount of emulative and creative behavior on the part of young Hispanic women, who formed numerous independent music groups and a host of formal and informal communication links' (p. 3).

Menudo sparked 'a resurgence of ethnic and national pride' amongst these young women, a contradiction which is set in the context of Menudo's international financial success as a 'market-driven commodity that attempted to target middle class, consumptionist values' (p. 15). For Rodriguez, the aims and implications of Menudo are eminently reactionary, yet the cultural and political implications for young working-class Puerto Rican women are potentially more radical. Rodriguez's study was relatively unusual in setting the operation of gender, 'race', and class relations in a specific youth culture within an international context, and in her reluctance to read off young women's cultural practices as either 'radical' or 'reactionary'.

As radical analyses examined the intersection of 'race', class, age, gender and sexuality in young people's lives, researchers were increasingly reluctant (and sometimes unable) to identify specific cultural practices as forms of resistance against (or collusion with) power relations structured by 'race' *or* class *or* gender. Feminist texts moved away from the construction of young people as resistant (or conformist) individuals within resistant (or conformist) lifestyles or cultural forms, towards representations of the negotiated and contested discursive configurations (e.g. Bhavnani, 1991), or textually-mediated cultural practices (Roman et al., 1988) through which young people operate in complex relations of domination and subordination. The focus on young women's lives which had been an early feminist strategy for undermining the 'gang of lads' model shifted to include critical analyses of young men's lives and the construction of hegemonic masculinities (e.g. Wood, 1984).

One of the key contributions of feminist analyses to work on young people's leisure was the focus on young women's lives and especially the *constraints* on their involvement in leisure activities (Deem, 1989; Henderson, 1991). In this sense young women are seen to have *less* leisure than young men, mainly due to domestic commitments, and young women also act as a form of leisure *for* men, especially through (hetero)sexual and emotional servicing (Griffin et al., 1982).

Feminist critiques of the male focus in studies of sport and leisure led to a growing concern over women's disproportionately low involvement in sporting and leisure activities in mainstream research as well as the 'boys' own' section of the radical literature (Wimbush and Talbot, 1989). A number of feminist social scientists examined young women's specific experiences of 'work' and 'leisure' (e.g. A. Campbell, 1984). Some studies looked at the various media aimed at young women and men, contrasting the pervasiveness of military themes in comics for boys and young men (e.g. O'Connor, 1986) with the close female friendships (and compulsory heterosexuality) reflected in school stories for girls and young women (e.g. Auchtermuty, 1987; E. Carter, 1984). Relatively few studies have focused on readers and their uses and understandings of these texts (one exception is Frazer, 1987).

Returning to the quote from Martin Kemp at the start of this chapter, youth gangs (usually male-dominated) have appeared as important elements in research around 'delinquency', youth and leisure in both the mainstream and radical analyses (Huff, 1989).

From Whyte's *Street Corner Society* onwards, the gang of young urban working-class men has exercised a gripping fascination for (male) youth researchers (Whyte, 1943; Adler et al., 1992). Relatively little attention has been paid to the position of women in male-dominated gangs (one exception is Hopper and Moore, 1990), and even less to all-female gangs (one exception is A. Campbell, 1984).

Hopper and Moore's analysis of women's involvement in US outlaw biker gangs set women's gang involvement in the context of their subordinated class and gender positions and their relative lack of alternative economic or social opportunities (Hopper and Moore, 1990). These women's circumstances must be desperate indeed if joining such a gang can come to constitute 'freedom'. Hopper and Moore argued that the position of biker women had increasingly 'solidified' since the late 1960s. The gangs of the 1980s were less racially and ethnically mixed; Anglo gangs were more racist, patriotic and conservative, and more frequently involved in illegal activities and the criminal underworld. These elements were seen to contribute to a growing level of 'sex segregation', male control of sexual activities and of women, and increasingly ritualized sexuality. The latter was seen to symbolize rituals of brotherhood and status (between men) rather than earlier constructions of sex as 'fun'.

In sharp contrast to biker gangs, urban street gangs are relatively younger, involving mainly young people of colour, with a greater interest in style, clothes and fashion. For young women in particular, street life can often come into conflict with family demands (A. Campbell, 1984; Huff, 1989). Involvement in gang life has gendered connotations, and both biker women and young women in street gangs are seen as 'deviant' and hence as unfeminine. Male bikers, like white working-class, Afro-Caribbean and African-American young men in street gangs, are often represented as hyper-masculine: their masculinity is seen as pre-eminently 'authentic', definitely heterosexual and also homosocial (Connell, 1989). The masculinity of other groups of young men is frequently represented as suspect, with overtones of effeminacy, including those with 'middle-class' values (e.g. Willis, 1977), or from Anglo-European middle-class backgrounds (e.g. Willis, 1978); young Asian-Americans and British Asians (Sinha, 1987; Bains, 1988); and gay and bisexual young men (Plummer, 1989).

The literature on young people and leisure has generally used the terminology of youth gangs and youth subcultures interchangeably and frequently with a marked lack of precision. Anne Campbell and Steven Muncer attempted to clarify this situation in a comparison of the conditions which produced North American gangs and British subcultures. They defined a gang as 'a group of recurrently associating individuals with identifiable leadership and internal organization, identifying with or claiming control over territory in the community, and engaging either individually or collectively in violent or other forms of illegal behavior' (Campbell and Muncer, 1989, P. 272, quoting Miller, 1975). Their own definition of youth subculture followed Pfantz, as 'a geographically diffuse social movement of teenagers and young people who share a common set of values, interests, and a tacit ideology but who are not necessarily dependent on face-to-face interaction with other members and do not have any rigid criteria of entry, membership or obligation' (p. 272; Pfantz, 1961).

Campbell and Muncer acknowledged that these definitions produce a polarization between two ideal types which appear in a far less clear cut form in the youth research literature, and amongst young people's social formations. They argued that the different conditions of US and British societies following the Second World War tended to encourage the growth of street gangs in the USA and successive waves of youth subcultures in Britain. Drawing on both radical and mainstream analyses, Campbell and Muncer suggested that in the USA, gangs 'sprang . . . from ethnic ghettos . . . embody[ing] many traditional mainstream values (consumerism, patriotism, elitism and competitive success) [and] recreating them in a distorted form on the street' (1989, p. 271). Conversely, British subcultures are represented as a 'response to a class-based society and . . . a ritual resistance to the status quo' (p. 271). Campbell and Muncer argued that 'the form which social deviance takes depends intimately upon the society which gives rise to them [youth subcultures]' (p. 271, my insertion), and they examined the class, 'race' and gender dimensions of youth cultures as important structural determinants of specific social formations.

Whilst the impact of feminist analyses on texts such as those of Hopper and Moore and Campbell and Muncer is clear, this is by no means a widespread phenomenon (Salmon, 1991). Responses to feminist critiques from the mainstream and radical literatures on young people's leisure have been diverse, but several common strategies can be identified. One strategy would mention a few examples of women's 'different' leisure experiences, without making any fundamental changes to the core theoretical framework and paying scant attention to the main arguments of feminist analyses (e.g. Muncie, 1984). Another strategy incorporates a more systematic examination of gender differences in the research design, bringing this into the text in a descriptive mode without launching any major deconstruction of existing notions of 'work', 'leisure', or their various meanings for young women and men (e.g. K. Roberts, 1983). A third strategy involves the simple tactic of ignoring the existence of such critiques and 'alternative' analyses altogether (e.g. Cubitt, 1990). Another strategy would include a few token references, paragraphs or chapters on 'race', 'the family', 'women's leisure' or 'black youth' in a manner which would not disturb the conceptual framework of the 'main' contributions (e.g. Brown and Sparks, 1989; Rojek, 1989).

Some texts have presented a dismissive patriarchal critique of feminist research on leisure (e.g. Moorhouse, 1989; see Deem, 1989, for review). Another strategy plays white feminists off against radical Black (usually male) scholars, thereby ignoring the work of Black feminists (e.g. Tomlinson, 1990). The synthesis between competing models strategy has seldom been adopted with regard to the work of feminist and radical Black scholars. Texts which take as their conceptual focus the intersection of 'race', class, sex/gender and age, or which examine the lives of young people of colour and/or young women are less likely to be treated as worthy of synthesis with Marxist analyses or the mainstream theories of young people and leisure. There are some texts within the radical perspective, however, which have incorporated feminist arguments at a theoretical level (e.g. Dorn and South, 1989; Aggleton and Whitty, 1985).

The three main approaches which have shaped my analysis of 1980s research on 'youth' can be identified in the key discursive configurations within research on young people and leisure (see chapter 1). The hegemonic ideology which permeates the mainstream perspective of youth research would construct young people outside the white middle-class heterosexual male norm as variously 'deficient', 'deviant' and/or 'dangerous' in terms of their uses of leisure time. Mainstream analyses (e.g. M.McDermott, 1986) present individualized accounts of psychological states of 'rebellion' or 'alienation', and such accounts obscure the social, economic and ideological conditions which might (according to radical analyses) have produced these very forms of 'rebellion' and 'resistance' (see Muncie, 1984).

Post-structuralist approaches would question the identification of specific cultural forms and social practices as 'resistance' or 'collusion' in debates over the relationship between structure, culture and agency, and the role of texts in mediating cultural practices within young people's leisure (e.g. Roman et al., 1988; Willis et al., 1990). Feminist analyses have challenged the 'gang of lads' model and the relative invisibility of young women which pervades both mainstream *and* radical research on young people and leisure (Wimbush and Talbot, 1989).

By the end of the 1980s, many feminist researchers shifted from critiques of the male-as-norm model towards an examination of young women's lives set in social and political context. These developments were most obvious in studies of peer group influence, including young women's involvement in gangs (Salmon, 1991; A. Campbell, 1984). In leisure studies, this phenomenon was more marked in research around courtship, romance and (hetero)sexuality (Beuret and Makings, 1986; Griffiths, 1988). Feminist and Marxist youth cultural studies examined young people's involvement in cultures of dance, fantasy, music, fashion and style in which the boundaries of 'resistance' and 'collusion' became increasingly blurred and dissolved altogether (Willis et al., 1990; Roman, 1988; McRobbie, 1984 and 1988). These studies operated on the boundary between the 'private' spheres of family life and sexuality, and the 'public' spheres of leisure, education and the job market.

Notes

1 I have drawn here on Margaret Sandelowski's notion of 'fault lines' in her study of infertility and imperilled sisterhood (Sandelowski, 1990).

2 One exception to this separation was the 1989 special issue of the mainstream journal *Marriage and Family Review*, which included articles on married lesbians and gay men, and lesbians and gay men as parents.

3 The white middle-class 'bohemian' youth cultures of the 1960s were also identified as resistant and 'radical'; the discourse of resistance was not confined to the cultural practices of their Black and working-class peers (Willis, 1978).

4 'Inarticulacy' has been used primarily in relation to subordinate groups such as working-class young people in mainstream analyses. The more convoluted texts of post-structuralism and post-modernism are seldom presented as 'inarticulate'. The 'inarticulacy' of academics is generally assumed to reflect conceptual sophistication (see Skeggs, 1991).

6
Young People and the 'Private Sphere': Family Life and Sexuality

The family and its maintenance really is the most important thing not only in your personal life but in the life of any community, because this is the unit on which the whole nation is built. (Margaret Thatcher interviewed by Julie Cockcroft, *Daily Mail*, 4 May 1989, quoted in Rutherford, 1990, p. 12)

By the mid-1980s, talk of family decay and decline seems to have waned in journalistic treatments of the family and even in political discourse, but expressions of concern from family social scientists were more conspicuous, and probably more frequent, than they were in the 1970s. (Norval Glenn, Editorial of the *Journal of Family Issues* volume on 'Continuity versus change: Views of the American Family in the 1980s', 1988, p. 348)

Much of the youth research literature discussed so far has focused on sectors of the 'public sphere', including education, the labour market, training and leisure, and most studies have been primarily concerned with young men's lives. An equally important area of youth research has dealt with what might be termed the 'private sphere', specifically family life and sexuality, and this literature has focused mainly on young women. The distinction between the 'private' and 'public' spheres is not clear-cut, since sectors of the 'private' sphere have played central roles in the narratives of research literature dealing with the 'public' sphere: the broken home thesis is a notable example in this respect (see chapter 4). Despite overlaps in the treatment of the 'public' and 'private' spheres, these literatures are still characterized by a degree of separation, such that family life and sexuality have frequently been dealt with in the clinical and medical domains as 'private' and beyond the realm of social, economic and political analysis, constrained like adolescence and sex/gender relations by the biological imperative (Haraway, 1989).

Both family life and sexuality have been crucial elements in discourses around adolescence. In the 1980s, the 'private' sphere took centre stage in moral panics about 'youth', notably the crisis over 'teenage pregnancy' (especially in the USA), 'adolescent sexuality' and AIDS, and threats to 'normal' family life. Many journals brought out special issues on topics relevant to young people, family life and sexuality during the 1980s.[1] The quote from Norval Glenn at the start of this chapter is taken from one such special issue, in which he distinguished between the representation of family life in journalistic and academic texts.

The so-called 'permissive society' of the 1960s has appeared as a frequent referent in media and academic panics over adolescence, family life and sexuality during the 1980s. By the end of the decade, Prime Minister Margaret Thatcher was quoted in a much-publicized speech arguing that 'there is no such thing as society, only family life' (Abbott and Wallace, 1989). She elaborated on this theme in the newspaper interview quoted at the start of this chapter, in which 'the family' was given central place as the very foundation of nationhood. Thatcherism denied the existence of any collective cultural (or sexual) life beyond the confines of the 'private' domestic sphere.[2]

In the radical literature the 1980s saw a rather different series of crises and concerns over young people, family life and sexuality. Feminist work took a critical look at the various Marxist analyses of youth cultures and subcultures which had focused primarily on the lives of young white working-class men in the 'public' sphere, arguing that such research ignored the diverse experiences of young women *and* the impact of gender and sexuality on *all* young people's lives (e.g. McRobbie, 1980). Radical Black and feminist scholars assessed the value of these analyses from the perspective of young people of colour, challenging myths about the 'matriarchal' African-American or Afro-Caribbean family, 'dysfunctional' working-class families, and the presumed sexual promiscuity and/or 'exotic sexuality' of young women of colour (e.g. Gibbs, 1988; Amos and Parmar, 1981). Feminist studies brought sexuality and family life from the arena of the 'private' and the personal into the political domain of radical analysis. This challenged the dominance of biological determinism which pervaded mainstream analyses of 'adolescent sexuality' through the storm-and-stress model.

One of the foundation stones of the storm-and-stress model, and indeed a key defining feature of 'adolescence' itself, has been the hormonal and physiological changes which occur during puberty (Muuss, 1968). Adolescence as a concept is distinctly sexualized,

lected most strongly in the clinical and psychological
tures. The ideological legacy of this bio-psychological
of adolescence is still evident in the force of the
sychological focus on individual young people as
lems, and the representation of adolescence as an
age stage which will inevitably involve forms of psychological
disturbance with a biological and/or physiological origin (Coleman, 1980). Library searches yield a considerable crop of references concerned with the emotional, psychological and social
'problems' of adolescence/adolescents and how to 'treat' them (e.g.
Leone, 1990). Adolescence is the only age stage (apart perhaps
from old age) which has been medicalized to such an extent. But
unlike old age, adolescence has also been sexualized (especially for
young women) and criminalized (especially for young men, working-
class and young people of colour).

Whilst biological determinism has been crucial to the construction of adolescence, it has been equally important within contemporary notions of sexuality. Dominant discourses around sexuality
still rely on the biological domain as a defining frame, although
the late 1970s and 1980s saw a series of radical analyses which
examined the social and historical construction of sexuality in a
political context (e.g. Faderman, 1981; Weeks, 1981). Such historical analyses represented sexuality as a social institution in which
heterosexuality was defined as normal, compulsory and a mark of
maturity, resting on the representation of femininity and masculinity as complementary opposites. This approach might seem to
have obvious benefits for radical youth research, but surprisingly
few texts have drawn on such analyses (see Griffin, 1985a, and
Plummer, 1989, for exceptions).

The 1980s was a period of resurgence for biological determinism
in New Right ideologies, alongside a series of panics over inter-
connections between 'biological' and 'social' discourses (Rose and
Rose, 1986). It is perhaps unsurprising that these moments of crisis
focused around such issues as 'teenage pregnancy', 'adolescent
sexuality', and 'the family', given that the 'private' sphere had
become something of a battleground between the New Right and
various radical ideologies (Abbott and Wallace 1989). The panic
over HIV and AIDS crystallized these various elements, concentrating on gay male sexuality, injecting drug users, and young
people's supposedly promiscuous sexual practices (both heterosexual and homosexual), all of which were presumed to pose serious
threats to the heterosexual nuclear family norm.

Moments of Crisis: Threats to the Heterosexual Nuclear Family Norm

Certain types of family life (generally called 'traditional') have long been represented as normal and ideal in western societies, rendering all other household forms or domestic practices as 'deviant' and as a potential source of 'social problems'. Several radical writers have argued that the illusory privacy of family life and the domestic sphere is no protection from external intervention; indeed the very ideology of privacy serves to obscure an unprecedented degree of state involvement and interference in family affairs, especially outside the realms of the white middle-class nuclear family form (Donzelot, 1977).

These constructions of 'normal' and 'deviant' family life did not originate in the era of Reagan and Thatcher: they can be traced through the twentieth century into the period since the Second World War, years which have been marked by a series of 'moral panics' over family life on both sides of the Atlantic (Lasch, 1977). One of the characteristics of these panics is a repeated concern with perceived threats to 'traditional' family life and the assumption that 'the family' as an institution is in danger of extinction. When the concept of 'the family' is used in this way, it usually operates as a universal term which refers to that which is taken to stand for 'normal family life': the nuclear family which is most prevalent amongst white middle-class groups in western industrialized societies.

By the 1980s it had become increasingly difficult for social scientists and policy-makers to talk in terms of one 'traditional' family form organized around the sole or main male breadwinner, a married heterosexual couple and two children (Berardo, 1990). Even mainstream texts were using terms such as 'family diversity' and 'wider families', moving from a concern with the question 'what is the family?' to 'what are families?' (see Marciano and Sussman, 1991; and Rowland, 1991, for an Australian perspective). Official statistics indicated that this pattern was very far from the norm, and feminist analyses had been pointing to the inadequacies of the patriarchal nuclear family model and the damage caused by the white middle-class norm for some time (e.g. Bhavnani and Coulson, 1986).

In terms of major demographic trends, the situations in the USA and Britain have been broadly similar, with a continuing tradition of relatively high rates of fertility, marriage and divorce in the USA (Wetzel, 1990; Bumpass, 1990). Andrew Cherlin and Frank Furstenberg have argued that 'the pivotal factor in postwar trends is the changing position of women in the economy and its consequences for gender roles in the family . . . [including] the increasing proportion of married women in the labour force and 'the growth of an ideology stressing independence and self-fulfillment' (1988, pp. 294–5, my insertion).

Feminist work around child sexual abuse and domestic violence has posed a serious challenge to the rosy picture of family life as a secure haven devoid of internal power differentials (e.g. Driver and Droisen, 1989). Panics over family life in the 1980s operated in the context of radical analyses which presented family life as oppressive for women and children, and as a source of potential support in the face of the intensified racism and rising unemployment which characterized working-class life under Thatcher and Reagan (e.g. Davis and Davis, 1986).

'Youth' entered this climate of panic in several different ways. Firstly, there was concern over the impact of assumed changes in patterns of family life (especially divorce and separation) on children and young people (e.g. Edwards, 1987); and secondly, over the time at which young people left the parental home (e.g. Bianchi, 1987). Thirdly, young people are frequently represented as the parents of the future, and so their sexuality and fertility as potential childbearers and child-rearers came under close scrutiny (e.g. Hayes, 1987). And finally, the presumed changes in 'traditional' family life have been represented as a potential influence on youthful 'delinquency' and 'deviance', notably via the broken home thesis (see chapter 4). Panics over family life in the 1980s revolved around the fear that the transition to 'normal' (hetero) sexuality and the nuclear family for young people had been disrupted to an irrevocable extent.

In a separate but expanding literature with a somewhat different agenda, radical Black scholars expressed concern over threats to the 'Black family', emphasizing the impact of unemployment, poverty and racism on African-American culture (e.g. Joe, 1987). Panics over 'the family' in the mainstream literature have generally operated with an Anglo- or Eurocentric model of family life (Phoenix, 1990). Debates about continuity versus change, selfish individualism versus communal family life, and the presumed dangers of female-dominated families are relatively common in mainstream analyses (Glenn, 1987; Aldous, 1987). Panics over the perceived threat to 'the family' coincided with various suggested 'solutions' to this 'problem'. These ranged from calls for a return to a mythical patriarchal past (Weiss, 1987); proposals for various educational initiatives (Landry et al., 1986); and more critical arguments that mainstream researchers and policy makers on family life should 'refocus our thinking', often as a response to feminist arguments (Scanzoni, 1987).

The 1980s also saw increasingly frequent but still uncommon appearances by the father, a shadowy figure who had been almost completely absent from such texts in previous decades. Despite (or perhaps because of) growing evidence of the damage done by fathers (and father figures) to women and children in family life, calls for a greater involvement by fathers in family life strengthened as the decade progressed, alongside continuing attacks on women's mothering abilities (Lewis and O'Brien, 1987; Chesler, 1986). This malestream concern over the presumed dangers of 'father-absent families' and 'female-dominated families' occured at a time when, as Glenn's review article put it, 'if any category of the population has benefited [from recent changes], or at least has not been substantially harmed, it is apparently the men' (Lewis and O'Brien, 1987, p. 353, my addition). Under a surface concern for the well-being of children and young people, malestream researchers appeared to hide considerable anxiety about a potential crisis for patriarchal control. The mainstream family studies literature brought an extra twist to the victim-blaming thesis, in that it also became possible to blame the victim's *mother* (and her cultural background) for any hypothetical misdemeanour by 'delinquent youth' (see chapter 4).

'Teenage Pregnancy'

In the USA, the mid-1980s brought a major moral panic over 'teenage pregnancy' which provided the focus for a more transitory stir in Britain during the early 1980s. In the USA, this panic coincided in the Reagan years with the upsurge of the 'Moral Majority', repeated bombing of abortion clinics, the growth of 'Operation Rescue' and other anti-abortion groups, restrictions on contraceptive advice, welfare provision and a concern over 'black teenage unwed mothers' which had distinctly eugenic overtones (Davis and Davis, 1986). In 1987, Thomas Espenshade, director of the Program in Development Studies at the Urban Institute argued that western industrialized nations faced a 'demographic dilemma' due to increasing fertility rates, and to the increase in immigrant populations from Third World countries (Espenshade, 1987). Espenshade was careful to deny the racist implications of his arguments, but he did not specify *why* such changes might be a matter for concern for *which* groups of people.

The moral panic over 'teenage pregnancy' was in part a crisis of national identification at a time when WASP America felt itself to be 'under threat' from a combination of external and internal forces. A veritable flood of dissertations, articles, books and conference papers concerned with 'teenage pregnancy' were produced throughout the 1980s and into the 1990s. Much of this concern centred around the 'fertility decision-making' of young working-class women and/or young women of colour (e.g. Miller and Dyk, 1990; see Loewenstein and Furstenberg, 1991, for a critique of this literature). Such texts aimed to discover why these young women became pregnant, especially outside marriage, with a view to preventing such pregnancies and any subsequent births. At a superficial level, the aim of this work appeared to be wholly benevolent, since babies born to low-income mothers are more likely to be premature, and to have poor health. However, this approach constructs and locates the 'problem' of 'teenage pregnancy' in young women's 'deficient' cultural backgrounds or 'inadequate' knowledge, not in the structural bases of poverty which produce the 'deprivations' mentioned above (Phoenix, 1990).

Fathers have been largely invisible in the mainstream literature on 'teenage pregnancy', with the spotlight fixed on young women who are usually poor, working-class, Black and single. They are frequently portrayed as inadequate, deviant, ignorant, deprived and/or promiscuous, as are their families of origin. Such young women are berated as the children of 'inadequate' parents, and as likely to make 'inadequate' parents themselves in a familiar set of stories about deprivation and deficiency (Phoenix, 1990). Whilst some writers have taken a more positive view of this literature, 'teenage pregnancy' is still treated relatively uncritically as a 'problem' which must be resolved regardless of whether researchers attribute it to 'early (hetero) sexual activity', 'inadequate' contraceptive use or teenage childbearing (Hayes, 1987).

In Britain, the research literature on 'teenage pregnancy' has not been so extensive as in the USA, but it reflects many of the same themes (e.g. Bury, 1984; Sims and Smith, 1986). US researchers like Frank Furstenberg and his colleagues have taken a closer look at the wealth of information on 'teenage pregnancy', arguing that the source of any 'problems' here is not the presumed inadequacies of (certain) young women, their families and friends, but the effects of poverty and the assumption that 'teenage pregnancy' represents an assault on normative family life (1987). Furstenberg and his colleagues considered 'the popular belief that early childbearing almost certainly leads to school drop-out, subsequent unwanted births and economic dependence': they found this notion to be 'greatly oversimplified, if not seriously distorted' (p. 142). This conclusion was confirmed and extended in the British context by Ann Phoenix's study of young women with children (1990). The panic over 'teenage pregnancy' reflects a crisis for the heterosexual system and for normative family life which is discussed in greater detail in chapter 7, and the concern over 'adolescent homosexuality' addresses many similar issues.

A Multiplicity of Causes: Young Lesbians and Gay Men

In the mainstream literature there has been a long history of concern over 'homosexual behaviour', especially amongst young men (Plummer, 1989). In the west gay men have been criminalized and dealt with through the judicio-legal system in conjunction with the medical profession (Weeks, 1981), whilst lesbianism has usually been ignored or 'treated' within the medical and clinical domain (Terry, 1990). For young people, 'adolescent homosexuality' is frequently represented in the mainstream literature via the distinction between a supposedly temporary form of homosexuality ('it's just a passing phase'), and the irrevocable form of 'true homosexuality' (Conger, 1979; see Griffin, 1987).

Radical historical analyses have traced the shift from the conceptualization of 'deviant' practices such as sodomy in the treatment of male homosexuality to the modern focus on 'deviant' (and therefore treatable and redeemable) individuals with specific sexual identities (Padgug, 1979). Lesbian feminist historical analyses examined women's 'romantic friendships' during the late nineteenth and early twentieth centuries and the construction of lesbianism (or 'female sexual inversion') as a form of deviant female sexual identity by western sexologists (Faderman, 1981, 1992). Most of these analyses have been Anglocentric, and not explicitly racialized, so there is an almost complete absence of information about the experiences of working-class lesbians (and gay men) of colour, and the diverse forms which heterosexism can take in different cultures (one exception is Moraga and Anzaldua, 1981).

These radical analyses had an uneven impact on the mainstream literature on 'adolescent homosexuality' during the 1980s, especially in the USA where this literature (and associated counselling services) are more extensive. Mainstream analyses would tend to explain 'adolescent homosexuality' (away) through bio-medical origin stories, but the more 'sympathetic' liberal humanist perspective has expanded in scope since the 1970s (Kitzinger, 1988). One example of the latter which adopts the integrative strategy of forging a synthesis between competing models is Ritch Savin-Williams's review of 'theoretical perspectives accounting for adolescent homosexuality' in a special issue of the *Journal of Adolescent Health Care* (1988). This text reviews origin stories on the 'etiology of homosexuality' which rest on evolutionary biology: psychoanalytic theory; social processes; and 'ethologic perspectives'.

Labelling theory has attributed psychological and social 'maladjustment' among young lesbians and gay men to the predominantly hostile reaction towards 'deviance', rather than a consequence of a pathology which is inherent in homosexuality or homosexuals (e.g. Gonsiorek, 1988). In contrast, biosocial learning theory would emphasize the opportunities created by the greater likelihood of same-sex contacts during adolescence (e.g. Niles, 1986). A biomedical account would represent 'adolescent homosexuality' as a consequence of physiological abnormality, whether genetic or hormonal (e.g. Green, 1987). Savin-Williams himself preferred an 'ethologic' perspective, arguing that 'all human behaviors are biologic phenomena shaped by both genetic and environmental influences, and that all behaviors have or have had direct or indirect adaptive significance' (1988, p. 101). His strategy was to 'balance' biological and social explanations in an attempt to forge a synthesis between competing origin stories about 'adolescent homosexuality'.

In all of these approaches, it is 'homosexuality' which must be explained: only radical gay, lesbian and feminist writers have turned the analytic spotlight onto *heterosexuality* as a dominant social institution through which 'normal' sexuality is defined and policed (e.g. Rich, 1981). The mainstream perspective has been far more interested in searching for the causes of 'adolescent homosexuality' as a means of defusing or obscuring the potential threat this might pose to the heterosexual nuclear family norm.

Discourses in 1980s Youth Research around Family Life and Sexuality

Youth in Transition: The Discourse of Development

The discourse of development combines the biological determinism which characterizes the storm-and-stress model with the social constructionism which represents adolescence as an age stage subject to particular (often conflicting) social and cultural pressures. The biological domain is generally constructed as a fundamental force, with the social realm as the more superficial 'icing on the cake' (Birke and Vines, 1987; see chapter 1 above). As a result, the discourse of development tends to emphasize the greater ideological force of the biological imperative, although social pressures may be allowed considerable space. The discourse of development has played a crucial role in shaping the psychology of adolescence, and in sociological texts it is represented in life course and life cycle theories as a meeting place of cultural, social, structural, physical and psychological elements (see chapter 5). This discourse is particularly prevalent in research concerning 'adolescent sexuality', especially studies on the antecedents and correlates of premarital sexual intercourse, and studies on the formation of 'homosexual identities'.

The Transition to Heterosexuality, Marriage and Parenthood

Apart from entry to full-time employment, marriage and parenthood are generally regarded as key signifiers of adult status, especially for young women, although the impact of feminism and rising youth unemployment have undermined this relationship to some extent (Wallace, 1987). All young people are presumed to be heterosexual until otherwise indicated, and the mark of 'mature' sexuality is taken to be the first experience of heterosexual intercourse, specifically penetration. Much of the concern of mainstream academics, policy-makers and other anxious adults focuses around the nature of this 'initiation', particularly for young women. This moment of initiation is presumed to mark the first step on the road to (monogamous) marriage and parenthood, so it is especially important that young women are not put off for life at this crucial stage.

Adolescence is represented via the storm-and-stress model as a period of unprecedented emotional and hormonal turmoil which is heavily sexualized, so that young people are assumed to be particularly prone to 'promiscuous' sexual behaviour. Adolescence is also constructed as a period of social and psychological ambiguity in the transition from a childhood, which is closer to the biological/animal, towards an adult status, which is represented as primarily social. The discourse of development constructs 'adolescent sexuality' as a force which must be 'guided' and controlled in order to channel such impulsive, though 'natural', energies into appropriate pathways, and to 'resolve' such psychological ambiguities through the 'crystallization' of 'mature' (i.e. heterosexual, married) identities (e.g. Thornton, 1990; J. S. Clausen, 1991).

The discourse of development operates on the blurred boundaries between childhood, youth and adult status. The difficult nature of this terrain is exemplified by the contradictory decisions of US courts over issues related to 'teenage pregnancy', contraception, abortion and the heterosexual activities of unmarried young people (especially young women) who are legally defined as 'minors'. US court decisions have been highly variable in such cases, quite apart from interstate variations, sometimes conferring rights of control to young people, their parents or to the state in different situations. Many of these cases have dealt with young women seeking abortions or contraception without their parents' consent. Reviewing this area, Battle and Battle argued that in such cases the interests of parents and the state have usually coincided in opposition to the interests of the 'minor' (Battle and Battle, 1987). The discourse of development blocks attempts to treat young people (especially female 'minors') as entitled to those constitutional rights provided for adults, since the former are constructed as less mature than adults. In a similar manner, the discourse of development undermines the potential threat posed to the heterosexual system by young lesbians and gay men through the 'passing phase' thesis.

Not Just a Passing Phase: The Development of 'Adolescent Homosexuality'

In the construction of penetrative heterosexual sex as normal and ideal, alternative forms of sexuality are rendered invisible (e.g. lesbianism, celibacy) or criminal (e.g. gay male sexuality), and always defined as deviant (Herdt, 1989). The 'passing-phase' thesis provides a powerful means by which rejections of heterosexuality by young people defining themselves as lesbian and gay (or bi-sexual or celibate) can be defused through the argument that this is likely to be merely a temporary phenomenon (e.g. Conger, 1979). In these terms, 'true homosexuality' is differentiated from the 'passing phase' of same-sex attraction, which is presented as a possible (though not automatic) element of 'adolescent sexual development'. The discourse of development does not always operate in conjunction with the passing-phase thesis. The relatively liberal approach taken by contributors to the special issue of the *Journal of Adolescent Health Care* (*JAHC*) on 'Adolescent Homo-sexuality' (1988) can be compared with the more radical analyses in the *Journal of Homosexuality* (*JHom*) special issue on 'Gay and Lesbian Youth' (1989).

Kourany's contribution to the *JAHC* dealt with the 'resolution of sexual identity', drawing on the discourse of development to argue that these 'choices about sexual orientation are thought to be made . . . during adolescence (1988, p. 114). In Kourany's text, the discourse of development constructed 'sexual orientation' as a (relatively) linear process in which individual subjects emerge as having a specific 'sexual identity'. There is no suggestion here that one might examine the causes and correlates of heterosexual 'object choice' in an equivalent manner: the latter is represented as the 'natural' end-point of psycho-sexual development and the epitome of sexual maturity: only 'homosexual object choice' must be explained, since it deviates from the heterosexual norm.

The sexual preference model puts the development of individuals' 'sexual object choice' at adolescence, rather later than the sexual orientation perspective of Gonsiorek, which located the formative moment of 'sexual object choice' in childhood (1988). The two approaches overlap and use interchangeable terminology, but the sexual preference model constitutes a greater degree of agency within the individual subject. The lack of a free 'object choice' is not always addressed in these texts, and both Gonsiorek and Kourany acknowledged the influence of homophobia in US so-ciety. For Gonsiorek it is impossible to change one's 'sexual orientation' once it has been developed, whilst for Kournay the latter is not an immutable condition nor a static sexual identity.

Kourany also cited Troiden's construction of 'a four-stage model for the attainment of 'gay identity' (Kourany, 1988, p. 115). Troiden contributed to both the *JAHC* and the *JHom* special issues, and whilst his texts drew on the discourse of development, he did not present the 'attainment of gay identity' in terms of a linear model of progressive stages. Troiden asked lesbians and gay men to 'recall having developed perceptions of themselves as homosexual' (1988, p. 105). Drawing on Erikson's theory of identity formation, Troiden's 'ideal-typical' model involved four stages: 'sensitization, identity confusion, identity assumption, and commitment' (p. 105). Troiden did not assume that this process would necessarily begin or occur during adolescence, and he argued that 'homosexual identity' 'is never fully determined in a fixed or absolute sense and is always subject to modification and further change' (p. 112). Troiden rejected the reliance of health professionals on the passing-phase thesis as a misguided strategy.

Troiden's rejection of the linear stage model which is central to the discourse of development was crucial to his reluctance to locate 'homosexual identity formation' in adolescence. This separation between the formation of lesbian and gay identities and 'adolescence' is even clearer in the literature on 'lesbian identity development' (e.g. Sophie, 1986). Only a few models of 'homosexual identity development' have recognized the specific experiences of young lesbians. Theories of 'lesbian identity development' have been more heavily influenced by feminist analyses compared to the literature on (male) 'homosexual identity development' described above (Schneider, 1989; Trenchard, 1984). Some writers have reversed the direction of the 'passing-phase' thesis, and examined the transition from heterosexuality to lesbianism (e.g. Kitzinger, 1991).

Theorists of 'lesbian identity development' have been more likely to critique and deconstruct the concept of 'identity' and specifically 'homosexual' or lesbian identity than their male counterparts (e.g. Cass, 1984). Beata Chapman and JoAnn Brannock for example, preferred to use the concept of 'lesbian self-labelling' rather than 'identity formation' or 'identity development' in their study of self-identified lesbians (1987). Lesbian self-labelling was not represented as a problem, a disease or a perversion, but a more positive process which involves defining oneself as Other and therefore as 'deviant' in a heterosexist and anti-lesbian society. Lesbian feminist theorists have made a more complete break with the discourse of development, and as a consequence research around lesbian identity has had fewer ties with youth research and its associated discursive configurations. In an ironic parallel to this, radical youth research has had relatively little to say about the lives of young lesbians and gay men, although the impact of pressures to become heterosexual on young women (and men) have been recognized in some of the feminist youth literature (e.g. Griffin, 1985a; Roman et al., 1988).

Studies like those of Chapman and Brannock have stressed the diversity of lesbian experience, although in common with the literature on 'homosexual identity formation', this work has been predominantly Anglocentric (Schneider, 1989). There is little mention of the particular experiences of young lesbians and gay men of colour, and the variety of forms which heterosexism, homophobia and anti-lesbianism can take in different cultures (one exception is Gerstel et al., 1989). This is in marked contrast to the mainstream literature on 'adolescent (hetero)sexuality', which has devoted considerable attention to young people of colour (and their white working-class peers), usually identifying these groups as 'delinquent' and 'deprived' through the discourse of sexual deviance.

'Perverted Youth': The Discourse of Sexual Deviance

The discourse of development lays out the path from childhood through adolescence to 'mature' adulthood, heterosexuality, marriage, parenthood, and (hopefully) a full-time job. This series of transitions marks out the 'normal' and 'ideal' pattern: it also defines any deviance from these norms as a 'problem' which must be explained, constructing 'deviants' as individuals to be dealt with, punished or 'helped'. 'Deviant youth' are more likely to be treated sympathetically within the radical perspective, since their deviance is frequently represented as a consequence of structural forces and/or as a form of resistance to those forces. Both mainstream and radical literatures have tended to adopt a voyeuristic gaze when discussing 'perverted youth', especially where the latter's 'deviance' is sexualized.

The mainstream British and US literatures have constructed specific groups of young women as potentially 'at risk' in heterosexual terms, or as exhibiting certain 'problem behaviours', especially those who are poor, working-class and/or young women of colour. Some studies have focused on young women's contraceptive use (or lack of it), or on their premarital (hetero)sexual behaviour. In other cases young women's pregnancy, regardless of marital status, is the primary focus; whilst for other researchers it is their *single* status which constitutes the main cause for concern. Other studies have focused on 'teenage prostitution' amongst young women and men, or 'adolescent homosexuality' (usually amongst young men) as forms of (sexual) deviance (see chapters 4 and 5). By the end of the 1980s, the panic around AIDS and HIV had been used to fuel and to challenge some of the founding assumptions of the discourse of sexual deviance.

Premarital Heterosexuality and 'Teenage Pregnancy'

The core of panics about premarital heterosexuality, especially amongst working-class young women and young women of colour, can be seen in fears over 'teenage pregnancy', which is usually represented as a consequence of 'uncontrolled adolescent (het-ero)sexuality' (e.g. Strassberg and Mahoney, 1988). Young women have provided the chief focus for academic anxiety partly because they have the babies (and the abortions), but mainly because this process of transition to heterosexuality, marriage and parenthood is crucial to the patriarchal control of female sexuality and fertility.

The literature on abortion forms one connection between concern over premarital heterosexuality (or 'early adolescent coitus'), contraceptive use and the panic over 'teenage pregnancy'. Since Britain's relatively liberal Abortion Act of 1967, there have been repeated attempts to restrict the availability of abortion. During the 1980s, a string of Bills galvanized a major national campaign to defend the 1967 legislation. In the USA, the picture was similar, with a militant anti-abortion movement which crossed the Atlantic to argue for the 'rights of the foetus' over those of pregnant women. In both countries, connections were made between the lack of abortion facilities and the sterilization of poor women and women of colour and the sterilization campaigns in the Third World funded by the World Health Organization (Mosher, 1990). Although the 'adolescent pregnancy rate' rose during the 1970s, peaked in 1980 and 1981, and has fallen ever since, this has had minimal impact on the climate of moral panic and the continuing focus on young women in the research literature (e.g. Henshaw, 1987).

Until the 1970s, official statistics and academic 'common sense' indicated that premarital heterosexual intercourse was primarily confined to the courtship sequence: i.e. that it was *pre*marital. After that time, mainstream researchers believed that such teenage heterosexual activity had become increasingly *non*-marital: i.e. that 'many teenagers began to have sexual intercourse while having no intention of marrying' (Furstenberg et al., 1987, p. 142). Initial concern focused on 'the black family', constructing 'teenage pregnancy' in the USA as a predominantly African-American phenomenon (Hayes, 1987). Frank Furstenberg attributed this concern to the fact that these changes happened first and were the most evident in African-American families, but radical Black scholars saw yet another attempt to pathologize African-American families and sexualities (e.g. Ladner, 1987).

A classic example of the use of the discourse of sexual deviance in a mainstream analysis of 'teenage pregnancy' is an article by Allan Abrahamse, Peter Morrison and Linda Waite, based at the Rand Corporation's Population Center in the USA (Abrahamse et al., 1988). Abrahamse and his colleagues distributed a questionnaire to 13,061 female high school sophomores in 1980 and again in 1982. They found that '41% of blacks, 29% of Hispanics and 23% of non-Hispanic whites said they either would or might consider having a child outside of marriage' (p. 13). This willingness was, they argued, higher amongst those 'at greater risk of teenage parenthood'. By this, Abrahamse and colleagues meant young women of 'low socio-economic status, poor academic ability, and parental family structure' (i.e. residence in female-headed family), since these were the factors on which they based their 'parenthood-at-risk' scale.

Abrahamse and colleagues represented 'teenage pregnancy' as part of a pattern which might include 'alcohol and drug use, misbehavior in school, criminal behavior, aggression, lying and stealing' (p. 16). 'Teenage pregnancy' was firmly located as a gendered, racialized and class-specific phenomenon which was a key indicator of female heterosexual 'deviance'. Researchers then set out to search for the causes of such 'deviance' and/or the 'risk factors' associated with it in order to prevent future increases in the rate of 'teenage pregnancy'. Abrahamse and his colleagues came down in favour of a combination of explanations for single parenthood amongst young women. These included a psychological explanation which located the cause of this 'problem' in the 'rebelliousness' of individual young women; an economic explanation, which emphasized the financial costs and benefits of becoming an 'unmarried mother'; and a further psychological thesis which linked depression and low self-esteem with single parenthood amongst young women.[3]

Not all mainstream analyses of 'teenage pregnancy' or 'single parenthood' have utilized the discourse of sexual deviance in the same way. Marianne Felice, Paul Schragg, Michelle James and Dorothy Hollingsworth investigated 'whether pregnant Mexican-American adolescents have psychosocial characteristics different from their pregnant white or black peers' (1987, p. 5). Felice and her colleagues argued that Mexican-American young women were more likely to be married at conception and/or delivery, and the fathers of their children were more likely to be full-time students or employed compared to their white or African-American peers. More young white women reported family histories of psychiatric illness, parental death or runaway behaviour.

Felice and her colleagues did not use this information to present a causal explanation of 'teenage pregnancy', nor to develop an identification of 'at risk' indicators. They recognized the possibility that such pregnancies might be the result of rape and/or sexual abuse, focusing their conclusions around the different *needs* and 'psychosocial problems' of young women from all three groups, rather than on those economic, social and psychological factors which had supposedly predisposed them to get pregnant in the first place. This text did not adopt the same discursive strategies as that of Abrahamse and his colleagues, but young pregnant women were still constructed as potential problems, cast as passive victims of abuse rather than as actively 'rebellious'.

The negative representations of 'adolescent mothers' through the discourse of sexual deviance has had repercussions beyond the literature on 'teenage pregnancy'. Pamela Pletsch examined substance use amongst pregnant adolescents, concluding that these young women 'demonstrated more positive health behaviors' than their non-pregnant peers (1988, p. 1). Pletsch was surprised by her results, since she admitted that the literature on 'teenage pregnancy' had led her to expect less positive health behaviours amongst pregnant young women. The discourse of sexual deviance does not enable mainstream researchers to contemplate the possibility that these young women might have 'chosen' to become pregnant outside marriage, or that their primary concerns might revolve around their poverty, inadequate housing or health care, rather than their marital status or their pregnancy. Only feminist analyses have presented such arguments (Phoenix, 1990; see chapter 7 below).

The other main area of concern in the research literature on young people and sexual deviance focuses on young people's involvement in prostitution. The nineteenth- and early twentieth-century literatures on adolescence represented young working-class women who left rural areas for the expanding cities as dangerous temptresses that might lure young men into 'vice' *and* as innocent victims of the pressures of urban life (e.g. Kett, 1977). Young women's involvement in prostitution has been less prevalent a theme in 1980s youth research texts compared to the scale of panics over 'teenage pregnancy' in the USA. There is a larger feminist literature on prostitution, but this has seldom focused on *young* women or addressed itself to the concerns of youth research (e.g. Barry, 1979).

Feminist work on prostitution generally has challenged dominant representations of prostitute women as deviant Others, undermining the discourse of sexual deviance. This has also struggled with the tension between constructing prostitute women and other sex industry workers as passive victims of patriarchal oppression (see N. Roberts, 1986, for critique) *or* as just another group of 'working women' (e.g. McLaughlin, 1991). Other feminist analyses have argued that female sexuality is still constructed as potentially dangerous and associated with prostitution if it is defined as 'excessive', and that representations of sexuality are often racialized as well as gendered (Young, 1990). Since young women's sexuality is so closely connected with notions of female deviance and is often represented as in need of adult (especially male) control, the discursive connections with prostitution are not difficult to find. There is one other area where links between young people's sexuality and prostitution have been made, and that is in research on 'adolescent homosexuality' or 'gay male prostitution', which has a focus on young *men*.

'Adolescent Homosexuality' and the AIDS Panic

The discourse of sexual deviance has also been central to the literature on 'adolescent homosexuality', and as Savin-Williams pointed out in his review article 'homosexuality is by definition deviant' (1988, p. 97). The discourse of sexual deviance is less concerned with the statistical incidence of specific sexual practices, and more involved in policing the boundary lines of the heterosexual norm. In mainstream youth research, specific groups of young people have been defined as sexually deviant. Young women have generally been represented as *too* heterosexual, as heterosexually involved with 'deviant' males, or as not heterosexual *enough* (Griffin, 1982a). Young men's sexuality has been constructed as deviant within the confines of 'adolescent homosexuality' (Gonsiorek, 1988). That is, deviant sexuality for young men is defined as gay sexuality: young gay men are represented as excessively sexual in a way that their heterosexual peers are not, and prostitution has close associations with any sexualities that are constructed as 'excessive' or 'deviant'. So it is scarcely surprising that young gay men should figure prominently in the research literature on male prostitution (Mathews, 1983).

The few studies which have not relied on the discourse of sexual deviance in their representations of young people and sexuality illustrate the limitations of the liberal strategy of tolerance in the context of the 'passing-phase' thesis. Aggleton and Whitty's neo-Marxist analysis examined the contradictory surveillance strategies of white, middle-class liberal parents over their daughters and sons (1985). Whilst parents 'openly welcomed gay men into their homes as friends, they viewed with considerable alarm the possibility of homosexual activity among their offspring', in one case actually threatening to invoke therapeutic counselling (p. 64). These British parents also adopted sharply divergent practices with regard to the degree of autonomy extended to their daughters and sons in heterosexual relationships. Sons were allowed, indeed encouraged, to practise far more latitude than were daughters.

From a practitioner's perspective, William Niles from New York's Residential School for Boys discussed various ways of 'managing episodic homosexual behaviour' amongst 'emotionally disturbed adolescents' in residential settings (1986). Niles lamented the lack of attention devoted to this issue, presenting such behaviour as 'a normative adolescent experience that will occur in congregate care facilities' (p. 15). He argued that such behaviour was a product of the single-sex institution in combination with adolescent male sexual expression, and should be accepted as such, rather than ignored or condemned. Niles was only able to challenge the dominant discourse of sexual deviance through the use of the 'passing-phase' thesis, since such 'homoeroticism' was relatively acceptable only if it could be constructed as temporary.

During the second half of the 1980s a moral panic of epidemic proportions resonated throughout western academia, the 'popular' media and amongst health care professionals and policy-makers around AIDS and HIV (Schwanberg, 1990). Much of this panic focused on sexual practices and sexualities, especially those of young people, gay men, sex industry workers, working-class and Black communities, all of whom were represented (in different ways) as promiscuous and sexually deviant (Redman, 1991). The sexuality of elite groups such as white heterosexual professional men was scarcely touched by the panic around AIDS and HIV.[4] This panic and the reactions to it both reinforced and challenged the discourse of sexual deviance. The panic around AIDS and HIV was a panic over 'deviant' sexualities in which 'perverted youth' formed an automatic constituency for adult concern through the sexualized construction of adolescence (Aggleton et al., 1988). Paradoxically, the AIDS panic produced a wave of intensified homophobia and anti-lesbianism *and* a space for radical researchers and practitioners to challenge such practices.

In his preface to a special issue of the *Journal of Adolescent Health Care* on 'Adolescent Homosexuality', Gary Remafedi argued that the crisis around AIDS and HIV forced 'adolescent health care professionals' to address the 'subject of homosexuality' (1987). For Remafedi, the spread of AIDS to heterosexuals provided a severe challenge to heterosexist assumptions about the separation between gay and straight cultures. AIDS and other 'gay enteric diseases' are presented as prime factors in the visibility – if not the acceptability – of 'homosexuality' in US life. Remafedi paid scant attention to the specific position of lesbians, or the complex and uneasy relations between lesbian feminists and those in the 'gay rights' movement. Remafedi urged all 'adolescent health care professionals to be actively involved in the care of young gays and lesbians and to promote understanding of their experiences and needs' (p. 93).

The AIDS panic did allow scope for challenges to many elements of the discourse of sexual deviance by radical academics and health care professionals working in a range of agencies. However, the British press was quick to label AIDS as 'the gay plague' and to increase the intensity of its homophobic content. The US press followed a similar pattern, and physical attacks on gay men and lesbians increased on both sides of the Atlantic. In 1988 Thatcher's Conservative government passed the Local Government Act, incorporating the infamous 'Section 28' which prohibited local authorities from 'intentionally promot[ing] homosexuality' or 'promot[ing] the teaching . . . of the acceptability of homosexuality as a pretended family relationship'.[5] For many young lesbians and gay men the lack of peer support and lack of access to more adult-oriented lesbian and gay communities can make life extremely difficult, increasing the likelihood of suicide attempts, drug and alcohol abuse (Kourany, 1987). In practice, most young lesbians and gay men were still likely to be referred to clinical psychologists and psychiatrists as part of that sector of western medicine which specializes in 'treating the problems of troubled youth'.

Treating 'Troubled Youth': The Clinical Discourse

As in so much of the literature on 'delinquency' and 'deviance' discussed in the previous chapters, the clinical discourse has played a key role in texts on young people, family life and sexuality. The construction of various categories of 'troubled youth' locates the source of particular 'problems' in the psychological states of (certain) individuals or groups of young people. Such discursive configurations have been a central element in the continued use of the victim-blaming thesis. The 'problems' to be 'treated' under this psychological, clinical and psychiatric regime include 'homo-sexuality', 'promiscuity' (i.e. an excess of heterosexuality directed at 'inappropriate' targets), 'teenage pregnancy', the effects of di-vorce on children, 'acting-out behaviours' and/or aggressive 'con-duct disorders' of various kinds. 'Treatment' is equally likely to be instigated, especially for young women, working-class and young people of colour, if they are deemed to be 'at risk' by welfare agencies and mental health professionals. Once the bound-ary lines have been drawn around 'normality', 'maturity' and 'deviance', young people who are seen as deviant or at risk of becoming deviant can be identified and 'treated'. The blame for youthful deviance is frequently laid at the door of their families (especially mothers), and the techniques and theories of family therapy have played a central role in this enterprise.

Family Therapy

'Family therapy' refers to a diverse set of approaches and practices which aim to 'treat' the 'disturbed' individual in the context of her/his immediate family. It unites progressive and traditional perspectives on clinical practice in a complex and contradictory cocktail. In the 'treatment' of 'troubled youth', family therapy has relied heavily on the clinical discourse (e.g. Fishman, 1988). Vari-ous forms of family therapy have been popular since the 1960s, especially in the USA, and their use has not been confined to clinical practitioners (Hoffman, 1981). Steven Schinke and his colleagues from the School of Social Work at Washington University for example, argued for 'a new definitional model and improved methods for human services prevention research with youth and families' (1986, p. 257). By 'prevention', they meant 'knowledge-based group intervention aimed at helping at-risk youth and families build skills and social supports to enhance interpersonal and environmental competence and manage stress' (p. 257). Schinke and his colleagues were concerned with 'at-risk' young people here, but similar points have been made when referring to young people who have been defined (or rather diagnosed) as exhibiting various 'problem behaviours'.

In Britain, the literature on family therapy has been less extensive, partly due to lack of institutional structures, finance for therapists and social workers, and fewer links with academic journals and research programmes (Dryden, 1988). However, Graham Bryce and David Baird described the use of family therapy with ten 'adolescent school refusers' in Scotland. This involved 'precipitating a crisis by insisting on the adolescents' early return to school' (1986, p. 199). A study on the effects of divorce on children and young people aged under sixteen or eighteen (i.e. legal minors) reviewed recent changes in the 'family counselling' field. Lydia Voight and William Thornton traced 'a shift from the "individual" to the family unit in terms of origination and treatment of problems' (1987, p. 1). They claimed that most family counsellors had failed to keep up with changes in family structure and dynamics as these affect young people, citing the relatively new phenomenon of the joint custody family as one example. Such calls for a shift from viewing young people as isolated individuals towards 'treating' them in the family context are not specific to the 1980s, but the series of panics over 'troubled youth', morality and family life during the 1980s did add considerable impetus to these arguments.

The progressive element of the family therapy approach lies in the shift of the clinical focus away from the individual subject towards the family setting. This rejection of the victim-blaming thesis found in some radical analyses has frequently involved the substitution of mother-blaming for victim-blaming (Chesler, 1986). It has also produced a wealth of texts on 'family dysfunction' which have pathologized working-class and Black family forms, reinforcing the nuclear family norm (Phoenix, 1988). Family therapy approaches are concerned to construct and prevent 'family dysfunction', and they must therefore operate with some model of a 'healthy family'. This has generally involved the heterosexual monogamous married couple and the nuclear family form, advocating specific patterns of intra-family relations which presume an egalitarian system of father–mother and parent–child relationships. Family therapy has also tended to locate young people's 'problems' within the family in preference to other social institutions such as the education system, the job market or the operation of the mental health professions.

The clinical family therapy literature also discusses the presumed need to explain 'adolescence' to parents, in order to enable them to 'cope' with their children's behaviour. Joyce Lohman provides a contemporary example of this phenomenon, writing in an American journal of Adlerian theory about the 'Toughlove' programme for 'parents of severely acting-out teenagers', the stated aim of which is to 'help parents cope with disruptive behavior', and to explain 'contemporary youth [and] society's effect on adolescents' to their parents (1986, p. 225). Programmes like Toughlove continue the practice of constructing adolescence and adolescents as Other, different from adults (and from children), as 'strange' beings whose culture, attitudes and behaviours are constructed as the subject of adult understanding, surveillance and control.

'The family' is treated as an institution which can (or should) operate along egalitarian lines: conflict is taken as evidence of 'dysfunction' within the clinical discourse. Frederick Lopes's review of the literature on depressed college students and family structure pointed to four features which have been linked to 'depression and maladjustment' in this population: '(1) parent–child overinvolvement, (2) parent–child role reversal, (3) marital instability, and (4) parent–child coalitions' (1986). This list must qualify almost every family in Britain and the USA as a possible source of 'depressed and maladjusted teenagers'.

'Treating the Problems of the Sexually Active Teenager'

Considerable research attention has been devoted to gay male sexuality and female heterosexuality as spheres of sexual deviance: young lesbians and heterosexual males are almost invisible in this literature as exemplars of 'deviance' and 'normality' respectively. The clinical discourse has taken a central place in constructing these related categories of sexual deviance. Most concern over 'adolescent (hetero)sexuality' has focused on young women, and this literature reflects the links between academic researchers and health care professionals.

Lawrence Neinstein and Jean Shapiro for example, interviewed 287 US pediatricians about their views on 'the medical and psychosocial problems of the adolescent, the problems of the sexually active teenager, and the pelvic examination' (1986, p. 18). This text is a valuable source of dominant clinical representations of 'adolescent female (hetero)sexuality', which set the boundaries between 'normal' and 'disturbed' behaviour. Another equally revealing study examined the circumstances in which US paediatricians might decide to ask young women about their sexual histories during clinical consultations. Andrew Hunt, Iris Litt and Mindy Loebner examined the medical records of sixty young women for evidence that paediatricians had asked questions (or at least recorded information) about their sexual histories (1988). All of these young women, aged between twelve and twenty, had been admitted to emergency or casualty departments with acute abdominal pains. Paediatricians were far more likely to ask working-class African-American and Chicana young women questions about heterosexual experience, contraceptive use or possible pregnancy compared to their white and middle-class peers. Hunt and his colleagues argued that this reflected a racialized rather than a class-based effect, and the gendered nature of such practices is evident.

A further example of the clinical discourse at work in the construction of young women 'at risk' can be found in an article by two Israeli researchers which drew on the British, US and Israeli research literatures (Berger and Schechter, 1989). This text demonstrates the ideological force of the US literature outside North America, and the related operation of class, 'race' and age relations alongside those of gender. Roni Berger and Yuta Schechter represented 'adolescent girls in distress' as at 'the intersection of three populations at risk: adolescents, females, and those experiencing socioeconomic difficulties' (p. 357). They characterized 'adolescent girls in distress' aged between thirteen and nineteen as having 'grown up in conditions of distress', and as showing behaviour which 'deviates from the accepted norms' (p. 358). These young women are defined as on the borderline of 'delinquency', since 'they tend . . . to harm themselves more than they do others' (p. 358). For Berger and Schechter, the main characteristic of 'adolescent girls in distress' was their 'severe difficulty, to the point of dysfunction, in the family, study and work systems' (p. 358).

The bulk of Berger and Schechter's article was devoted to a six-page literature review in tabular form which ran through various aspects of 'adolescent development', highlighting those phenomena which are apparently common to all young people, those which are specific to 'adolescent boys', 'adolescent girls' and 'adolescent girls in distress' (pp. 364–9). The latter group are represented as a problem since, for example, 'mutual father–daughter attraction is perceived as threatening'; they have 'difficult' mother–daughter relations, and 'a high frequency of incestual relations and running away in order to avoid confrontation' (p. 365). Two pages further on 'mother–daughter rejection' appears as one component in the incidence of incest amongst these young women. Abusive fathers or male relatives are largely invisible in this text, as far as their patriarchal status is concerned: *his* 'dysfunctional' behaviour is attributed instead through the clinical discourse to deficient cultural practices and limited educational and economic opportunities in those 'families [who] suffer from the distress syndrome' (p. 371). So young women are blamed for viewing 'father–daughter attraction' as threatening, *and* blamed (along with their mothers and their cultural backgrounds) when sexual abuse occurs (see Driver and Droisen, 1989).

The source of these young women's distress is not assumed to lie in the exercise of patriarchal power through sexual abuse, as feminist analyses would argue, but in the 'mixed messages' which young women receive in such 'dysfunctional families', especially around the status of women. In these families, young women are apparently expected to do well in school and the job market, but (unlike their male peers) they are discouraged from taking up any opportunities in these spheres, and are expected instead to become good wives and mothers. Feminist writers have presented this phenomenon as a common element in women's subordinated position (e.g. Barrett and McIntosh, 1982), but the use of the clinical discourse in Berger and Schechter's text presents this phenomenon as specific to 'dysfunctional families' which are predominantly poor, working-class and of African or Asian descent.

Less frequently, studies have examined the role of health care practitioners as problematic in the construction of specific young people's sexualities. George Realmuto and William Erikson, for example, discussed 'the special problems presented by disturbed adolescents confined to inpatient treatment for the management of sexual behaviors' (1986, p. 347). The 'problems' encountered by adult staff members turned out to be based on the staff's own 'sexual anxiety . . . caused by societal stereotypes of adolescents' (p. 347). Other problems amongst the staff included inexperience with the intervention techniques used, 'ignorance of normal adolescent development' and countertransference. This text is relatively unusual: in most cases the spotlight remains on young people as potential sources of sexual deviance.

The clinical discourse constructs the 'problems' of heterosexual and 'homosexual' young people differently. In the 'treatment' of young people with heterosexual 'problems', there is at least a norm to which they can be steered: the acceptance and practice of heterosexual penetrative intercourse within a monogamous marital relationship. The sexuality of young lesbians and gay men is represented as a problem *in itself*: there is no acceptable or normal sexual practice here. John Gonsiorek did not use the clinical discourse to pathologize young lesbians and gay men (1988). He represented 'homosexuality [as] a nonpathologic variant on the continuum of sexual orientation' (p. 114), and he was interested in preventing mental health problems amongst young lesbians and gay men, not in the prevention of 'homosexuality' *per se*. Gonsiorek identified three barriers to 'understanding homosexuality in adolescence': the problematic concepts of adolescence; homophobia; and erotophobia. He argued that the trend towards lengthening the upper limit of adolescence which is most marked in the more affluent socio-economic strata in the USA is in sharp contrast to the lowering of the age of puberty onset.

Gonsiorek defined homophobia as 'an irrational and distorted view of homosexuality or homosexual persons' (p. 125). He stated that 'youthful sexual expression has been construed as an institutional problem requiring a response . . . It is to be understood, categorized, legislated, pathologized, cured and ultimately suppressed' (p. 125). In heterosexuals, this is usually manifested as prejudice or general discomfort with homosexuals: in gay men and lesbians, this can be reflected in a complex form of 'internalized homophobia'. For Gosiorek, it is particularly important for health care professionals to recognize the existence and effects of homophobia – especially in themselves.

Gonsiorek devoted some attention to erotophobia, or the way in which US culture is 'obsessed with sex, yet phobic and deeply distrustful of sexuality' (p. 125). Gonsiorek had less to say about the specifically gendered nature of this uneasy combination of obsession and phobia, and the link between violence and sexuality (see Coveney et al., 1984). He did identify social pressures to be acceptably feminine and masculine as part of the problems faced by young lesbians and gay men, and the different psychological, social and cultural problems faced by young lesbians and gay men during the process of 'coming out'.

Gonsiorek's text examined clinical concerns without recourse to the clinical discourse. He was not searching for the causes or correlates of 'homosexuality', and his work provides a powerful rejection of the 'passing-phase' thesis. Gonsiorek stated from clinical experience that 'professionals cannot alter an adolescent's sexual orientation, but can merely obscure it by cooperating in avoidance, denial and shame' (p. 129). The aim of therapy or counselling should not to be to try and change young lesbians and gay men into heterosexuals, but to help them to deal with their sexuality and the problems of living in a heterosexist society (see Schneider and Tremble, 1986).

'Deficient Youth': The Discourse of Education and Training

Once adolescence has been constructed as an age stage involving some degree of psychological and social disturbance via the discourse of development, (certain) groups of young people can then be defined as 'troubled' through the clinical discourse. Others (sometimes similar groups or individuals) may also be positioned as 'perverted' or 'deviant' through the discourse of sexual deviance; or as coming from 'inadequate' or 'disadvantaged' families or cultural backgrounds through the use of the victim-blaming thesis in stories of deprivation. Whilst the clinical discourse would advocate the 'treatment' of 'troubled youth' within the medical regime, the allied discourse of education and training emphasizes the need to educate such 'deficient youth' out of their 'problem behaviours'.

Heterosexual Education: Learning 'Pregnancy Avoidance'

Research on young people's attitudes towards, and knowledge about sexuality concentrates on *heterosexual* education, although this restriction is seldom recognized outside the feminist literature (e.g. Holly, 1989). Marvin Eisen and Gail Zellman for example, carried out a fifteen-hour sex education programme using a health belief model, with 126 female and 77 male Texan thirteen- to seventeen-year-olds (1986). These young people were interviewed about their 'sexual and contraceptive knowledge, attitudes towards pregnancy and contraception, and prior sex education and sexual activity experiences' (p. 9). Gender and age were not associated with variations in these scores, whilst 'minority ethnic status was consistently associated with less sexual and contraceptive knowledge' (p. 9). According to the authors, the aim of such (hetero)sexual education programmes should be to increase knowledge and 'motivation for pregnancy avoidance and contraception [use]' (p. 9). In this case, as in many other similar texts, young people of colour were defined as the most deficient in terms of their knowledge and behaviour, and they were therefore constructed as the focus for change.

One of the key elements in the discourse of education and training concerns the representation of specific young people as deficient, with the implication that educational initiatives should be directed at these individuals or groups, who are predominantly young working-class women and young women of colour. Debra Kalmuss of Columbia University's Center for Population and Family Health distinguished between 'ever- and never-pregnant adolescents' in her study on the effects of 'teenage pregnancy on contraceptive behavior of adolescent females' (1986, p. 332). This sharp distinction between young women in terms of their pregnancy history appears to ignore the role played by young men, and it led Kalmuss to search for differences between the two groups. Kalmuss argued that 'the negative effect of pregnancy history may occur because ever-pregnant teens hold more positive attitudes about pregnancy than their never-pregnant peers' (p. 332).

Researchers or health care professionals have seldom asked young women about *their* primary concerns and needs: adults are assumed to know best, especially where 'pregnant teens' are concerned. Dana Schwartz and Katherine Darabi, for example, admitted that whilst most family planning clinics routinely gather information on referral sources and primary reasons for visits, 'little is known about the "precipitating events" that motivate young women to attend a clinic' (1986, p. 1). Only a few studies have examined the practices of adult professionals from young women's standpoint. Phyllis Levenson, Peggy Smith and James

Morrow surveyed the views of forty-six physicians and 146 'pregnant teens' with regard to the main information needs of the latter group (1986). They found considerable agreement, but two key areas of mismatch. Physicians expressed a greater interest in birth control information and psychosocial concerns than did the young women, indicating perhaps that adult professionals' concern over contraception and the psychological state of 'pregnant teens' was not shared by the young women themselves.

One of the hallmarks of the discourse of education and training is that 'deficient' young people are assumed to lack knowledge and to hold 'inappropriate' attitudes about contraception, sexuality and parenthood (Furstenberg et al., 1987). When researchers have subjected this assumption to closer scrutiny many young people have *not* been found to lack information on contraception (e.g. Phoenix, 1990; Landry et al., 1986). This overturns the argument that 'teenage pregnancy' can be attributed to ignorance about contraception on the part of young people, and the notion that rates of 'teenage pregnancy' can be reduced by educational initiatives based solely on providing information.[6]

A second strand of the discourse of education and training is its reliance on a rational decision-making model. George Loewenstein and Frank Furstenberg criticized the value of such a model on three grounds: '(a) because the decision-makers are teenagers, (b) because the decision concerns sexual behavior, and (c) because the costs of contraception and abstinence are immediate and certain, while the benefits are delayed and uncertain' (1991, p. 957). I would argue that it is the rational decision-making framework which poses the major problem here, as in all its psychosocial applications, since it constitutes a unitary rational individual subject as the location of rational choices (Venn, 1984).

Poor and working-class young women and young women of colour are especially likely to be defined as 'deficient' in the mainstream literature, and many studies have constructed these groups of young women as particular 'social problems'. Evelyn Landry and her colleagues at Tulane University School of Public Health and Tropical Medicine for example, looked at 'teen pregnancies' in New Orleans in terms of 'factors that differentiate teens who deliver, abort and successfully contracept' (1986, p. 259). Only young African-American women were included in the participating group for this study, and the dimensions selected for inclusion in the questionnaire were 'family background, sociodemographic characteristics, attitudes towards school, knowledge of contraception, sexual experiences, and best friend's experiences with pregnancy' (p. 259). Landry and her colleagues concluded that 'teen childbearers are more likely to live with a parent, have a best friend who had been pregnant, and know less about contraception, [whereas] aborters were typically living with a parent and planning to go to college' (p. 259). This research design provided a snapshot of three pre-selected groups of young Black women, with the intention of preventing 'teenage pregnancy' amongst this group (Griffin, 1992).

Beck and Davies's review of US research on 'pregnancy prevention' has demonstrated the prevalence of the discourse of education and training and the victim-blaming thesis in this literature (1987). They began by pointing to the 'near epidemic rates of teenage pregnancy' in the USA, and the particular concern expressed over specific groups (e.g. Mexican-Americans and African-Americans). Beck and Davies argued that most studies have lacked theoretical guidance and most research on 'pregnancy prevention' has focused on 'compliance with contraception', trying to identify 'factors that predict consistent contraceptive use and on designing interventions to enhance adherence' (p. 338). They also reported widespread inconsistencies across studies in recording relevant dimensions of adherence to birth control.

Turning to those studies which have tried to identify predictive factors in 'contraceptive compliance', Beck and Davies examined three perspectives used in this literature: the biomedical, behavioural and self-control models. In the former case, patients are labelled as 'noncompliant' due to 'inadequate' personal characteristics. Much of this research has aimed to identify the demographic characteristics associated with 'noncompliance', and 'race' or ethnicity have appeared repeatedly despite conflicting evidence on the differences between the contraceptive use of various ethnic groups. In research using the behavioural model, terminology shifts from 'compliance' to 'adherence', with an emphasis on 'norms' rather than 'rules'. Within the behavioural model, attention has moved from intra-individual variations to 'behaviour–attitude–environment interactions' (p. 356). Most studies have used self-reports of behaviour within a range of different questionnaire formats. Failure to adhere to or comply with 'appropriate' contraceptive use is defined as just that: failure. Thirdly, studies adopting self-control models of contraceptive compliance derived from a systems perspective have focused on individual motivations within the context of 'goal-directed behaviour'. Unlike the biomedical model, this approach constructs the individual as an active agent, able to define her own goals and motivate her own behaviour.

The discourse of education and training is only part of an ideological framework which has constructed young working-class women, and especially young women of colour in the USA, as deficient, feckless and in need of training in 'responsible' contraceptive use, heterosexuality and parenthood. In the British literature, the discourse of education and training operated in similar ways, with a focus on white, Asian and Afro-Caribbean working-class young women as particularly 'deficient' and 'deviant' (Burrage, 1986). Radical Black scholars have adopted a very different perspective on the issue of 'teenage pregnancy' which will be examined in the final chapter.

Welfare and Workfare: The Discourse of Dependence

Dependence and independence are crucial to constructions of adolescence as a transition point between the dependency of childhood and the economic, social and psychological independence which is associated with adult status. Such transitory states of independence position the individual subject in relation to her/his immediate family of origin, specifically the parents. This process of transition is also gendered, since only young men are expected to move into total independence: young women are presumed to shift over from the control and 'protection' of the father to that of the husband. Where notions of dependence have appeared in youth research and in youth policy it is scarcely surprising that concern has focused on young women, and especially young working-class women of colour with 'dependents' of their own.

On both sides of the Atlantic, the New Right mobilized fears over welfare dependence to justify major cuts in welfare provision which led to substantial increases in the incidence of poverty. During the era of Thatcher and Reagan welfare was viewed not as a right or a means of distributing wealth in a more egalitarian fashion, nor even as a safety net for the poor and needy, but as a continual threat, like a dangerously addictive drug (Brown and Sparks, 1989). In the USA, the 'New Consensus' proposed that the major problem in social welfare was not poverty, but dependency. As the 1980s wore on, a growing body of evidence appeared to challenge this assumption, indicating that welfare cuts did *not* reduce poverty or dependency (Schram, 1991). Young people, working-class and Black communities were the hardest hit by these welfare cuts, especially in combination with rising unemployment rates (Malveux, 1988; Pope, 1988). The discourse of dependence played a central role in Thatcherite and Reaganite ideologies, and this was also reflected in the mainstream research literature on young people, sexuality and family life.

Young women with children have been studied as actual or potential recipients of welfare benefits, especially in terms of their being 'at risk of becoming welfare dependent' (e.g. Chambre, 1982; Rudd et al., 1990). New Right ideology defined welfare payments as an incentive to single parenthood amongst young working-class women in Britain and the USA, and these arguments entered mainstream youth research through studies on the antecedents of 'teenage pregnancy'. In the USA, the discourse of dependence castigated welfare payments and Medicaid for producing increases in rates of 'teenage pregnancy', births and abortions. In Britain, some Conservatives called for the abolition of all benefits for single parents (i.e. mainly young working-class women), arguing that many single young women become pregnant in order to improve their chances of getting public housing (Phoenix, 1990).

The discourse of dependence was used to justify massive cuts to the US AFDC (Aid to Families with Dependent Children) pro-gramme and restrictions in the availability of Medicaid during the 1980s (Schram, 1991; Pope, 1988). In Britain a series of changes to the Social Security system in 1988 cut benefits to sixteen- and seventeen-year-olds even if they were homeless. Government-sponsored youth training programmes were also used throughout the 1980s to keep young people's wages low and to maintain young people's dependent status (Finn, 1987).

Some mainstream studies challenged the central arguments of the discourse of dependence. Susheela Singh for example, examined the considerable interstate variations in US rates of 'teenage pregnancy', birth and abortion, considering the impact of local policy measures as well as social and economic factors (1986). Singh argued that states with high official birthrates tended to have low abortion rates, so pregnancy rates varied less than birth and abortion measures. That is, 'in states with very high pregnancy rates, the adolescent abortion rate is higher than the birthrate and abortion rate combined in states with low pregnancy rates (p. 210). This challenged the Reaganite thesis that welfare payments and programmes like Medicaid lead to increases in teenage birth, pregnancy and abortion rates.

In the spheres of training, education and the job market, similar arguments have arisen around Reagan's 'workfare' and 'learnfare' programmes, in which young people must enter specified schemes or lose their welfare benefits. A similar system based on compulsion was operating in Britain by the end of the 1980s (Brown and Sparks, 1989). Jacqueline Pope produced a critical analysis of Reagan's welfare 'reforms,' arguing that changes to the AFDC programme tended to be 'biased against the poor', with many families below the poverty line being unable to claim assistance (1988). The twin themes of population control and maintaining power over low-wage workers were united under the umbrella of 'workfare'. Single women on AFDC have been a particular target for US conservatives in their recommendations about who should go on 'workfare'. Workfare is a compulsory programme, and it has served to depress wages, deunionizing major sectors of the US workforce. As Jacqueline Pope pointed out, workfare is *not* a cost-efficient programme, although advocates have presented it as such. Its *raison d'être* is not economic, but political and ideological (1988).

One of the central contradictions of the Thatcher and Reagan era was the use of pervasive and 'common-sense' discursive configurations stressing 'enterprise and efficiency', alongside practices which had the opposite effects (S. Hall, 1988). Jacqueline Pope, like others working from a radical perspective, was criticizing the mainstream research literature and government policies regarding workfare and welfare. Her objections to what I have termed the discourse of dependence stemmed from a different set of concerns than those found in the bulk of the mainstream literature.

Radical Analyses and the Discourse of Resistance

Radical research on young people, sexuality and family life has included (amongst others) feminist analyses, youth subcultural research, lesbian and gay studies and the work of radical Black scholars. These various approaches overlap to a considerable extent, and they are all marked by an opposition to the mainstream representation of (certain) young people as 'deviant', 'deficient' and/or 'troubled' in relation to their sexualities or their family lives. Many radical analyses especially in youth cultural studies have used the discourse of resistance to identify those cultural forms through which young people are seen to reject or negotiate the conditions of their oppression.

Young people are not constructed as 'problems' in the radical literature, but as victims or survivors of oppressive social and economic conditions. The discourse of resistance represents young people as active social agents capable of negotiating, challenging and/or rejecting such conditions. Feminist work from the late 1970s and into the 1980s focused particularly on the lives of young women, bringing issues of sexuality and the domestic world into the domain of radical youth studies (e.g. Holly, 1989). Feminist researchers are more likely to address young women's lives in the bedroom or the kitchen than the traditional haunt of the (male) ethnographers: the street corner (e.g. McRobbie and Garber, 1975).

Feminist analyses have had a particularly powerful impact on the literature concerning young people, family life and sexuality, challenging the dominant representation of young women (especially young working-class women and young women of colour) within mainstream research as sexually deviant, morally deficient and/or as inadequate mothers. Some radical texts have examined the position of young men in relation to the panic over young women's entry into parenthood, whilst others sought to portray 'teenage pregnancy' not as a sign of 'deviance' or 'family dysfunction', but as a mark of resistance to oppressive economic and social conditions. Many such analyses used the discourse of resistance to rescue young women from the position of passive victims or promiscuous delinquents to which they had been relegated within the mainstream literature.

The mainstream argument was that unemployed young single women (especially if they were working-class and Black) became pregnant as a consequence of their ignorance of contraceptive methods, their presumed 'promiscuity' or as a cynical manipulation of the welfare system. Some feminist analyses turned these arguments around to propose that young working-class women had 'babies on the dole' as a form of *resistance* to the pressures of unemployment, poverty and dependence on men (e.g. B. Campbell, 1984; Beuret and Makings, 1986).[7] Several studies have contradicted Campbell's proposition however, arguing that the transition to motherhood does not necessarily involve one straightforward decision, and that it may not even be experienced as a decision over which young women have exercised conscious 'choice' (Bhavnani, 1991). The most important question for these researchers is the way in which 'teenage pregnancy' came to be *constructed* as such a crisis for traditional family life and monogamous heterosexuality (Phoenix, 1990).

Apart from using the discourse of resistance as a means of turning the tables on mainstream analyses of young people, family life and sexuality, feminists and other radical researchers have a different ideological agenda. Radical research also looked at absences in the mainstream youth literature, such as the invisible fathers in many studies of 'teenage pregnancy', and at silenced voices, such as those of young lesbians and gay men, young people with disabilities or sex industry workers. Feminist work on family life also drew attention to sexual abuse, child abuse and domestic violence.

Absences and Silenced Voices

There has been an almost complete absence of young lesbian and gay voices in the mainstream and radical youth research literatures, with only a few exceptions (Plummer, 1989). These young people have not been represented as part of 'normal youth', apart from a few isolated studies which have usually involved retrospective interviews with older people (e.g. Schneider, 1989; Trenchard and Warren, 1987). The voices of young people with disabilities have been even less visible in the mainstream and radical research literatures, apart from patronizing texts on 'genetic counselling for handicapped adolescents'. These young people are not represented as sexual beings outside such arguments for sterilization, with the exception of the campaigning literature of disability rights groups, which has had minimal impact on academic youth research (Shearer, 1981; Fine and Asch, 1989).

One area in which radical (and some mainstream) texts have attempted to fill an existing gap is in their treatment of young men's position as fathers, particularly with respect to the 'teenage pregnancy' literature (Phoenix, 1990). Few studies have even recognized the existence of fathers or potential fathers, but Sandra Danziger and Charles Nagatoshi of the Institute of Research on Poverty at Madison, Wisconsin did focus on the child–father relationship (1987). Their concern was for the relationships of those almost 50 per cent of 'teen mothers' who are unmarried when they have their first child. In a related study, Danziger and Radin argued that 'father absence' is not equivalent to non-involvement in 'teen mother families' (1990). Most studies which have looked at young men's family responsibilities have tended to consider their involvement in childcare with respect to their position in the job market (e.g. Payne, 1989). The numerous studies of 'teenage pregnancy' have seldom mentioned young women's employment status; the emphasis is usually on their educational or domestic commitments (Burrage, 1986).

One of the relatively rare projects to consider young men's involvement (or lack of it) in childcare was Simon Lalonde's study on the effects of employment and unemployment on young white working-class fathers' childcare responsibilities in the British context (1987). Lalonde presented the decision to devote their time and energies to employment or to continuing participation in childcare if they managed to get a job as a dilemma for these young men. Most young women have no such 'choice', since childcare and domestic work are treated as their primary responsibilities, irrespective of their employment status. There is little evidence to suggest that most young men (or men of *any* age) do take a greater part in domestic work if they become unemployed (Wallace, 1987). However, several studies have argued that families of African and Caribbean descent in Britain and the USA tend to be more egalitarian with regard to the distribution of housework and childcare responsibilities compared to their white counterparts (Mirza, 1992; Danziger and Radin, 1990).

Discourses of Defence and Survival: Radical Research on Young People, Sexuality and Family Life in the Post-modern Age

In the latter half of the 1980s several critical examinations of the discourse of resistance emerged from within the radical perspective as the impact of post-structuralist arguments began to be felt in radical youth research following their effects within literary studies (Lather, 1990). Some radical researchers argued that 'resistance theory' invested them with the power of naming certain cultural practices as 'resistance' against or as 'collusion' with oppressive forces (Aggleton and Whitty, 1985; see chapters 3 and 4 above). Researchers were therefore imbued with magisterial authority, turning their moralizing (if sympathetic) and voyeuristic gaze upon 'deviant youth': a practice which they abhorred when conducted by mainstream youth researchers. The discourse of resistance also carried the possibility of romanticizing specific cultural practices as 'resistant' which might also be sexist or racist or both (McRobbie, 1980).

British sociologists Kris Beuret and Lynn Makings' study of 'women, class and courtship in a recession' in Britain during the early 1980s, for example, avoided the discourse of resistance, preferring not to speculate about whether young women's involvement in heterosexual relationships took the form of collusion or resistance. Beuret and Makings were interested in the impact of unemployment on courtship and marital relationships (1986; see Wallace, 1987). They constructed young women's relationships in terms of negotiations and strategies which operated in a depressed and restrictive job market through a powerful ideology of heterosexual romance. Beuret and Makings argued that both the young white working-class and middle-class women they interviewed operated strategies designed to 'save their boyfriends' face', especially when the latter were unemployed (p. 15).

A key area of debate within radical youth research concerns the tension between the construction of young people as passive victims of oppression and or as active social agents who are capable of resisting and transforming the conditions of that oppression. In the feminist research literature this debate has been especially relevant to the construction of sex industry workers. Some feminist analyses represented young women working in the sex industry in the passive mode as subjects of oppressive economic, political and ideological forces (Cain, 1989). Other feminist analyses, including sex industry workers themselves, rejected the notion that they were passive victims any more than supposedly 'respectable' wives and mothers, presenting their work as just that: a means of surviving in a situation with few possibilities for economic independence for women, especially young working-class women and young women of colour (e.g. N. Roberts, 1986; Lowman, 1989).

The discourses of resistance and suffering were rejected in this feminist literature on female sex industry workers in favour of a discourse of defence and survival (see chapter 5). In the feminist literature on sexual abuse and harassment, this tension between the construction of young women as victims or survivors was resolved in texts which represented young women as capable of adopting strategies of resistance, coping and/or survival (e.g. Halston, 1989). By the late 1980s, many radical texts had jettisoned the discourse of resistance, representing young working-class people and young people of colour as trapped within a state of crisis by the policies of Thatcher and Reagan. Other radical analyses addressed the debate over the relationships between structure, culture and agency, and between subjects and texts (e.g. Roman et al.,

1988; Willis et al., 1990). These discursive moves and the implications of my analysis for youth research in the 1990s will be examined in the final chapter.

Notes

1   The US-based *Journal of Adolescent Research* for example, launched in the 1980s, promoted itself by highlighting ten key areas in which the journal published material. Several of these areas are relevant to family life and sexuality, including 'social influences on sexual behavior; teenage pregnancy; [and] parenting styles'.

2   The defence of patriarchal nuclear family life has not been confined to the Right. The British Labour Party and Trade Union movement placed 'the family' at the centre of their plans for the post Second World War welfare state in the 1940s, and the defence of the 'family wage' for the male breadwinner has formed the centrepiece of numerous industrial disputes (Women's Studies Group, 1978).

3   Abrahamse and colleagues based this conclusion on a correlation between responses to *one* question on self-reported depression and others on self-esteem and the incidence of single parenthood amongst white and Chicana young women.

4   In 1988, British Airways refused to include an educational advertisement comprising a cautionary tale about the dangers of unsafe sex in their in-flight travellers' magazine, on the grounds that it might offend their customers, many of whom would be professional businessmen.

5   This Act was not challenged in court, but before the end of the decade many local authorities (including Labour-controlled councils) had cut their funding to lesbian and gay self-help organizations. Section 28 was only one of several legislative changes which reinforced the heterosexual basis of the nuclear family norm during the 1980s (Comely, 1991).

6   Several studies have argued that information-based education programmes have had little impact in the field of education around AIDS and HIV; some have even been counter-productive (Aggleton et al., 1988).

7   This is distinct from the mainstream argument that young women become pregnant as a means of developing their own sense of positive social identity (see Stiffman et al., 1990 for review).

7
Recovery and Survival: Youth Research after Thatcher and Reagan

A selection of young people's responses to the question 'What's it like to be young in the 1980s?' asked at an Open Day for school students, Birmingham University, March 1987:

> 'I can't wait to be over 20.'
>
> 'The day I turn 21 I'll go into hibernation.'
>
> 'There are too many pressures to grow up too quickly, exam and career pressures. It is also easy to get depressed, especially at the restrictive attitudes of adults towards young people. If you can get away from this and enjoy yourself it can be fantastic. Your free to form your own ideas and views without being thought insipid or pretensous [sic].'

> Young people no longer have the attention span to cope with serious ideas. (Verity Lambert, British TV producer, quoted by Patrick Stoddart in *The Times*, 10 March 1992)

The influential television producer Verity Lambert was referring in the above quote to the emergence of a specific 'youth TV' format in Britain during the 1980s. This was characterized by a series of short segments, often with simultaneous and different messages written on the screen and spoken by the presenter. The effect was one of rapid shifts between brief 'punchy' and inevitably superficial visual and graphic representations. This was the antithesis of the in-depth discussions between talking heads which epitomized 'serious' TV for (intellectual) adults. One of the ironies of the 1980s was that the format of 'youth TV', which could be (and was) constructed in creative opposition to the 'serious' adult norm, might then be re-appropriated by that same constituency as evidence of the feckless superficiality of contemporary adolescence.

The 1980s were marked by some profound ideological and political shifts, as discursive configurations appeared at times to move beneath one's feet and realign themselves in new and contradictory constellations. The sixteen- to seventeen-year-olds quoted at the start of this chapter to whom I spoke in 1987 also expressed this sense of contradiction. 'Being young in the 1980s' was represented both as a period of restriction and dread *and* in terms of a potential 'freedom to be yourself'. To some extent these parallel strands run through 'common-sense' and academic representations of adolescence over most of the past four decades. However there are several distinctive elements of youth research texts during the 1980s which are characteristic of the particular economic, political, cultural and ideological conditions of the period. As I have argued in this book, it is through considering the precise ways in which various discourses are mobilized and juxtaposed that we can examine mainstream and radical representations of 'youth' and 'adolescence' in the 1980s.

Philip Cohen makes this point in his foreword to Robert Hollands's study of class, culture and youth training in Britain, *The Long Transition* (Hollands, 1990): 'The importance of the youth question has nothing to do with demography or deviance. It is a site of discourses and institutions which play a key role in shaping the society we all live in–condensing certain strategic contradictions which are otherwise hidden or displaced' (P. Cohen, 1990, p. xii).

Representations of Youth originated as an examination of the impact of youth cultural analysis and other radical critiques on mainstream youth research. It developed into a far larger project, partly because the impact of radical research needs to be set in relation to the wider political context of the 1980s, a decade of New Right ascendancy. This book examines the range of discourses, representations and arguments which have been used to construct and explain 'youth' and 'adolescence' in British and US texts, and to make distinctions between different groups of young people and the representation of certain behaviours as actual or potential 'social problems'.

Adolescence was 'discovered' by G. Stanley Hall at the end of the last century, and many of the discursive hallmarks of this ideological construction can still be identified in contemporary research texts (see chapter 1). None of the dimensions of nineteenth-century representations of 'adolescence' have remained untouched by subsequent economic, political and ideological conditions, and many additional discursive configurations have entered the picture since G. Stanley Hall's time. 'Youth' is still treated as a key indicator of the state of the nation itself: it is expected to reflect the cycle of booms and troughs in the economy; shifts in cultural values over sexuality, morality and family life; and changes in class relations, concepts of nationhood, and occupational structures. To some extent the nation itself is produced and understood through representations of 'youth'. The treatment and management of 'youth' is expected to provide the solution to a nation's 'problems', from 'drug abuse', 'hooliganism' and 'teenage pregnancy' to inner city 'riots'. The young are assumed to hold the key to the nation's future: if official levels of unemployment rise or the incidence of violent crime increases, this can be attributed to 'problem youth', and a whole series of 'respectable fears' have been dealt with in this way (Pearson, 1983).

Although to some extent the division into decades is always a matter of convenience, there are some good reasons for treating the 1980s as a relatively discrete entity, at least in Britain and the USA. It would be foolish to deny the crucial influences of the post-Second World War period on the political climate of the 1980s, just as it is impossible to ignore the disastrous legacies of Thatcher and Reagan in the 1990s (Hall and Bailey, 1992). However, several discursive moves are characteristic of youth research in the 1980s, and these are examined in detail throughout this book.

The 1980s were characterized by a constellation of New Right policies and ideologies under Thatcher and Reagan which had a specific impact on young people and on research around 'youth' and 'adolescence' (see chapter 2). In Britain, the era of the New Right brought a reassertion of inequalities around class, 'race', gender and sexuality as education became a market-place founded on 'enterprise', competition and the wealth and wishes of parents (Ball, 1990; Brown, 1989). The USA entered the 1980s with many of its citizens experiencing a worse standard of living than thirty years previously. Severe cuts in social and welfare programmes, public housing projects and rising poverty levels produced a situation in which young people, and especially working-class young people and young people of colour were suffering more than at any time since the Second World War (Center on Budget and Policy Priorities, 1986).

Representations of Youth concentrates on British and US youth research texts since they have played a major role in shaping international representations of 'youth'. However irrelevant these western Anglocentric theoretical frameworks might be for the position of young people in other parts of the world, the discursive dominance of British and US texts makes them a valuable focus for study. Whilst there were many similarities between the political situations in Britain and the USA during the 1980s, it would be a mistake to minimize the differences between the two societies. The rise of the New Right is common to 1980s Britain and the USA, but the pattern of youth unemployment, the diversity of the two labour markets, variations between British and US economic and political systems, welfare provision and educational institutions all contribute to the many differences between Thatcher's Britain and Reagan's USA (Levitas, 1986; Hall and Jacques, 1983). Forms of opposition, negotiation and survival have also varied on both sides of the Atlantic.

Representations of Youth sets out to identify those discourses through and within which 'youth' was framed in British and US research texts of the 1980s. I present two related arguments about the main narrative and rhetorical forms through which the main discursive configurations are organized. Firstly, research texts are shaped by mainstream and radical perspectives which are constructed in opposition to one another. I have characterized the mainstream perspective in terms of the search for the putative causes of specific constructed social problems, the tendency to use the victim-blaming thesis, and to represent certain groups or individual young people as 'deviant', 'deficient' or otherwise inadequate. Mainstream analyses also tend to psychologize inequalities, obscuring structural relations of domination behind a focus on individual 'deficient' working-class young people and/or young people of colour, their families or cultural backgrounds. Within the radical perspective, researchers tend to ask different questions, beginning from an explicitly politicized socialist, feminist and/or anti-racist commitment, and usually presenting a structuralist or post-structuralist analysis which is constructed in opposition to the (supposedly 'apolitical') mainstream approach (see chapter 1). Radical analyses are more likely to know 'whodunit', refusing the search for causes and deconstructing 'social problems' such as 'delinquency' or 'football hooliganism'. The focus here is on the individual or collective cultural practices of particular young people as forms of resistance, defence and/or survival.

Secondly, British and US research texts of the 1980s were marked by a series of moral panics and constructed crises over young people and issues related to 'youth', such as 'teenage pregnancy' (see chapter 6) and youth unemployment (see chapter 3). The financial constraints introduced by right-wing governments also had a significant impact on social science research with young people, especially radical projects. These crises had different implications for mainstream and radical perspectives in youth research. Radical analyses during the 1980s reflected a specific set of crises for the Left in a period of triumphant New Right expansion. In response to internal debates emerging from feminist analyses and the work of radical Black, lesbian and gay scholars, radical analyses began to concentrate on the relation between culture, structure and agency, the value of resistance theory, and the role of the researcher. In *Representations of Youth*, I reclaim the notion of 'radical' youth research to include analyses of 'difference' and 'diversity' which move away from a narrow focus on class and age to examine intersections between 'race', ethnicity, gender, sexuality and (less frequently) disability.

Key Discourses in British and US Youth Research of the 1980s

This book identifies a range of discourses through which 'youth' is constructed in British and US research texts in relation to constructed crises including youth unemployment, 'teenage pregnancy', 'drug abuse' and 'delinquency'. A particularly close discursive constellation can be identified in mainstream analyses, revolving around the discourses of education and training, the clinical discourse and the discourse of criminality. Each of these discourses rests on the construction of individual young people, their families and/or cultural backgrounds as 'deficient', 'deviant' or otherwise inadequate, and each discourse carries with it a set of associated prescriptions for 'dealing with' these presumed inadequacies. So the discourse of education and training constructs working-class young people and/or young people of colour as 'deficient' in various ways which are assumed to affect their academic performance or their orientation to school. Such young people can be represented as individually inadequate or culturally 'disadvantaged', but in either case the solution will be seen to lie in remedial programmes aimed at 'deficient youth' (see chapter 2). It is young people (and/or their families or cultural backgrounds) which are expected to change, not the structural or ideological dimensions of the British or US education systems.

The clinical discourse identifies specific young people as psychologically 'troubled', usually in terms of diagnostic criteria laid down in standardized professional systems (e.g. Cantwell and Baker, 1988). Some degree of psychological disruption is seen as an inevitable part of adolescence, but the clinical discourse differentiates between 'normal' and 'troubled' young people, juggling the ideological tensions within the definitions of psychological 'normality' and 'deviance' (see chapter 4). Therapeutic interventions follow from the clinical discourse, rather than the rehabilitative programmes associated with the discourse of education and training.

The discourse of criminality represents certain young people as particularly prone to 'delinquency' or other forms of 'deviance'. Like all of these discourses, the former is gender-, class- and 'race'-specific, in that young working-class men and young men of colour are especially likely to be constructed as 'deviant' in criminal terms (see chapter 3). The discourse of criminality advocates the use of corrective forms of intervention within the judicial system. These three discourses are frequently used in concert, drawing on each other in a pattern of mutual reinforcement. The term 'at risk' for example, which has medical and psychiatric connotations, is frequently used to forge connections between the clinical discourse, the discourse of criminality and the discourse of education and training (Winfield, 1991). This avoids the awkward problem of having to identify certain young people as actual criminals or school refusers, enabling researchers to discuss 'deviant youth' in terms of the *likelihood* that they may become involved in a whole range of unacceptable activities or psychological orientations. The introduction of educational, clinical and/or corrective interventions can then be justified in the absence of any evidence of actual 'deviance' or 'deficiency' on the part of young people (see chapter 6).

These three discourses frequently operate in conjunction with the discourse of sexual deviance and that of disaffection. Such discursive configurations rest on a range of conceptual assumptions about the effects of particular social conditions for young people, including the unemployment/mental-health thesis, the unemployment/crime thesis, and the leisure/boredom thesis (see chapters 3, 4 and 5). In this context, youth unemployment is presumed to increase the 'risk' of criminal involvement and mental disturbance and the likelihood of youthful boredom, therefore leading to 'disaffection' and 'delinquency'. The concept of 'disaffection' marks a particular, danger, since it signifies a youthful disillusion with the key institutions and practices of adult society, notably the education system, waged work and family life. Once again, we see the careful demarcation between that degree of 'rebelliousness' which is seen as normal, and even expected in young people (especially young men), and the 'disaffection' which appears as a problem and a threat to the dominant social order (e.g. M. McDermott, 1986).

All of the above discourses are heavily gendered, anticipating a greater likelihood of criminalized 'deviance' and 'disaffection' amongst young men, especially if they are working-class and/or Black. The discourse of sexual deviance has a particular focus on the feminine, shaping panics over young women's sexuality and the path to heterosexuality, marriage and motherhood. 'Premarital adolescent (hetero)sexuality' and 'teenage pregnancy' are two constructed crises which have close associations with young female (hetero)sexuality, whilst the panic over 'adolescent homosexuality' concentrates mainly on young men, and young lesbians are rendered invisible in both of these discourses (see chapters 4, 5 and 6). It is scarcely surprising that sexuality should provide a central element of youthful 'deviance', since adolescence itself has been defined around the onset of puberty (see chapter 1). It is never possible to overlook the gendered nature of that connection, nor the construction of heterosexuality (preferably penetrative and monogamous within a marital relationship) as a crucial mark of normal mature femininity – and masculinity.

Two further discourses have a particularly close association with the ideology of adolescence: the discourse of development and that of dependence. 'Adolescence' is defined as a discrete age stage in a linear path of physiological, psychological and social maturation into 'normal' adulthood. This process is represented in psychological terms, such that adulthood is signified by a whole, coherent and unitary identity, whilst adolescence is marked by a 'natural' period of hormonal and psychological turbulence and confusion. The move from the supposed turmoil of adolescence to the idealized stability of adulthood is reflected most clearly in the literature on the psychology of adolescence in which biological and social discourses combined in the discourse of development.

The discourse of development retained its dominant position in the youth research literature of the 1980s. It appeared in two contexts within the mainstream approach: the crisis over rising youth unemployment and disrupted transitions to full-time waged work and family life, and panics over 'teenage pregnancy' and the transition to 'normal' penetrative heterosexuality, monogamous marriage and parenthood (see chapters 3 and 6). The discourse of development does allow considerable space for social constructionist explanations of 'adolescence' and youthful instability, but this frequently retains a foundation in biological determinism. Texts which suggest that adolescence is not necessarily characterized by psychological or social turmoil rest uneasily with the discourse of development, as do analyses which argue that the move from youth to adulthood is seldom a linear transition or series of transitions (e.g. Coleman and Hendry, 1990; Willis, 1984; Phoenix, 1990).

In the 1980s the discourse of dependence took on an additional dimension with New Right ideologies and policies around 'welfare dependence' and the reduction of state provision for people living in poverty. Such ideologies constructed 'welfare dependence' in predominantly negative terms, defining state benefits as a problem rather than a right (see chapter 6). As with other dominant discourses in 1980s youth research texts, the locus of problems, risks or crises is usually concentrated on particular groups of young people, especially young working-class people, young people of colour and/or young women.

Studies of young people, crime and leisure incorporated a set of discourses around freedom and consumption. Dominant ideologies of adolescence construct young people as particularly prone to 'rebelliousness'. 'Having a fling while you're young' is represented as a normal part of this age stage, which, provided that it can be contained, is assumed to present no actual or potential threat to the dominant social system. Whilst the search for 'freedom' is represented as a normal part of adolescence, young people are also constructed as particularly malleable subjects in contemporary mass consumerist culture. 'Leisure' is the primary site in which patterns of consumption are located for young people, and mainstream texts are concerned that the latter should be educated to use their leisure time in appropriate and socially acceptable ways (see chapter 5). The adult capacity to exercise 'choice' of lifestyles, products and leisure activities, must be used in a 'responsible' manner. Many 1980s research texts reflected a series of panics around young people and particular disorders of consumption, such as 'drug abuse' and eating disorders, which link young people into discourses of delinquency, criminality and regimes of medical/psychiatric disease (see chapter 4).

The above discourses are found mainly in mainstream analyses, shaping and reinforcing the victim-blaming thesis and the search for causes of specific constructed social problems. The 1980s also saw a series of realignments between mainstream and radical perspectives as the former reacted to the radical analyses of the

1970s in the political context of Thatcherism and Reaganomics. The chief discursive strategy here, apart from a straightforward backlash and calls for a return to the mainstream psychology of adolescence, involved attempts to construct a synthesis between competing models (see chapters 2 and 4). In research on education for example, several texts presented a synthesis between mainstream arguments and radical explanations of 'problems' such as 'minority school failure' or 'educational underachievement'. This discursive strategy attempted to integrate arguments which were originally constructed in opposition to one another. It operated within the terms of mainstream analyses, retaining the use of terms such as 'minority school failure' for example, which had been heavily criticized in radical analyses (see chapter 2).

In research operating from the radical perspective the picture is different, since debates take place within the discursive framework of radical arguments. Radical analyses have challenged the construction of specific social problems such as 'delinquency' or 'football hooliganism' through various forms of labelling theory, refusing to search for the causes of these 'problems of youth'. Radical researchers would claim already to *know* the causes of 'real' social problems such as youth unemployment or 'educational underachievement': the operation of exploitative systems within racially structured capitalist patriarchy (see chapters 2 and 3).

The predominant discourse in the radical analyses of the 1970s was that of resistance. The discourse of resistance turned the ideological tables on mainstream analyses, presenting the activities and attitudes of particular young people not as evidence of 'deficiency' or 'deviance', but as resistance to their subordinated social positions (e.g. Murdock and McCron, 1975). The stress was on *collective* cultural forms rather than idiosyncratic individual behaviour. As in mainstream analyses, radical youth cultural studies have tended to focus on young white working-class heterosexual men, with minimal consideration of the gender, sexual and/or racial dimensions of their lives. Radical approaches encompassed a considerable diversity of theoretical frameworks and explanatory models, although the predominant approach has been a form of Marxist cultural analysis which concentrated on the structuring force of class in shaping young people's lives (e.g. Willis, 1977; Hall and Jefferson, 1975).

By the 1980s, the radical perspective incorporated a growing body of work by feminists, radical Black, lesbian and gay scholars which led to a series of debates over the nature of 'difference' and 'diversity' between young people. The predominance of the 'gang of lads' model came under considerable critical scrutiny as feminist researchers argued that the diverse experiences of young women needed to be reflected in radical youth research (e.g. McRobbie, 1980; see chapters 4 and 5). In addition, some studies about young working-class women and men began to move beyond a narrow focus on age and class towards an examination of the nexus of power relations around gender, sexuality, 'race' and ethnicity (e.g. Moffatt, 1986; Hollands, 1990; see chapter 2 above). Research studies with young women of colour presented this group as occupying a distinctive position which has implications for analyses of all young people's lives (Mirza, 1992). The specific experiences of young women of colour have usually been lost in the gap between feminist studies that concentrated on the lives of young white women and the work of radical Black scholars which focused on young men of colour.

These are two debates in which young people have occupied a central position and around which radical researchers have their own particular perspective and agendas: those over the 'Black underclass' and 'teenage pregnancy'. These debates had considerable impact on the academic and popular literatures during the 1980s and into the 1990s, with resonances on both sides of the Atlantic, but especially in the USA. These two issues represent areas of potential crisis in the 1980s youth research literature: youth unemployment and adolescent (hetero)sexuality and fertility. Whilst the position of young Black (especially African-American) women and men appears at the centre of these debates, the latter have implications for the representation of all young people. What is relevant here is the way in which *particular* groups of young people became the focus of academic concern in mainstream and radical analyses, and the political context in which this process took place.

Radical Analyses of 'Teenage Pregnancy' and the 'Black Underclass' Debate

In 1981 Douglas Glasgow's book *The Black Underclass* was published in the USA, providing a focus for the 'Black underclass' debate, and the status of young African-Americans occupied a key position in this text. Glasgow defined the 'Black underclass' in terms of a lack of socio-economic mobility; the existence of a 'survival culture'; a social preference for the ghetto as a reference point; and maintenance by welfare, law enforcement and health agencies (Glasgow, 1981). The June 1988 issue of the radical US journal *The Black Scholar* reviewed the literature on the 'Black underclass', and several articles represented the 'Black underclass' debate as a means of dealing with the growing poverty which characterized the Reagan years, and negating the legacy of the Civil Rights and Black Power movements as forms of organized resistance in what was and still is a racist society (George, 1988). Troy Duster argued that young African-Americans had been shifted from their traditional position as a source of cheap unskilled labour to a situation in which 'the new generation faces for the first time both the rejection and massive irrelevance of their labor' (Duster, 1988, p. 3). For Duster, this accounted for the increasing levels of welfare dependence amongst young women of colour, and for the growing involvement of young African-Americans (especially young men) in violent crimes, both as victims and as perpetrators, as 'legitimate' occupations dried up (Duster, 1988). For Julianne Malveux, the notion of a 'Black underclass' represented the victim-blaming thesis in another guise. The construction of young and poor African-Americans as 'problems' obscured and reinforced the inherent structural inequalities within US society (Malveux, 1988).

The perspective of radical Black scholars on the mainstream panic over the 'Black underclass' relied on a form of Marxist structural analysis which drew on Gramscian theory and feminist work to different degrees. Both radical and mainstream approaches to the 'Black underclass' debate have located young people of colour (notably young African-American men) at the centre of a project with major ideological implications beyond the boundaries of youth research. In a related panic over 'teenage pregnancy', mainstream analyses turned the spotlight onto young African-American women.

The existence of the 'problem' of 'teenage pregnancy' has been taken for granted in much of the mainstream literature (Furstenberg, 1976, is one exception). For most radical researchers, 'teenage pregnancy' has been *constructed* as a 'social problem' for ideological and political reasons, and the 'problem' of 'teenage pregnancy' lies not with 'deviant youth', but with the effects of poverty or social and economic disadvantage (e.g. Stiffman et al., 1990; Phoenix, 1990). The critical perspective on this particular moral panic has, with a few exceptions, been developed by Black scholars, feminists and health care professionals concerned over the tendency to pathologize and blame Black or other 'minority' families for the incidence of 'teenage pregnancy' within the mainstream literature (see chapter 6). As in the radical literature on the 'Black underclass', discourses of suffering and survival have predominated in radical analyses of 'teenage pregnancy'.

In the USA the debate over 'teenage pregnancy' (like the 'Black underclass' debate) has been more intense and more overtly racialized, and this has been reflected in both the mainstream and radical research literatures. One example of the latter was the 1987 special issue of the *Children and Youth Services Review* (*CYSR*) on 'The Black Adolescent Parent'.[1] Several contributors to this special issue argued that as adult Black scholars, their reasons for trying to understand the phenomenon of 'Black teenage pregnancy' were not the same as those of their white peers (Correia, 1987; Battle, 1987). In the absence of any substantial understanding of African-American culture, white researchers and health care professionals rush to make 'deviant' clinical assessments: they lack the conceptual tools to do otherwise (Taborn, 1987). The primary aim of Black scholars was not to develop the most effective interventions in order to reduce or eliminate 'Black teenage pregnancy', but to consider these young people and their offspring as a positive resource for African-Americans in 'the relentless struggle against the negative effects of racism and oppression' (H. Jones, 1987, p. ix).

Donna Franklin argued that the mainstream literature on 'black adolescent pregnancy' tended to 'circumvent the concerns of race, gender and socio-economic class', relying on a psychological approach which blamed individual young women for the constructed problem of 'teenage pregnancy' (1987, p. 15). Dominant representations of the sexually 'loose' African-American woman and the 'matriarchal' Black family continue to pervade the mainstream literature (see Weinberg and Williams, 1988). In the mid-1980s nearly 60 per cent of African-American children were born out of marriage; young African-American women aged between fifteen and nineteen had the most children of any young women in that age group in the industrialized world; and half of all young African-American women were likely to become pregnant (H. Jones, 1987). For radical researchers such statistics did not reflect the 'promiscuity' or 'deficiency' of young African-Americans, but the oppressive conditions in which many young people of colour were struggling to survive during the 1980s in the world's most affluent nation.

Radical analyses saw the panic over 'teenage pregnancy', like that over the 'Black underclass' debate, partly as a dominant response to the organized opposition of oppressed communities during the 1960s, and partly as part of mainstream attempts to obscure the continued existence of structural inequalities in US and British societies during the 1980s and into the 1990s. Such analyses owe a considerable debt to Gramscian theory on the role of hegemonic ideology which provided one of the three interrelated 'starting points' for the analysis presented in this book, along with post-structuralist and feminist approaches (see chapter 1). In the final section I will review the contributions made by these three approaches to the present analysis, drawing out some of the main issues facing radical youth research in the 1990s.

Recovery and Survival: Issues for Radical Youth Research in the 1990s

A Gramscian perspective enables us to look at the processes through which hegemonic ideologies around 'youth' and 'adolescence' operate to conceal forms of opposition and oppression. Mainstream analyses of 'teenage pregnancy' and 'premarital adolescent sexuality' for example, have represented the path to marriage, monogamous heterosexuality and parenthood (preferably in that order) as 'natural' and 'normal' (see chapters 5 and 6). Any 'deviations' from this path are construed as evidence of 'deficiency' and/or 'alienation' on the part of individual young women, their families and/or cultural backgrounds, especially for young working-class women and young women of colour. Such discursive configurations are shaped and reinforced by the institutions of the welfare and social services, the medical and psychiatric professions and the education system.

In Gramscian terms the construction of certain forms of heterosexuality and family life as 'natural' have been used in the mainstream literature on 'teenage pregnancy' to obscure the impact of poverty and victimize young women of colour and young working-class women (e.g. Franklin, 1987). From a feminist perspective, dominant constructions of sexuality and family life play an important part in the social control of young women's lives, and especially the representation of monogamous heterosexuality within marriage as a mark of 'mature' and 'normal' femininity (e.g. Lees, 1986; Phoenix, 1990). Such constructions are shaped by dimensions of 'race', class and culture as well as gender, sexuality and age, and particular young women are especially likely to be defined as 'deviant' and 'deficient'. A post-structuralist approach would tend to deconstruct concepts such as 'teenage pregnancy' and the representation of certain forms of sexuality as 'natural' and 'normal', examining the ways in which particular young women are located within discourses of sexual deviance and deficiency (see chapters 5 and 6).

It would be more accurate to represent these three approaches as interrelated rather than as distinct and autonomous perspectives. None emerged in ideological and political isolation, and the combination of the three approaches has shaped radical youth research in significant ways. During the 1980s some radical analyses began to place an increasing emphasis on discourses, texts and representations rather than the identification of specific cultural practices as 'resistant' or 'conformist' (e.g. McRobbie, 1988). Radical youth research informed by feminist and/or post-structuralist approaches developed a critical perspective on resistance theory, the complexity of analysing power relations around gender, sexuality, 'race', class and age for different groups of young people in particular contexts, the role of the researcher and the debate over the relationship between culture, structure and individual agency (McRobbie, 1991). These are some of the issues facing radical youth research in the 1990s.

During the 1980s the discourse of resistance lost some ground in radical texts in favour of discourses of defence and survival (see chapters 4, 5 and 6). In part this arose from the specific economic and political conditions faced by young working-class people and young people of colour in Britain, the USA and other western industrialized societies during this period of New Right expansionism. It also reflected the various critiques of the conceptual basis of resistance theory which had emerged from feminist and post-structuralist work during the 1970s and into the 1980s. By the mid-1980s the discourse of resistance (or the theory of cultural reproduction) was being represented as overly simplistic, with a tendency to romanticize working class youth cultures (e.g. J. C. Walker, 1986a).

This is not to imply that the discursive frameworks of radical youth research texts reflected the conditions of young people's lives in any straightforward way, or that no subordinated groups of young people were engaging in forms of resistance during the 1980s. The conditions of young people's lives cannot be 'read off' from research texts in such a simplistic manner, but nor do they exist in a completely autonomous relationship to one another. My perspective, like that of some post-structuralists, dissolves the distinction between representations and the real (see Game, 1991). The discourse of resistance predominated in radical youth research of the 1970s, and the shift towards the discourses of suffering, defence and survival represented a whole series of ideological and political changes during the 1980s both on the Left and the (New) Right.

Radical analyses which revolve around the discourse of resistance rest on an opposition between the oppressed but resisting individual subject (who is usually white, working-class, heterosexual and male), and the dominant structures of (capitalist) society. There is no straightforward way in which researchers (even radical researchers) can read off specific cultural forms as evidence of 'resistance', since this often ignores the perspective of the young people concerned, casting the researcher in the role of expert – and voyeur. Some feminist researchers have also argued that the concept of cultural resistance is too narrow and gender-specific, since young women might adopt less 'visible' forms of resistance or negotiation such as silence or giggling (e.g. Holly, 1989; Griffin, 1982b).

The main issue in these debates concerns the relationship between notions of culture, structure and individual agency. Some radical texts have examined 'textually-mediated cultural practices', attempting to avoid the scenario in which radical researchers (however self-reflexive) identify individual young people or specific cultural practices as 'resistant' or 'conformist' (e.g. Roman et al., 1988). Others have focused on the relationship between texts and cultural practices in analyses of symbolic activity and creativity amongst different groups of young people (e.g. Willis et al., 1990). The boundary lines between oppositional or dominant cultures, social structures and the arena of individual agency or identity have become increasingly blurred in radical youth research texts of the late 1980s, although radical researchers are not attempting to undermine the notion that young people operated within and through sets of social relations structured in dominance (Bhavnani, 1991).

I do not wish to suggest that the above texts exemplify the 'correct' approach to untangling the relationship between culture, structure and agency, nor that they provide evidence of systematic academic progress towards a resolution of these issues. There are no 'correct' answers to these questions, and the whole debate reverberates with contradictory and complex arguments drawn from post-structuralism and from feminist and other radical perspectives, shaped by the rise of the New Right and the crisis which faced the Left during the 1980s. The issues raised by these debates over the role of radical researchers, over the relationship between cultures, texts, structure and individual agency and over discourses of resistance, defence and survival are unlikely to disappear during the 1990s.

The second set of issues facing radical youth research in the 1990s concerns some of the wider political resonances of academic research with young people. The work of feminist researchers, radical Black, lesbian and gay scholars and others has produced a major shift away from a focus on the lives of young white, heterosexual working-class men and the operation of social relations structured around class and age. It was not simply that many groups of young people were being ignored in most radical analyses, but that the latter had produced a theoretical framework which rested on an implicit and unexamined norm. The position of young white heterosexual working-class men in advanced capitalist societies dominated the conceptual and political space in radical work around 'youth'. In addition, the concentration on structural relations of class and age meant that few texts examined the dynamics of relations around gender, sexuality or 'race' (and almost never dis/ability) for these groups of young men (exceptions include Wood, 1984; and Moffatt, 1986).

By the late 1980s, radical texts in and outside youth research were looking at questions of 'difference' and 'diversity', something which radical women of colour had already been discussing for several years (e.g. Bhabha, 1990; see Amos and Parmar, 1981, and Moraga and Andalzua, 1981). This concern with 'difference' highlighted a set of absences in radical youth research which included the relative paucity of radical analyses concerned with the position of young people with disabilities. The majority of work was located within the mainstream perspective, and especially within a medical framework. Young people with disabilities have generally been represented as 'deficient' in clinical terms, confined to the margins of the education system, the job market, family life and sexuality. Minimal attention has been paid to the experiences of young people with disabilities or to the role of dis/ability as a structural force in shaping dominant representations of masculinity and (especially) femininity for *all* young people.

Another notable absence in radical youth research has been the lack of work concerned with the lives of young lesbians, gay men and bisexuals, who still remain relatively invisible in the radical literature. This is ironic given the considerable impact of feminist perspectives which have brought the analysis of power relations around gender and sexuality into the realm of radical youth research. The growing international literature on young women's friendship groups, for example, still tends to assume that all young women are heterosexual unless specified otherwise, and it stops short of examining the processes through which the transition to heterosexuality is policed in the arena of friendships between young women (e.g. Naber, 1992; Griffiths, 1992; Eder, 1992).

Just as the start of the 1980s marked something of a political and ideological transition point in Britain and the USA, the end of the decade also saw a moment of disjuncture. The economic, political and ideological legacy of the 1980s is still visible in the 1990s, as an increasing proportion of research texts can testify (e.g. St Pierre, 1991), but there *is* a sense in which the 1990s brought a certain break with what has come to be signified by the terms 'Thatcherism' and 'Reaganomics' (Hall and Bailey, 1992).

The issues mentioned above will continue to be discussed in radical youth research during the 1990s, but there are other issues which have been relatively absent from 1980s research. Changing discursive configurations around 'youth' and 'adolescence' during the 1980s reflect a series of crises in contemporary western cultures which resonate around questions of development and maturity, nationality, struggles over power and citizenship, resistance and survival, domination and the relationship between culture, structure and agency (Bhabha, 1990). At the broadest level harsher policies on immigration and asylum in Britain and the USA will have the greatest impact on young people of colour, and at a more local level questions of citizenship and enfranchisement affect all of the most marginal groups of young people. As Kum-Kum Bhavnani has argued, a sense of disenfranchisement amongst young people may not reflect a state of 'dysfunctional' psychological alienation, but a politicized analysis of their position which produces a form of conscious disengagement (Bhavnani, 1987). Why should such young people feel any obligation towards a society which relegates them to a form of social and economic scrap heap (Duster, 1988)?

Young people's positions in education, training, the job market, sexuality and family life will continue to be a central concern of academic research during the 1990s, and few radical analyses have addressed the question of young people's enfranchisement and empowerment within these areas. One exception is a British study based in the city of Wolverhampton, which was co-ordinated by Paul Willis during the late 1980s (Willis, 1985). Funded by a Labour-controlled local council, and adopting a combination of research methods, this project aimed to involve local youth workers and young people in the research process. Significantly this was not a solely academic initiative, and the links with the local authority produced a set of recommendations which called for greater involvement (and not just consultation) of young people in the decision-making process of the local state and for a coherent 'policy for youth' which covered areas such as housing and social services as well as education, training and leisure provision (Willis, 1985). This project is not cited as a model of ideal practice, but as one example of the direction in which radical youth research might move in the 1990s. Developing closer links between academic research 'practitioners' and young people themselves is only one possible route, and the funding strategies of major grant-giving agencies are unlikely to be any more sympathetic to the interests of radical researchers than they were during the 1980s.

Representations of Youth was written in a spirit of critique and refusal: a refusal to accept the arguments of some mainstream youth research texts that radical analyses could be either disregarded or assimilated within the mainstream perspective. My main thesis is that radical analyses have their own political and conceptual agendas, and their own (relatively) distinctive discursive frameworks. Far from declining or becoming incorporated within the dominant perspective, radical youth research in Britain and the USA was continually remaking itself during the decade of the New Right.

The spirit of critique in which this book was written is both constructive and deconstructive. It presents a critical analysis of discourses which takes the form of a refusal of the 'apolitical' mainstream project in contemporary youth research, rather than a recipe for 'doing better research'. As Foucault argued:

> Critique doesn't have to be the premise of a deduction which concludes: this then is what needs to be done. It should be an instrument for those who fight, those who resist and refuse what is. Its use should be in processes of conflict and confrontation, essays in refusal. It doesn't have to lay down the law for law. It isn't a stage in programming. It is a challenge directed at what is. (1981, p. 13)

My aim is not to present an alternative model of good practice for radical youth research in the 1990s, but to throw a conceptual spanner into the workings of most mainstream and some radical youth research by examining the discursive processes through which 'youth' and 'adolescence' were represented during the 1980s. I would borrow Luce Irigaray's notion of 'jamming the theoretical machinery' here, since the present analysis is primarily a project of deconstruction (Irigaray, 1985, p. 78).

I have deconstructed some of the key elements in mainstream and radical perspectives on 'youth' and 'adolescence', unravelling the discursive implications of specific arguments and constructed crises over the state of British and US 'youth'. Like the editors of *Becoming Feminine*, I have treated youth research texts as *'constructs* subject to undoing or deconstruction' (Roman and Christian-Smith, 1988, p. 21, original emphasis). Like Leslie Roman and Linda Christian-Smith, my feminist materialist analysis:

> do[es] not go so far as a post-structuralist might in defining what constitutes a deconstructive reading. [I] do not, for example, claim that all meaning is anarchically unstable. Nor do [I] deny the possibility that some meanings are selected more often, given more weight, and hence become dominant over others . . . [my] notion of deconstruction defines the text . . . to include social relations and their conflicting divisions by gender, class, race, age and sexual[ity]. (1988, p. 22, my insertions)

I have not set out to present an alternative or 'correct' approach to the project of radical youth research in the 1990s. My main intention is that this analysis of 1980s research texts should raise issues for current youth research work by examining the discursive representation of 'youth' and 'adolescence' in Britain and the USA during a distinctive period of political realignment.

Notes

1 The arguments raised in these articles were markedly different from the mainstream perspective on 'teenage pregnancy' reflected in *Family Planning Perspectives* or the *Journal of Adolescent Health Care*.

References

Abbott, P. and Wallace, C. 1989: The family. In Brown and Sparks, *Beyond Thatcherism*.

Abrahamse, A., Morrison, P. and Waite, L. 1988: Teenagers willing to consider single parenthood: who is at greatest risk? *Family Planning Perspectives*, 20, 1, 13–18.

Abrams, M. 1959: *The Teenage Consumer*. LPE paper 5, London: Routledge and Kegan Paul.

Adelson, J. 1964: *The Universal Experience of Adolescence*. New York: John Wiley.

Adler, P. A., Adler, P. and Johnson, J. M. 1992: Street Corner Society revisited: new questions about old issues. *Journal of Contemporary Ethnography*, 21, 1, 3–10.

Aggleton, P., Homans, H. and Warwick, I. 1988: Young people, sexuality education and AIDS. *Youth and Policy*, 23, 5–13.

Aggleton, P. and Whitty, G. 1985: Rebels without a cause? Socialization and subcultural style among the children of the new middle class. *Sociology of Education*, 58, 60–72.

Ainley, P. 1986: Shades of the prison house: working class resistance to state intervention in the transition from school to work. Paper presented at British Sociological Association conference, Loughborough.

Aldous, J. 1987: American families in the 1980s: individualism run amok? *Journal of Family Issues*, 8, 4, 422–5.

Allen, S. 1968: Some theoretical problems in the study of youth. *Sociological Review*, 16, 3, 10–15.

Alpert, G. and Dunham, R. 1986: Keeping academically marginal youths in school. *Youth and Society*, 17, 4, 346–61.

Amos, V. and Parmar, P. 1981: Resistances and responses: the experiences of Black girls in Britain. In A. McRobbie and T. McCabe (eds), *Feminism for Girls: An Adventure Story*. London: Routledge and Kegan Paul.

Anthias, F. 1990: Race and class revisited: conceptualizing race and racisms. *Sociological Review*, 38, 19–42.

Apple, M. 1982: *Education and Power*. London: Routledge and Kegan Paul.

Ariès, P. 1962: *Centuries of Childhood*. Harmondsworth: Penguin.

Ashton, D. N. 1973: The transition from school to work: notes on the development of different frames of reference among young male workers. *Sociological Review*, 21, 101–25.

Ashton, D. N. 1986: *Unemployment under Capitalism*. Brighton: Harvester Wheatsheaf.

Ashton, D. N. and Field, D. 1976: *Young Workers*. London: Hutchinson.

Auchtermuty, R. 1987: You're a dyke, Angela! *Trouble and Strife*, 10, 23–30.

Bailey, G. W. 1989: Current perspectives on substance abuse in youth. *Journal of American Academy of Child and Adolescent Psychiatry*, 28, 2, 151–62.

Bains, H. 1988: Southall youth: an old-fashioned story. In Cohen and Bains, *Multi-Racist Britain*.

Ball, S. 1990: Education, inequality and school reform: values in crisis! Inaugural lecture, Centre for Educational Studies, King's College, London (October).

Banks, M., Bates, I., Breakwell, G., Bynner, J., Emler, N., Jamieson, L. and Roberts, K. 1991: *Careers and Identities*. Milton Keynes: Open University Press.

Baron, S. W. 1989: The Canadian west coast punk subculture: a field study. *Canadian Journal of Sociology*, 14, 3, 289–316.

Barrett, M. and McIntosh, M. 1982: *The Anti-social Family*. London: Verso.

Barry, K. 1979: *Female Sexual Slavery*. Englewood Cliffs, NJ: Prentice Hall.

Bates, I., Clarke, J., Cohen, P., Finn, D., Moore, R. and Willis, P. (eds) 1984: *Schooling for the Dole? The New Vocationalism*. London: Macmillan.

Battle, S. F. 1987: Introduction. *Children and Youth Services Review*, special issue on 'The Black Adolescent Parent', xv–xvii.

Battle, S. F. and Battle, J. L. R. 1987: Adolescent sexuality: cultural and legal implications. *Children and Youth Services*, special issue on 'The Black Adolescent Parent', 125–36.

Beck, G. and Davies, D. 1987: Teen contraception: a review of perspectives on compliance. *Archives of Sexual Behavior*, 16, 4, 337–69.

Becker, B. and Hills, S. 1981: Youth attitudes and adult labor market activity. *Industrial Relations*, 20, 1, 60–70.

Becker, H. 1963: *Outsiders: Studies in the Sociology of Deviance*. New York: Free Press.

Beegley, C. and Sellers, C. 1986: Adolescents and sex: a structural theory of premarital sex in the United States. *Deviant Behavior*, 7, 4, 313–36.

Bensman, J. and Vidich, A. J. 1976: The crisis of contemporary capitalism and the failure of nerve. *Sociological Inquiry*, 46, 3/4, 207–17.

Berardo, F. M. 1990: Trends and directions in family research in the 1980s. *Journal of Marriage and the Family*, 52, 809–17.

Berger, R. and Schechter, Y. 1989: Adolescent girls in distress: a high-risk intersection. *Adolescence*, 24, 94, 357–74.

Beuret, C. and Makings, L. 1986: Love in a cold climate: women, class and courtship in a recession. Paper presented at British Sociological Association conference, Loughborough.

Bhabha, H. (ed.) 1990: *Nation and Narration*. London: Routledge.

Bhavnani, K.-K. 1987: Disaffection or disenfranchisement? Paper presented at British Psychological Society conference, Oxford University.

Bhavnani, K.-K. 1991: *Talking Politics: A Psychological Framing for Views from Youth in Britain*. Cambridge: Cambridge University Press.

Bhavnani, K.-K. 1992: Talking racism and the editing of Women's Studies. In D. Richardson and V. Robinson (eds), *Introductory Women's Studies*. London: Macmillan.

Bhavnani, K.-K. and Coulson, M. 1986: Transforming socialist feminism: the challenge of racism. *Feminist Review*, 23, 81–92.

Bianchi, S. 1987: Living at home: young adults' living arrangements in the 1980s. Paper presented at American Sociological Association conference.

Birke, L. and Vines, G. 1987: Beyond nature versus nurture: process and biology in the development of gender. *Women's Studies International Forum*, 10, 6, 555–70.

Blos, P. 1962: *On Adolescence*. London: Collier-Macmillan.

Blue, A. 1988: *Grace under Pressure: The Emergence of Women in Sport*. London: Sidgwick and Jackson.

Borman, K. 1988: Playing on the job in adolescent work settings. *Anthropology and Education Quarterly*, 19, 163–96.

Borman, K. and Riesman, J. (eds) 1986: *Becoming a Worker*. Norwood, NJ: Apex Publishing Corporation.

Bowlby, J. 1969: *Attachment and Loss*, vol. 1. London: Hogarth Press.

Bowles, S. and Gintis, H. 1976: *Schooling in Capitalist America*. London: Routledge and Kegan Paul.

Bowman, P. J. 1984: A discouragement-centred approach to studying unemployment among Black youth: hopelessness, attributions and psychological distress. *International Journal of Mental Health*, 13, 1/2, 68–91.

Box, S. and Hale, C. 1982: Economic crisis and the rising prisoner population in England and Wales. *Crime and Social Justice*, 17 (July), 10–21.

Boyer, D. K. 1986: Male prostitution: a cultural expression of male homosexuality. University of Washington, Seattle: unpublished Ph.D. thesis.

Brah, A. 1988a: Review article. *British Journal of the Sociology of Education*, 9, 1, 25–34.

Brah, A. 1988b: Black struggles, equality and education. *Critical Social Policy*, 8, 3, 83–9.

Brah, A. and Minhas R. 1985: Structural racism or cultural difference: schooling for Asian girls. In G. Weiner (ed.), *Just a Bunch of Girls*. Milton Keynes: Open University Press.

Brake, M. 1984: *Comparative Youth Cultures: The Sociology of Youth Culture and Youth Subcultures in America, Britain and Canada*. London: Routledge and Kegan Paul.

Breakwell, G. 1985: Abusing the unemployed: an invisible injustice. *Journal of Moral Education*, 14, 1, 56–62.

Breakwell, G., Harrison, B. and Propper, C. 1984: Explaining the psychological effects of unemployment for young people: the importance of specific situational factors. *British Journal of Guidance and Counselling*, 12, 132–40.

Brenner, M. H. 1978: Impact of economic indicators on crime indices. In *Unemployment and Crime* (hearing before Subcommittee on the Judiciary: US House of Representatives) 59th Congress, first and second sessions, serial no. 47, 20–54.

Bresnick, D. 1984: *Youthjobs: Toward a Private/Public Partnership.* Westport: Quorum Books.

Brewer, D. D. and Miller, M. L. 1990: Bombing and burning: the social organization and values of hip hop graffiti writers and implications for policy. *Deviant Behavior*, 11, 345–69.

Bright, H. 1987: Confined and silenced: how do schoolgirls manage? *Women in Management Review*, 3, 2, 90–3.

Brown, L. 1986: Moralizing community services for adolescents in trouble. *Social Work with Groups*, 9, 1, 107–19.

Brown, P. 1989: Education. In Brown and Sparks *Beyond Thatcherism*.

Brown, P. and Sparks, R. (eds) 1989: *Beyond Thatcherism: Social Policy, Politics and Society.* Milton Keynes: Open University Press.

Bryan, B., Dadzie, S. and Scafe, S. 1985: *The Heart of the Race: Black Women's Lives in Britain.* London: Virago.

Bryce, G. and Baird, D. 1986: Precipitating a crisis: family therapy and adolescent school refusers. *Journal of Adolescence*, 9, 3, 199–213.

Bullivant, B. 1987: *The Ethnic Encounter in the Secondary School: Ethnocultural Reproduction and Resistance: Theory and Case Studies.* Lewes: Falmer Press.

Bumpass, L. L. 1990: What's happening to the family? Interactions between demographic and institutional change. *Demography*, 27, 4, 483–98.

Burchell, G. 1979: A note on juvenile justice. *Ideology and Consciousness*, 5, 125–35.

Burrage, H. 1986: 'Premature' pregnancy and parenthood: a working paper on socioeconomic variables associated with the fertility of young people in the city. Paper presented at British Sociological Association conference, Loughborough.

Burt, C. 1925: *The Young Delinquent* London: University of London Press.

Bury, J. 1984: *Teenage Pregnancy in Britain.* London: Birth Control Trust.

Bush, D. M. 1987: The impact of family and school on adolescent girls' aspirations and expectations: the public–private split and the reproduction of of gender inequality. Paper presented at American Sociological Association conference.

Cain, M. (ed.) 1989: *Growing up Good: Policing the Behaviour of Girls in Europe.* London: Sage.

Calabrese, R. and Seldin, C. 1986: Adolescent alienation: an analysis of the female response to the secondary school. *High School Journal*, 69, 2, 120–5.

Campbell, A. 1984: *Girls in the Gang.* New York: Basil Blackwell.

Campbell, A. and Muncer, S. 1989: Them and us: a comparison of the cultural context of American gangs and British subcultures. *Deviant Behavior*, 10, 271–88.

Campbell, B. 1984: *Wigan Pier Revisited*. London: Virago.

Canaan, J. 1990: Individualizing Americans: the making of middle class teenagers. Unpublished Ph.D. thesis, University of Chicago.

Cantwell, D. and Baker, L. 1988: Issues in the classification of child and adolescent psychopathology. *Journal of the American Academy of Child and Adolescent Psychiatry*, 27, 5, 521–33.

Carby, H. 1982: White women listen! Black feminism and the boundaries of sisterhood. In Race and Politics Group, *The Empire Strikes Back*.

Carlen, P. (ed.) 1985: *Criminal Women*. Cambridge: Polity Press.

Carnoy, M. 1974: *Education as Cultural Imperialism*. New York: David McKay.

Carter, E. 1984: Alice in consumer wonderland. In A. McRobbie and M. Nava (eds), *Gender and Generation*. London: Macmillan.

Carter, M. 1962: *Home, School and Work: A Study of the Education and Employment of Young People in Britain*. London: Pergamon Press.

Carter, M. 1966: *Into Work*. Harmondsworth: Penguin.

Cashmore, E. and Troyna, B. (eds) 1982: *Black Youth in Crisis*. London: Allen and Unwin.

Cass, V. C. 1984: Homosexual identity: a concept in need of definition. *Journal of Homosexuality*, 9, 2/3, 105–26.

Center on Budget and Policy Priorities, 1986: Falling behind: a report on how Blacks have fared under Reagan. *Journal of Black Studies*, 17, 2, 148–72.

Chambre, S. M. 1982: Welfare use as status attainment: similarities between factors influencing socio-economic status and welfare use. *Journal of Social Service Research*, 5, 3/4, 17–32.

Chapman, B. E. and Brannock J. 1987: Proposed model of lesbian identity development: an empirical examination. *Journal of Homosexuality*, 14, (3/4), 69–80.

Cherlin, A. and Furstenberg, F. F. 1988: The changing European family: lessons for the American reader. *Journal of Family Issues*, 9, 3, 291–7.

Chesler, P. 1986: *Mothers on Trial: The Battle for Children and Custody*. New York: McGraw-Hill, Harcourt Brace Jovanovich.

Chigwada, R. 1987: Not victims – not superwomen. *Trouble and Strife*, 11, 19–22.

Christian, B. 1988: The race for theory. *Feminist Studies*, 14, 1, 67–80.

Clarke, J. and Critcher, C. 1985: *The Devil Makes Work: Leisure in Capitalist Britain*. London: Macmillan.

Clarke, J., Hall, S., Jefferson, T. and Roberts, B. 1975: Subculture, cultures and class. In Hall and Jefferson, *Resistance through Rituals*.

Clausen, J. A. 1986: Early adult choices and the life course. Paper presented at American Sociological Association conference.

Clausen, J. S. 1991: Adolescent competence and the shaping of the life course. *American Journal of Sociology*, 96, 4, 805–42.

Cloward, R. A. and Ohlin, L. E. 1960: *Delinquency and Opportunity: A Theory of Delinquent Gangs*. New York: Free Press.

Cockburn, C. 1987: *Two-Track Training*. London: Macmillan.

Coffield, F., Borrill, C. and Marshall, S. 1986: *Growing Up at the Margins*. Milton Keynes: Open University Press.

Cohen, A. K. 1955: *Delinquent Boys: The Culture of the Gang*. Glencoe: Free Press.

Cohen, G. and Nixon, J. 1981: Employment policies for youth in Britain and the USA. *Journal of Social Policy*, 10, 3, 331–51.

Cohen, P. 1982: Schooling for the dole. *New Socialist*, 3, 12–15.

Cohen, P. 1986: Rethinking the youth question. London University Institute of Education: Post-16 Education Centre and *Youth and Policy* pamphlet.

Cohen, P. 1988: The perversions of inheritance: studies in the making of multi-racist Britain. In Cohen and Bains, *Multi-Racist Britain*.

Cohen, P. 1990: Foreword. In R. G. Hollands, *The Long Transition*.

Cohen, P. and Bains, H. (eds) 1988: *Multi-racist Britain*. London: Macmillan.

Cole, M. (ed.) 1988: *Bowles and Gintis Revisited: Schooling and Capitalism Ten Years After*. Lewes: Falmer Press.

Coleman, J. 1980: *The Nature of Adolescence*. Harmondsworth: Penguin.

Coleman, J. and Hendry, L. 1990: *The Nature of Adolescence* (2nd edn). London: Methuen.

Comely, L. 1991: Lesbian and gay teenagers at school: how can educational psychologists help? Paper presented at British Psychological Society conference, Bournemouth.

Conger, J. 1979: *Adolescence: A Generation Under Pressure*. London: Harper and Row.

Connell, R. W. 1989: Cool guys, swots and wimps: the interplay of masculinity and education. *Oxford Review of Education*, 15, 3, 291–303.

Connell, R. W., Ashenden, D. J., Kessler, S. and Dowsett, G. W. 1982: *Making the Difference: Schools, Families and Social Division*. Sydney: Allen and Unwin.

Connolly, M. and Torkington, N. P. K. 1990: Black youth and politics in Liverpool. Social Statistics Research Unit, London University: ESRC 16–19 Initiative Occasional Paper.

Correia, P. 1987: Preface. *Children and Youth Services Review*, special issue on 'The Black Adolescent Parent', xi–xii.

Coveney, L., Jackson, M., Jeffreys, S., Kaye, L. and Mahoney, P. (eds) 1984: *The Sexuality Papers*. London: Hutchinson in association with the Explorations in Feminism Collective.

Cowie, C. and Lees, S. 1981: 'Slags or drags' *Feminist Review*, 9, 17–31.

Cowie, J., Cowie, V. and Slater, E. 1968: *Delinquency in Girls*. London: Heinemann.

Cross, M. and Smith, D. I. (eds) 1987: *Black Youth Futures*. Leicester: National Youth Bureau.

Cubitt, S. 1990: Innocence and manipulation: censorship, consumption and freedom in Britain. In A. Tomlinson (ed.), *Consumption, Identity and Style*. London: Routledge, for Comedia.

Curry, T. J. 1991: Fraternal bonding in the locker room: a pro-feminist analysis of talk about competition and women. *Sociology of Sport Journal*, 8, 119–35.

Danziger, S. and Nagatoshi, C. 1987: Adolescent welfare mothers and the fathers of their children: legal ties, family relationships and economic prospects. Paper presented at American Sociological Association conference.

Danziger, S. and Radin, N. 1990: Absent does not equal uninvolved: predictors of fathering in teen mother families. *Journal of Marriage and the Family*, 52, 636–42.

Davis, A. Y. 1982: *Women, Race and Class* London: The Women's Press.

Davis, A. and Davis, F. 1986: The Black family and the crisis of capitalism. *The Black Scholar* (September–October), 33–40.

DelaCoste, F. and Alexander, P. 1987: *Sex Work: Writings by Women in the Sex Industry*. New York: Cleis Press.

Deem, R. 1989: Feminism and leisure studies: opening up new directions. In Wimbush and Talbot, *Relative Freedoms*.

Demaine, J. 1989: Race, categorisation and educational achievement. *British Journal of Sociology of Education*, 10, 2, 195–214.

Department of Education and Science, 1983: *Young People in the 1980s: A Survey*. London: HMSO.

Donovan, A. and Oddy, M. 1982: Psychological aspects of unemployment: an investigation into the emotional and social adjustment of school leavers. *Journal of Adolescence*, 5, 1, 15–30.

Donzelot, J. 1977: *The Policing of Families*. London: Hutchinson.

Dorn, N. and South, N. 1983: Of males and markets: a critical review of 'youth culture' theory. Centre for Occupational and Community Research, Middlesex Polytechnic: Research Paper 1.

Dorn, N. and South, N. 1989: Drugs and leisure, prohibition and pleasure: from subculture to the drugalogue. In Rojek, *Leisure for Leisure*.

Douvan, E. and Adelson, J. 1966: *The Adolescent Experience*. New York: John Wiley.

Driver, E. and Droisen, A. (eds) 1989: *Child Sexual Abuse: Feminist Perspectives*. London: Macmillan.

Dryden, W. (ed.) 1988: *Family Therapy in Britain*. London: Sage.

DuBois, W. E. B. 1987: The Negro criminal. *Review of the Black Political Economy*, 16, 1/2, 17–31: first published 1899.

Duster, T. 1988: Social implications of the 'new' Black urban underclass. *The Black Scholar* (May/June), 2–9.

Dyhouse, C. 1981: *Girls Growing up in Late Victorian and Edwardian England*. London: Routledge and Kegan Paul.

Eberley, D. J. 1977: National Service: alternative strategies. *Armed Forces and Society*, 3, 3, 445–56.

Eder, D. 1992: Girls talk about romance and sexuality. Paper presented at First International Conference on Girls and Girlhood, Amsterdam.

Edwards, J. N. 1987: Changing family structure and youthful well-being. *Journal of Family Issues*, 8, 4, 355–72.

Eichler, M. 1985: And the work never ends: feminist contributions to anglophone sociology. *Canadian Review of Sociology and Anthropology*, 22, 5, 619–44.

Eisen, M. and Zellman, G. 1986: The role of health belief attitudes, sex education and demographics in predicting adolescents' sexuality knowledge. *Health Education Quarterly*, 13, 1, 9–22.

Eisenstadt, S. N. 1956: *From Generation to Generation: Age Groups and Social Structure*. Glencoe: Free Press.

Ellis, L. 1987: Criminal behavior and r/K selection: an extension of gene-based evolutionary theory. *Deviant Behavior*, 8, 149–76.

Erickson, F. 1987: Transformation and school success: the politics and culture of educational achievement. *Anthropology and Education Quarterly*, 18, 4, 335–56.

Erikson, E. 1951: *Childhood and Society*. London: Imago.

Erikson, E. 1968: *Identity: Youth and Crisis*. New York: Norton.

Espenshade, T. J. 1987: Population replacement and immigration adaption: issues facing the west. *Family Planning Perspectives*, 19, 3, 115–18.

Ettore, B. 1989: Women and substance use/abuse: towards a feminist perspective or how to make dust fly. *Women's Studies International Forum*, 12, 6, 593–602.

Factor, F. and Stenson, K. 1989: Community control and the policing of Jewish youth. Paper presented at British Criminology conference, Bristol Polytechnic (July).

Faderman, L. 1981: *Surpassing the Love of Men: Romantic Friendships and Love between Women from the Renaissance to the Present*. New York: Junction Books.

Faderman, L. 1992: *Odd Girls and Twilight Lovers: A History of Lesbian Life in Twentieth-Century America*. New York: Penguin.

Featherman, D. and Willhelm, S. 1979: Controversies: social mobility. *Society*, 16, 3, 4–17.

Felice, M., Schragg, P., James, M. and Hollingsworth, D. 1987: Psychological aspects of Mexican-American, white and black teen pregnancy. *Journal of Adolescent Health Care*, 8, 4, 330–5.

Fine, G. 1987: *With the Boys: Little League Baseball and Preadolescent Subculture*. Chicago: University of Chicago Press.

Fine, M. and Asch, A. (eds) 1989: *Women with Disabilities: Essays in Psychology, Culture and Politics*. Philadelphia: Temple University Press.

Fineman, S. (ed.) 1987: *Unemployment: Personal and Social Consequences*. London: Tavistock.

Finn, D. 1987: *Training without Jobs: New Deals and Broken Promises*. London: Macmillan.

Finn, D. and Ball, L. 1991: *Unemployment and Training Rights Handbook*. London: Unemployment Unit.

Fishman, H. C. 1988: *Treating Troubled Adolescents: A Family Therapy Approach*. London: Harper Collins Academic.

Fleming, D. and Lavercombe, S. 1982: Talking about unemployment with school-leavers. *British Journal of Guidance and Counselling*, 10, 1, 22–33.

Foreman, A. 1977: *Femininity and Alienation: Women and the Family in Marxism and Psychoanalysis*. London: Pluto Press.

Foucault, M. 1981: Questions of method: an interview with Michel Foucault. *Ideology and Consciousness*, 8, 7–26.

Franklin, D. L. 1987: Black adolescent pregnancy: a literature review. *Children and Youth Services Review*, special issue on 'The Black Adolescent Parent', 15–38.

Frazer, E. 1987: Teenage girls reading 'Jackie'. *Media, Culture and Society*, 9, 4, 407–25.

Freeman, R. B. and Holzer, H. (eds) 1986: *The Black Youth Unemployment Crisis*. Chicago: University of Chicago Press.

Freeman, R. B. and Wise, D. A. 1982: *The Youth Labor Market Problem: Its Nature, Causes and Consequences*. Chicago: University of Chicago Press.

Freire, P. 1970: *Pedagogy of the Oppressed*. New York: Seabury Press.

Frith, S. 1983: *Sound Effects: Youth, Leisure and the Politics of Rock 'n' Roll*. London: Constable.

Fryer, D. 1987: Monmouthshire and Marienthal: sociographies of two unemployed communities. In Fryer and Ullah, *Unemployed People*.

Fryer, D. and Ullah, P. (eds) 1987: *Unemployed People: Social and Psychological Perspectives*. Milton Keynes: Open University Press.

Furlong, V. J. 1991: Disaffected pupils: reconstructing the sociological perspective. *British Journal of Sociology of Education*, 12, 3, 293–307.

Furstenberg, F. 1976: *Unplanned Parenthood: The Social Consequences of Teenage Parenthood*. New York: Free Press.

Furstenberg, F., Brooks-Gunn, J. and Morgan, S. P. 1987: *Adolescent Mothers in Later Life*. Cambridge: Cambridge University Press.

Gallatin, J. E. 1975: *Adolescence and Individuality*. New York: Harper and Row.

Game, A. 1991: *Undoing the Social: Towards a Deconstructive Sociology*. Milton Keynes: Open University Press.

Garibaldi, A. M. and Bartley, M. 1987: Black school pushouts and dropouts: strategies for reduction. *Urban League Review*, 11, 1/2, 227–35.

Gaston, J. C. 1986: The destruction of the young black male: the impact of popular culture and organized sports. *Journal of Black Studies*, 16, 4, 369–84.

George, H. 1988: The 'Black underclass' thesis and the legacy of Civil Rights and Black Power movements. *The Black Scholar* (June), 23–31.

Gerstel, C. J., Feraios, A. J. and Herdt, G. 1989: Widening circles: an ethnographic profile of a youth group. *Journal of Homosexuality*, 17, 1/2, 75–92.

Gibbs, J. T. 1988: Conceptual, methodological and socio-cultural issues in black youth suicide: implications for assessment and early intervention. *Suicide and Life-Threatening Behavior*, 18, 1, 73–81.

Gilbert, M. J. and Alcocer, A. M. 1988: Alcohol use and Hispanic youth: an overview. *The Journal of Drug Issues*, 18, 1, 33–48.

Gilchrist, L. D., Schinke, S. P., Trimble, J. E. and Cvetkovich, G. T. 1987: Skills enhancement to prevent substance abuse among American Indian adolescents. *The International Journal of the Addictions*, 22, 9, 869–79.

Gillis, J. 1974: *Youth and History: Tradition and Change in European Age Relations. 1770–Present*. New York: Academic Press.

Gilroy, P. 1982: You can't fool the youths: race and class formation in the 1980s. *Race and Class*, 23, 2/3, 207–22.

Gilroy, P. 1987: *Ain't No Black in the Union Jack: The Cultural Politics of Race and Nation*. London: Hutchinson.

Gilroy, P. and Lawrence, E. 1988: Two-tone Britain: white and Black youth and the politics of anti-racism. In Cohen and Bains, *Multi-Racist Britain*.

Glasgow, D. 1981: *The Black Underclass: Poverty, Unemployment and the Entrapment of Ghetto Youth*. San Fransisco: Jossey Bass.

Glenn, N. 1987: Continuity versus change, sanguineness versus concern: views of the American family in the late 1980s. *Journal of Family Issues*, 8, 4, 348–54.

Gold, J. H. 1984: Unemployed youth: developmental and psychotherapeutic considerations. *Journal of the University of Ottawa*, 9, 3, 138–41.

Golding, P. and Middleton, S. 1983: *Images of Welfare*. Oxford: Martin Robertson.

Gonsiorek, J. 1988: Mental health issues of gay and lesbian adolescents. *Journal of Adolescent Health Care*, 9, 123–32.

Good, D. H. and Pirog-Good, M. A. 1987: A simultaneous probit model of crime and employment for Black and white teenage males. *Review of the Black Political Economy*, 16, 1/2, 109–27.

Goodwin, L. 1980: Poor youth and employment: a social psychological perspective. *Youth and Society*, 11, 3, 311–51.

Gottlieb, E. 1989: Discursive construction of knowledge: the case of radical education discourse. *International Journal of Qualitative Studies in Education*, 2, 2, 131–44.

Gramsci, A. 1971: *Selections from the Prison Notebooks*. London: Lawrence and Wishart.

Green, R. 1987: *The 'Sissy Boy Syndrome' and the Development of Homosexuality*. New Haven: Yale University Press.

Greif, G. L. and Porembski, E. 1987: Significant others of IV drug abusers with AIDS: new challenges for drug treatment programs. *Journal of Substance Abuse Treatment*, 4, 151–5.

Griffin, C. 1982a: The good, the bad and the ugly: images of young women in the labour market. CCCS, Birmingham University: Occasional Paper.

Griffin, C. 1982b: Cultures of femininity: romance revisited. CCCS, Birmingham University: Occasional Paper.

Griffin, C. 1985a: *Typical Girls? Young Women from School to the Job Market*. London: Routledge and Kegan Paul.

Griffin, C. 1985b: Qualitative methods and cultural analysis: young women and the transition from school to un/employment. In R. Burgess (ed.), *Field Methods in the Study of Education*. Lewes: Falmer Press.

Griffin, C. 1986: Black and white youth in a declining job market: unemployment amongst Asian, Afro-Caribbean and white young people in Leicester. Centre for Mass Communication Research, Leicester University: Research Report Series.

Griffin, C. 1987: Broken transitions: schooling to the scrap heap. In P. Allatt, T. Keil, A. Bryman and B. Blytheway (eds), *Women and the Life-Cycle: Transitions and Turning Points*. London: Macmillan.

Griffin, C. 1988: Youth research: young women and the 'gang of lads' model. In J. Hazekamp, W. Meeus and Y. te Poel (eds), *European Contributions to Youth Research*. Amsterdam: Free University Press.

Griffin, C. 1989: 'I'm not a women's libber, but . . .': feminism, consciousness and identity. In Deborah Baker and Suzanne Skevington (eds), *The Social Identity of Women*, London: Sage.

Griffin, C. 1992: Fear of a Black (and working class) planet: young women and the racialisation of reproductive politics. *Feminism and Psychology*, 2, 3, 491–4.

Griffin, C. (forthcoming): Short-term palliatives and placebos: youth training programmes in Britain and the USA.

Griffin, C., Hobson, D., MacIntosh, S. and McCabe, T. 1982: Women and leisure. In J. Hargreaves (ed.), *Sport, Culture and Ideology*. London: Routledge and Kegan Paul.

Griffiths, V. 1988: From 'playing out' to 'dossing out': young women and leisure. In Wimbush and Talbot, *Relative Freedoms*.

Griffiths, V. 1992: Willingly to school? Girls' groups and girls' cultures. Paper presented at First International Conference on Girls and Girlhood, Amsterdam.

Grootings, P. and Adamski, W. 1986: Sociology of youth and sociology of work and the study of the transition from school to work. Paper presented at International Sociological Association conference, Austria.

Hagan, J., Gillis A. R. and Simpson, J. H. 1985: The class structure of gender and delinquency: toward a power-control theory of common delinquent behavior. *American Journal of Sociology*, 90, 1151–78.

Hall, G. Stanley 1904: *Adolescence: Its Psychology and Its Relation to Physiology, Anthropology, Sociology, Sex, Crime, Religion and Education*, 2 vols. New York: D. Appleton and Co.

Hall, S. 1988: Thatcher's lessons. *Marxism Today* (March), 20–7.

Hall, S. and Bailey, D. 1992: Radical Black photography. Seminar presented at CCCS, Birmingham University.

Hall, S., Critcher, C., Jefferson, T., Clarke, J. and Roberts, B. 1977: *Policing the Crisis: Mugging, the State and Law and Order*. London: Macmillan.

Hall, S. and Jacques, M. (eds) 1983: *The Politics of Thatcherism*. London: Lawrence and Wishart/Marxism Today.

Hall, S. and Jefferson, T. (eds) 1975: *Resistance through Rituals: Youth Sub-cultures in Post-war Britain*. London: Hutchinson.

Halsey, A. H., Heath, A. F. and Ridge, J. M. 1980: *Origins and Destinations*. Oxford: Clarendon Press.

Halston, J. 1989: The sexual harassment of young women. In Holly, *Girls and Sexuality*.

Hamilton, S. and Powers, J. L. 1989: Failed expectations: working-class girls' transition from school to work. *Youth and Society*, 22, 2, 241–62.

Haraway, D. 1989: *Primate Visions: Gender, Race and Nature in the World of Modern Science*. New York: Routledge, Chapman and Hall.

Hare, B. R. 1987: Structural inequality and the endangered status of Black youth. *Journal of Negro Education*, 56, 1, 100–10.

Hartnagel, T. F. and Krahn, H. 1989: High School dropouts, labor market success, and criminal behavior. *Youth and Society*, 20, 4, 416–44.

Hayes, C. (ed.) 1987: *Risking the Future: Adolescent Sexuality, Pregnancy and Childbearing*, vol. 1. Washington, DC: National Academy Press.

Hayes, J. and Nutman, P. 1981: *Understanding the Unemployed: The Psychological Effects of Unemployment*. London: Tavistock.

Haynes, R. 1992: Marching on together: a reappraisal of Leeds, the lads, and the meeja. Manchester Polytechnic Unit for Law and Popular Culture: Working Paper.

Hazekamp, J., Meeus, W. and te Poel, Y. 1987: *European Contributions to Youth Research*. Amsterdam: Free University Press.

Hebdige, D. 1987: *Cut 'n' Mix: Culture, Identity and Caribbean Music*. London: Comedia.

Hemmings, S. (ed.) 1982: *Girls are Powerful: Young Women's Writings from Spare Rib*. London: Sheba Press.

Henderson, K. A. 1991: The contribution of feminism to an understanding of leisure constraints. *Journal of Leisure Research*, 23, 4, 363–77.

Henry, S. (ed.) 1981: *Can I Have it in Cash? A Study of Informal Institutions and Unorthodox Ways of Doing Things*. London: Astragal Books.

Henshaw, S. 1987: Characteristics of US women having abortions. *Family Planning Perspectives*, 18, 1, 5–9.

Henwood, F. and Miles, I. 1987: The experience of unemployment and the sexual division of labour. In Fryer and Ullah, *Unemployed People*.

Herdt, G. 1989: Introduction: gay and lesbian youth, emergent identities and cultural scenes at home and abroad. *Journal of Homosexuality*, 17, 1/2, 1–42.

Hirschi, T. 1969: *Causes of Delinquency*. Berkeley: University of California Press.

Hofferth, S., Kahn, J. and Baldwin, W. 1987: Pre-marital sexual activity among US teenage women over the past three decades. *Family Planning Perspectives*, 19, 2, 46–53.

Hoffman, L. 1981: *Foundations of Family Therapy: A Conceptual Framework for Systems Change*. London: Harper Collins Academic.

Hoggart, R. 1957: *The Uses of Literacy*. London: Chatto and Windus.

Hollands, R. G. 1990: *The Long Transition: Class, Culture and Youth Training*. London: Macmillan.

Hollin, C. 1989: *Psychology and Crime: An Introduction to Criminological Psychology*. London: Routledge.

Hollingshead, A. 1949: *Elmtown's Youth: The Impact of Social Class on Adolescents*. New York: John Wiley.

Hollway, W. 1989: *Subjectivity and Method in Psychology: Gender, Meaning and Science*. London: Sage.

Holly, L. (ed.) 1989: *Girls and Sexuality: Teaching and Learning*. Milton Keynes: Open University Press.

Honess, T. 1989: Personal and social enabling conditions for the 16-year-old school leaver: a transactional model for understanding the school leaving transition. *Research Papers in Education*, 4, 2, 28–52.

Hopper, C. B. and Moore, J. 1990: Women in outlaw motor cycle gangs. *Journal of Contemporary Ethnography*, 18, 4, 363–87.

Horne, J. 1986: Continuity and change in the state regulation and schooling of unemployed youth. In S. Walker and L. Barton (eds), *Youth, Unemployment and Schooling*. Milton Keynes: Open University Press.

Horowitz, R. and Pottieger, A. E. 1991: Gender bias in juvenile justice handling of seriously crime-involved youths. *Journal of Research in Crime and Delinquency*, 28, 1, 75–100.

Huff, C. R. 1989: Youth gangs and public policy. *Crime and Delinquency*, 35, 4, 524–37.

Humphries, S. 1981: *Hooligans and Rebels: An Oral History of Working-Class Childhood and Youth 1889–1939*. Oxford: Basil Blackwell.

Hundleby, J. 1986: Personality and the prediction of delinquency and drug use: a follow-up study of training school boys. *British Journal of Criminology*, 26, 2, 129–46.

Hunt, A., Litt, I. and Loebner, M. 1988: Obtaining a sexual history from adolescent girls: a preliminary report of the influence of age and ethnicity. *Journal of Adolescent Health Care*, 9, 52–4.

Hutson, S. and Jenkins, R. 1989: *Taking the Strain: Families, Unemployment and the Transition to Adulthood*. Milton Keynes: Open University Press.

Iadicola, P. 1981: Desegregation: the assimilation of a minority population. *Sociological Focus*, 14, 3, 193–206.

Iadicola, P. 1983: Schooling and symbolic violence: the effect of power differences and curriculum factors on Hispanic students' attitudes toward their own ethnicity. *Hispanic Journal of Behavioral Sciences*, 5, 1, 21–43.

Irigaray, L. 1985: *This Sex which is not One*. Ithaca: Cornell University Press.

Iso-Ahola, S. E. and Crowley, E. D. 1991: Adolescent substance abuse and leisure boredom. *Journal of Leisure Research*, 23, 3, 260–71.

Jackson, M. 1985: *Youth Unemployment*. London: Croom Helm.

Jahoda, M., Lazarsfeld, P. F. and Zeisel, H. 1972: *Marienthal: The Sociography of an Unemployed Community*. London: Tavistock.

James, J. and Thornton, W. E. 1980: Women's liberation and the female delinquent. *Journal of Research in Crime and Delinquency*. 17, 230–44.

Jencks, C. 1973: *Inequality: A Reassessment of the Effect of Family and Schooling in America*. London: Allen Lane.

Jenkins, R. 1983: *Lads, Citizens and Ordinary Kids: Working-Class Youth Life Styles in Belfast*. London: Routledge.

Joe, T. 1987: The other side of Black female-headed families: the status of adult black men. *Family Planning Perspectives*, 19, 2, 74–6.

Jones, A. 1991: '*At school I've got a chance*'. *Culture/Privilege: Pacific Islands and Pakeha Girls at School*. Palmerston North, New Zealand: Dunmore.

Jones, H. 1987: Foreword. *Children and Youth Services Review*, special issue on 'The Black Adolescent Parent', ix–x.

Jones, S. 1988: *Black Culture, White Youth: The Reggae Tradition from JA to UK*. London: Macmillan.

Jordan, B. 1982: *Mass Unemployment and the Future of Britain*. Oxford: Basil Blackwell.

Junankar, P. (ed.) 1987: *From School to Unemployment? The Labour Market for Young People*. London: Macmillan.

Kalmuss, D. S. 1986: Contraceptive use: a comparison between ever- and never-pregnant adolescents, *Journal of Adolescent Health Care*, 7, 5, 332–7.

Kandel, D., Simcha-Fagan, O. and Davies, M. 1986: Risk factors for delinquency and illicit drug use from adolescence to young adulthood. *Journal of Drug Issues*, 16, 1, 67–90.

Katz, M. 1980: Missing the point: National Service and the needs of youth. *Social Policy*, 10, 4, 36–40.

Kelvin, P. and Jarrett, J. 1985: *Unemployment: Its Social Psychological Effects*. Cambridge: Cambridge University Press.

Kett, J. 1977: *Rites of Passage: Adolescence in America, 1790 to the Present*. New York: Basic Books.

Kettle, M. and Hodges, L. 1982: *Uprising! The Police, the People and the Riots in Britain's Cities*. London: Pan.

King, E. W. 1984: Studies of schooling: a cross-cultural perspective. *Social Science Journal*, 21, 3, 123–6.

Kitzinger, C. 1988: *The Social Construction of Lesbianism*. London: Sage.

Kitzinger, C. 1991: Making lesbians of ourselves: the transition from heterosexuality to lesbianism. Paper presented at British Psychological Society conference, Bournmouth.

Kornhauser, R. R. 1978: *Social Sources of Delinquency: An Appraisal of Analytic Models*. Chicago: University of Chicago Press.

Kourany, R. 1987: Suicide among homosexual adolescents. *Journal of Homosexuality*, 13, 4, 111–17.

Kourany, R. 1988: Gay and lesbian youth and the resolution of sexual identity. *Journal of Adolescent Health Care*, 9, 114–22.

Kozicki, Z. 1986: Why do adolescents use substances (drugs/alcohol)? *Journal of Alcohol and Drug Education*, 32, 1, 1–7.

Ladner, J. 1971: *Tomorrow's Tomorrow: The Black Woman*. New York: Doubleday.

Ladner, J. 1987: Black teenage pregnancy: a challenge for educators. *Journal of Negro Education*, 56, 1, 53–63.

Lalonde, S. 1987: The young father's dilemma: employment or participation. Paper presented at British Psychological Society conference (Social Psychology section), Oxford.

Landry, E., Bertrand, J. T., Cherry, F. and Rice, J. 1986: Teen pregnancy in New Orleans: factors that differentiate teens who deliver, abort and successfuly contracept. *Journal of Youth and Adolescence*, 15, 3, 259–74.

Lasch, C. 1977: *Haven in a Heartless World*. New York: Basic Books.

Laslett, P. 1971: Age of menarche in Europe since the eighteenth century. *Journal of Interdisciplinary History*. 2, 2, 221–36.

Lather, P. 1990: Review of *Critical Redogogy and Cultural Power* by D. Livingstone et al. (1987), *International Journal of Qualitative Studies in Education*, 3, 1, 90–4.

Lawrence, E. 1982: Just plain common sense: the roots of racism. In Race and Politics Group, *The Empire Strikes Back*.

Lees, S. 1986: *Losing Out: Sexuality and Adolescent Girls*. London: Hutchinson.

Lemert, E. 1967: *Human Deviance, Social Problems and Social Control*. Englewood Cliffs, NJ: Prentice Hall.

Lemle, R. and Mishkind, M. E. 1989: Alcohol and masculinity. *Journal of Substance Abuse Treatment*, 6, 213–22.

Leone, P. E. (ed.) 1990: *Understanding Troubled and Troubling Youth*. Newbury Park, CA: Sage.

Levenson, P., Smith, P. and Morrow, J. 1986: A comparison of physician–patient views of teen prenatal information needs. *Journal of Adolescent Health Care*, 7, 1, 6–11.

Levitas, R. 1986: *The Ideology of the New Right*. Cambridge: Polity Press.

Lewin-Epstein, N. 1986: Effects of residential segregation and neighborhood opportunity structure on the employment of Black and white youth. *Sociological Quarterly*, 27, 4, 559–70.

Lewis, C. and O'Brien, M. 1987: *Reassessing Fatherhood*. London: Sage.

Leyton, E. 1979: *The Myth of Delinquency: An Anatomy of Juvenile Nihilism*. Ontario: McClelland and Stewart.

Little, A. and Westergaard, J. 1964: The trend of class differentials in educational opportunity. *British Journal of Sociology*, 15, 4, 301–16.

Loewenstein, G. and Furstenberg, F. 1991: Is teenage sexual behavior rational? *Journal of Applied Social Psychology*, 21, 12, 957–86.

Lohman, J. 1986: Comparison of the York's Toughlove concepts with Adlerian theory and practice. *Individual Psychology: Journal of Adlerian Theory, Research and Practice*, 42, 2, 225–33.

Lopes, F. 1986: Family structure and depression: implications for the counseling of depressed college students. *Journal of Counselling and Development*, 64, 8, 508–11.

Lowman, J. 1989: *Street Prostitution. Assessing the Impact of the Law: Vancouver.* Ottawa: Department of Justice.

Luttrell, W. 1989: Working-class women's ways of knowing: effects of gender, race and class. *Sociology of Education*, 62, 33–46.

Mac an Ghaill, M. 1988: *Young, Gifted and Black: Student–Teacher Relations in the Schooling of Black Youth.* Milton Keynes: Open University Press.

Macaulay, R. 1923: *Told by an Idiot.* London: Hogarth Press.

MacDonald, R. and Coffield, F. 1990: Youth enterprise and business start-up in a depressed area of Britain. City University, London: Social Statistics Research Unit.

Maizels, J. 1970: *Adolescent Needs and the Transition from School to Work.* University of London: Athlone Press.

Malveux, J. 1988: Poverty, Black youth and the 'Black underclass'. *The Black Scholar* (June), 37–42.

Mannheim, K. 1952: The problem of generations. In P. Kecskmeti (ed.), *Essays in the Sociology of Knowledge.* Oxford: Oxford University Press.

Marchant, H. and Smith, H. 1977: *Adolescent Girls at Risk.* London: Pergamon Press.

Marciano, T. and Sussman, M. B. 1991: Wider families: an overview. In T. Marciano and M. B. Sussman (eds), *Wider Families: New Traditional Family Forms.* New York: Haworth Press.

Mare, R. D. and Winship, C. 1984: The paradox of lessening racial inequality and joblessness among Black Youth: enrollment, enlistment and employment, 1964–1981. *American Sociological Review*, 49, 1, 39–55.

Marks, J. B. and Glaser, E. M. 1980: The antecedents of chosen joblessness. *American Journal of Community Psychology*, 2, 2, 173–201.

Marshall, R. 1984: Selective employment programs and economic policy. *Journal of Economic Issues*, 18, 1, 117–42.

Marsland, D. 1986: The theory of youth in sociology and in practice. Paper presented at British Sociological Association annual conference, Loughborough University.

Massey, D. and Meegan, R. 1982: *The Anatomy of Job Loss.* London: Methuen.

Mathews, P. W. 1983: *Male Homosexual Prostitution.* Unpublished Sociology honours thesis, University of New South Wales, Sydney.

Matsueda, R. L. and Heimer, K. 1987: Race, family structure, and delinquency: a test of differential association and social control theories. Paper presented at American Sociological Association conference.

McCarthy, C. 1988: Marxist theories of education and the challenge of a cultural politics of non-synchrony. In Roman and Christian-Smith, *Becoming Feminine.*

McCarthy, C. 1989: Rethinking liberal and radical perspectives on racial inequality in schooling: making the case for non-synchrony. Paper presented at International Sociology of Education conference, Birmingham, UK.

McDermott, M. 1986: Rebelliousness in adolescence and young adulthood: a two dimensional model. Paper presented at British Psychological Society conference, London.

McDermott, R. P. 1987: The explanation of minority school failure, again. *Anthropology and Education Quarterly*, 18, 4, 361–4.

McGahey, R. 1987: Crime and employment research: a continuing deadlock? *Review of the Black Political Economy*, 16, 1/2, 223–30.

McLachlan, P. 1981: Teenage experiences in a violent society. *Journal of Adolescence*, 4, 4, 285–94.

McLaren, P. 1989: On ideology and education: Critical pedagogy and the politics of resistance. In H. Giroux and P. McLaren (eds), *Critical Pedagogy, the State and Cultural Struggle*. New York: State University of New York Press.

McLaughlin, L. 1991: Discourses of prostitution/discourses of sexuality. *Critical Studies in Mass Communication*, 8, 249–72.

McLeod, E. 1982: *Women Working: Prostitution Now*. London: Croom Helm.

McLorg, P. A. and Taub, D. E. 1987: Anorexia nervosa and bulimia: the development of deviant identities. *Deviant Behavior*, 8, 177–89.

McRobbie, A. 1978: Working class girls and the culture of femininity. In Women's Studies Group, *Women Take Issue*.

McRobbie, A. 1980: Settling accounts with subcultures: a feminist critique. *Screen Education*, 34, 37–49.

McRobbie, A. 1984: Dance and social fantasy. In A. McRobbie and M. Nava (eds), *Gender and Generation*. London: Macmillan.

McRobbie, A. (ed.) 1988: *Zoot Suits and Second-Hand Dresses: An Anthology of Fashion and Music*. London: Macmillan.

McRobbie, A. 1991: Moving cultural studies on: post-marxism and beyond. *Magazine of Cultural Studies*, 4, 18–21.

McRobbie, A. 1992: From youth to pop culture: changing modes of femininity. Paper presented at First International Conference on Girls and Girlhood, Amsterdam.

McRobbie, A. and Garber, J. 1975: Girls and subcultures: an exploration. In Hall and Jefferson, *Resistance through Rituals*.

Mead, M. 1928: *Coming of Age in Samoa: A Study of Adolescence and Sex in Primitive Societies*. London: Cape.

Messner, M. 1990: Boyhood, organized sports, and the construction of masculinities. *Journal of Contemporary Ethnography*, 18, 4, 416–44.

Miller, B. C. and Dyk, P. H. 1990: Adolescent fertility-related behavior in the 1990s: risking the future continued. *Journal of Family Issues*, 11, 3, 235–8.

Miller, B. C. and Moore, K. 1990: Adolescent sexual behavior, pregnancy and parenting: research through the 1980s. *Journal of Marriage and the Family*, 52, 1025–44.

Miller, W. B. 1975: *Violence by Youth Gangs and Youth Groups as a Crime Problem in Major American Cities*. Washington, DC: Government Printing Office.

Millman, M. and Kantor, R. (eds) 1975: *Feminist Perspectives on Social Life and Social Science*. New York: Anchor Press.

Minor, K. 1987: Toward an integrated theory of youth crime: a contribution to progress in criminological theory construction. Paper presented at American Sociological Association conference.

Mirza, H. S. 1992: *Young, Female and Black*. London: Routledge.

Moffatt, M. 1986: The discourses of the dorm: race, friendship and 'culture' among college youth. In H. Varenne (ed.), *Symbolizing America*. Lincoln, NB: University of Nebraska Press.

Moll, L. C. and Diaz, S. E. 1987: Change as the goal of educational research. *Anthropology and Education Quarterly*, 18, 4, 300–11.

Moorhouse, H. F. 1989: Models of work, models of leisure. In Rojek, *Leisure for Leisure*.

Moraga, C. and Andalzua, G. (eds), 1981: *This Bridge Called My Back: Radical Writing by Women of Color*. Watertown, MA: Persephone Press.

Morris, A. 1987: *Women, Crime and Criminal Justice*. Oxford: Basil Blackwell.

Mosher, W. D. 1990: Contraceptive practice in the United States, 1982–1988. *Family Planning Perspectives*, 22, 5, 198–205.

Moynihan, D. P. 1977: The most important decision-making process. *Policy Review*, 1 (Summer), 89–94.

Muncie, J. 1984: *The Trouble with Kids Today: Youth and Crime in Post-war Britain*. London: Hutchinson.

Munene, J. C. 1983: Understanding juvenile unemployability: an exploratory study. *Journal of Adolescence*, 6, 3, 247–61.

Mungham, G. and Pearson, G. 1975: *Working Class Youth Cultures*. London: Routledge and Kegan Paul.

Murdock, G. and McCron, R. 1975: Consciousness of class and consciousness of generation. In Hall and Jefferson, *Resistance through Rituals*.

Murphy, J. 1989: Race, education and intellectual prejudice. In F. Macleod (ed.), *Parents and Schools: The Contemporary Challenge*. Lewes: Falmer Press.

Muuss, R. E. 1968: *Theories of Adolescence* (2nd edn). New York: Random House.

Myers, S. L. 1987: Introduction. *Review of the Black Political Economy*, 16, 1/2, 5–15.

Myrdal, G. 1987: Inequality of justice. *Review of the Black Political Economy*. 16, 1/2, 81–98 (first published 1944).

Naber, P. 1992: Friendship between young women. Paper presented at First International Conference on Girls and Girlhood, Amsterdam.

Neinstein, L. and Shapiro, J. 1986: Pediatrician's self-evaluation of adolescent health care training skills and interest. *Journal of Adolescent Health Care*, 7, 1, 18–21.

Newcomer, S. and Udry, R. 1986: Parental marital status effects on adolescent sexual behavior. Paper presented at American Sociological Association conference.

Newton, J. 1990: Historicisms new and old: 'Charles Dickens' meets Marxism, feminism and West Coast Foucault. *Feminist Studies*, 16, 3, 449–70.

Niles, W. 1986: Managing episodic homosexual behavior of adolescents in residential settings. *Child Care Quarterly*, 15, 1, 15–26.

O'Connor, D. 1986: The pervasiveness of military themes in the early male culture. *Dissertation Abstracts International*, 47, 3, 840-A.

Ogbu, J. 1987: Variability in minority school performance. *Anthropology and Education Quarterly*, 18, 4, 312–34.

Ogbu, J. 1989: The individual in collective adaptation: a framework for focussing on academic underperformance and dropping out among involuntary minorities. In L. Weis, E. Farrar and H. Petrie (eds), *Issues, Dilemmas and Solutions*. Albany, NY: State University of New York Press.

Okazawa-Rey, L. 1989: Review of L. Weis (1988). *Journal of Negro Education*, 58, 1, 118–21.

Oliver, M. 1988: The social and political context of educational policy: the case of special needs. In L. Barton (ed.). *The Politics of Special Educational Needs*. Lewes: Falmer Press.

Omi, M. and Winant, H. 1986: *Racial Formation in the United States*. Boston: Routledge and Kegan Paul.

Osterman, P. 1980: *Getting Started: The Youth Labor Market*. Cambridge, MA: MIT Press.

Outwrite. 1988: Editorial (December), 1, 4–5.

Padgug, R. A. 1979: Sexual matters: on conceptualizing sexuality in history. *Radical History Review*, 20, 3–23.

Pahl, R. 1982: Family, community and unemployment. *New Society* 21 January, 91–6.

Parker, I. 1989: *The Crisis in Modern Social Psychology – And How to End It*. London: Routledge.

Parsons, T. 1942: Age and sex in the social structure of the United States. *American Sociological Review*, 7, 604–16.

Payne, J. 1989: Unemployment and family formation among young men. *Sociology*, 23, 2, 171–91.

Pearson, G. 1983: *Hooligan: A History of Respectable Fears*. London: Macmillan.

Petrie, C. 1986: *The Nowhere Girls*. Aldershot: Gower.

Pfantz, H. W. 1961: Near-group theory and collective behavior: a critical reformulation. *Social Problems*, 9, 167–74.

Phillips, L. and Votey, H. L. 1987: Rational choice models of crimes by youth. *Review of the Black Political Economy*, 16, 1/2, 183–5.

Phoenix, A. 1988: Theories of gender and black families. In Weiner and Arnot, *Gender Under Scrutiny*.

Phoenix, A. 1990: *Young Mothers?* Cambridge: Polity Press.

Pinchbeck, I. 1930: *Women Workers and the Industrial Revolution: 1750–1850*. London: Routledge (republished 1981).

Pletsch, P. 1988: Substance use and health activities of pregnant adolescents. *Journal of Adolescent Health Care*, 9, 38–45.

Plummer, K. 1989: Lesbian and gay youth in England. *Journal of Homosexuality*, 17, 3/4, 45–63.

Pope, J. 1988: Women and welfare reform. *The Black Scholar* (May/June), 22–30.

Presdee, M. 1985: Agony or ecstasy: broken transitions and the new social state of working-class youth in Australia. South Australian Centre for Youth Studies: Occasional Papers, no. 1.

Pugh, M. D., De Maris, A., Giordano, P. C. and Groat, H. T. 1990: Delinquency as a risk factor in teenage pregnancy. *Sociological Focus*, 23, 2, 89–100.

Race and Politics Group (eds) 1982: *The Empire Strikes Back: Race and Racism in '70s Britain*. London: Hutchinson.

Raskin White, H. and LaGrange, R. 1987: An assessment of gender effects in self-report delinquency. *Sociological Focus*, 20, 3, 195–214.

Realmuto, G. and Erikson, W. 1986: The management of sexual issues in adolescent treatment programs. *Adolescence*, 21, 82, 347–56.

Reckless, W. C. and Dinitz, S. 1967: Pioneering with the self-concept as a vulnerability factor in delinquency. *Journal of Criminal Law, Criminology and Police Science*, 58, 515–23.

Redhead, S. 1991: *Football with Attitude*. Manchester: Wordsmith.

Redman, S. 1991: Invasion of the monstrous others: identity, genre and AIDS. *Cultural Studies*, 1, 8–28.

Reicher, S. and Potter, J. 1985: Psychological theory as intergroup perspective: a comparative analysis of 'scientific' and 'lay' accounts of crowd events. *Human Relations*, 38, 2, 167–89.

Remafedi, G. J. 1987: Preventing the sexual transmission of AIDS during adolescence. *Journal of Adolescent Health Care*, 9, 139–43.

Renwick, S. and Emler, N. 1991: The relationship between social skills deficits and juvenile delinquency. *British Journal of Clinical Psychology*, 30, 61–71.

Rich, A. 1981: Compulsory heterosexuality and lesbian existence. London: Onlywomen Press pamphlet.

Riley, D. 1978: Development psychology: biology and Marxism. *Ideology and Consciousness*, 4, 73–91.

Roberts, K. 1983: *Youth and Leisure*. London: Allen and Unwin.

Roberts, K. 1984: *School Leavers and their Prospects*. Milton Keynes: Open University Press.

Roberts, K. 1986: Current changes in the process of entering employment. Paper presented at International Sociological Association conference, USA.

Roberts, K. and Parsell, G. 1988: Opportunity structures and career trajectories from age 16–19. Social Statistics Research Unit, City University, London: ESRC 16–19 Initiative Occasional Papers.

Roberts, N. 1986: *Frontline: Women in the Sex Industry Speak*. London: Grafton Books.

Rodriguez, C. 1986: 'Menudo': popular culture and the Puerto Rican community. Paper presented at American Sociological Association conference.

Rojek, C. (ed.) 1989: *Leisure for Leisure: Critical Essays*. London: Macmillan.

Roman, L. 1988: Intimacy, labor and class: ideologies of feminine sexuality in the punk slam dance. In Roman and Christian-Smith, *Becoming Feminine*.

Roman, L. and Christian-Smith, L. with Ellsworth, E. (eds) 1988: *Becoming Feminine: The Politics of Popular Culture*. New York: Taylor and Francis.

Rose, N. 1977: The psychological complex: mental measurement and social administration. *Ideology and Consciousness*, 5, 5–68.

Rose, S. and Rose, H. 1986: Less than human nature: biology and the new right. *Race and Class*, 27, 3, 47–66.

Ross, D. 1972: *G. Stanley Hall: The Psychologicst as Prophet*. Chicago: University of Chicago Press.

Rowland, D. T. 1991: Family diversity and the life cycle. *Journal of Comparative Family Studies*, 22, 1, 1–14.

Rubin, G. 1975: The traffic in women: notes on the political economy of sex. In R. Reiter (ed.), *Towards An Anthropology of Women*. New York: Monthly Review Press.

Rudd, N. M., McKenry, P. C. and Nah, M. 1990: Welfare receipt among Black and White adolescent mothers. *Journal of Family Issues*, 11, 3, 315–29.

Rumberger, R. W. 1987: Dropouts: a review of issues and evidence. *Review of Educational Research*, 57, 101–21.

Rushton, J. P. 1985: Differential K theory and race differences in E and N. *Personality and Individual Differences*, 6, 769–70.

Russell, D. (ed.) 1989: *Exposing Nuclear Phallacies*. New York: Pergamon Press.

Rutherford, J. 1990: A place called home: identity and the cultural politics of difference. In J. Rutherford (ed.), *Identity: Community, Culture, Difference*. London: Lawrence and Wishart.

Rutter, M. 1972: *Maternal Deprivation Reassessed*. Harmondsworth: Penguin.

Rutter, M. and Giller, H. 1983: *Juvenile Delinquency*. Harmondsworth: Penguin.

Ryan, W. 1969: *Blaming the Victim*. New York: Random House.

Said, E. 1978: *Orientalism*. London: Routledge and Kegan Paul.

Salmon, P. 1991: The peer group. In J. C. Coleman (ed.), *The School Years*. London: Routledge.

Sandelowski, M. 1990: Fault lines infertility and imperiled sisterhood. *Feminist Studies*, 16, 1, 33–52.

Sarup, M. 1986: *The Politics of Multi-racial Education*. London: Routledge and Kegan Paul.

Savin-Williams, R. 1988: Theoretical perspectives accounting for adolescent homosexuality. *Journal of Adolescent Health Care*, 9, 95–104.

Sayers, J. 1982: *Biological Politics: Feminist and Anti-feminist Perspectives*. London: Tavistock.

Scanzoni, J. 1987: Families in the 1980s: time to refocus our thinking. *Journal of Family Issues*, 8, 4, 394–421.

Schinke, S. P., Schilling, R. F., Gilchrist, L. D., Whittaker, J. K., Kirkham, M. A., Senechal, V. A., Snow, W. H. and Maxwell, J. S. 1986: Definition and methods for prevention research with youth and families. *Children and Youth Services Review*, 8, 3, 257–66.

Schneider, M. 1989: Sappho was a right-on adolescent: growing up lesbian. *Journal of Homosexuality*, 1/2, 111–30.

Schneider, M. and Tremble, B. 1986: Training service providers to work with gay or lesbian adolescents: a workshop. *Journal of Counselling and Development*, 65, 2, 98–9.

Schram, S. 1991: Welfare spending and poverty: cutting back produces more poverty, not less. *American Journal of Economics and Sociology*, 50, 2, 129–42.

Schwanberg, S. L. 1990: Attitudes towards homosexuality in American health care literature: 1983–1987. *Journal of Homosexuality*, 19, 3, 117–36.

Schwartz, D. and Darabi, K. 1986: Motivations for adolescents' first visit to a family planning clinic. *Adolescence*, 21, 83, 535–45.

Serna, L. A. Schumaker, J. B. Hazel, J. S. and Sheldon, J. B. 1986: Teaching reciprocal social skills to parents and their delinquent adolescents. Special issue: 'Social Skills training', *Journal of Clinical Child Psychology*, 15, 1, 64–77.

Seydlitz, R. 1990: The effects of gender, age and parental attachment on delinquency: a test for interactions. *Sociological Spectrum*, 10, 209–25.

Shaw, A. 1968: *Sinatra: A Biography*. New York: W. H. Allen.

Shearer, A. 1981: *Whose Handicap?* London: Croom Helm.

Sims, M. and Smith, C. 1986: *Teenage Mothers and Their Partners*. London: HMSO Report no. 15.

Singh, S. 1986: Adolescent pregnancy in the U.S. *Family Planning Perspectives*, 18, 5, 210–20.

Sinha, M. 1987: Gender and imperialism: colonial policy and the ideology of moral imperialism in 19th century Bengal. In M. Kimmel (ed.), *Changing Men: New Directions in Research on Men and Masculinity*. Newbury Park, CA: Sage.

Sivanandan, A. 1982: *A Different Hunger*. London: Pluto Press.

Skeggs, B. 1991: Postmodernism: what is all the fuss about? *British Journal of Sociology of Education*. 12, 2, 225–67.

Smith, B. 1982: Racism and Women's Studies. In G. T. Hull, P. B. Scott and B. Smith (eds), *All the Women are White, All the Blacks are Men, But Some of Us are Brave*. New York: The Feminist Press.

Smith, D. 1991: Writing women's experience into social science. *Feminism and Psychology*, 1, 1, 155–70.

Snedeker, B. 1982: *Hard Knocks: Preparing Youth for Work*. Baltimore: Johns Hopkins University Press.

Snyder, J., Dishion, T. J. and Patterson, G. R. 1986: Determinants and consequences of associating with deviant peers during pre-adolescence and adolescence. *Journal of Early Adolescence*, 6, 1, 29–43.

Sophie, J. 1986: A critical examination of stage theories of lesbian identity development. *Journal of Homosexuality*, 12, 2, 39–51.

Spaights, E. and Dixon, H. E. 1986: Black youth unemployment: issues and problems. *Journal of Black Studies*, 16, 4, 385–96.

Spinner, D. and Pfeifer, G. 1986: Group psychotherapy with ego-impaired children: the significance of peer group culture in the evolution of a holding environment. *International Journal of Group Psychotherapy*, 36, 3, 427–46.

Spivak, G. C. 1987: Displacement and the discourse of woman. In M. Krupnick (ed.), *Displacement: Derrida and After*. Bloomington: Indiana University Press.

Sprecher, S., McKinney, K. and Orbuch, T. 1986: Has the double standard disappeared? An experimental test. Paper presented at American Sociological Association conference.

Springhall, J. 1986: *Coming of Age: Adolescence in Britain. 1860–1960.* Dublin: Gill and Maomillan.

Squire, C. 1988: Stories of gender: feminism and social psychology. Paper presented at British Psychology Society conference (Social Psychology Section), University of Kent at Canterbury.

St Pierre, M. 1991: Reaganomics and its implications for African-American family life. *Journal of Black Studies*, 21, 3, 325–40.

Stanworth, M. 1983: *Gender and Schooling: A Study of Sexual Divisions in the Classroom*. London: Hutchinson, with the Explorations in Feminism Collective.

Starr, J. 1986: American youth in the 1980s. *Youth and Society*, 17, 4, 323–45.

Stephenson, S. P. 1979: From school to work: a transition with job search implications. *Youth and Society*, 11, 1, 114–32.

Stern, J. 1982: Does unemployment really kill? *New Society*, 10 June, 421–2.

Stevenson, R. B. and Ellsworth, J. 1991: Dropping out in a working class high school: adolescent voices on the decision to leave. *British Journal of Sociology of Education*. 12, 3, 277–91.

Stiffman, A. R., Powell, J., Earls, F., and Robins, L. N. 1990: Pregnancies, childrearing, and mental health problems in adolescents. *Youth and Society*, 21, 4, 483–95.

Stokes, G. 1984: Out of school – out of work: the psychological impact. *Youth and Policy*, 2, 2, 27–9.

Strange, P. 1983: It'll make a man of you: a feminist view of the arms race. Nottingham: Peace News/Mushroom Press.

Strassberg, D. L. and Mahoney, J. M. 1988: Correlates of the contraceptive behavior of adolescents/young adults. *Journal of Sex Research*, 25, 4, 531–6.

Summerfield, P. 1984: *Women Workers in the Second World War*. London: Croom Helm.

Taborn, J. M. 1987: The Black adolescent mother: selected, unique issues. *Children and Youth Services Review*, special issue on 'The Black Adolescent Parent', 1–13.

Taylor, I. and Jamieson, R. 1983: Young people's response to the job crisis in Canada – a framework for theoretical and empirical research. Department of Sociology, Carleton University, Ottawa: unpublished paper.

Taylor, I., Walton, P. and Young, J. 1973: *The New Criminology*. London: Routledge and Kegan Paul.

Terry, J. 1990: Lesbians under the medical gaze: scientists search for remarkable differences. *Journal of Sex Research*, 27, 3, 317–39.

Thompson, E. P. 1967: Time and industrial work discipline. *Past and Present*, 38, 45–54.

Thornton, A. 1990: The courtship process and adolescent sexuality. *Journal of Family Issues*, 11, 3, 239–73.

Thrasher, F. M. 1927: *The Gang*. Chicago: University of Chicago Press.

Tomlinson, A. (ed.) 1990: *Consumption, Identity and Style: Marketing, Meanings and the Packaging of Pleasure*. London: Routledge, for Comedia.

Trenchard, L. 1984: Talking about young lesbians. London: London Gay Teenage Group pamphlet.

Trenchard, L. and Warren, H. 1987: Talking about school: the experiences of young lesbians and gay men. In Weiner and Arnot, *Gender Under Scrutiny*.

Troiden, R. R. 1988: Homosexual identity development. *Journal of Adolescent Health Care*. 9, 105–13.

Trueba, H. 1988: Culturally based explanations of minority students' academic achievement. *Anthropology and Education Quarterly*, 19, 3, 270–87.

Trueba, H. 1990: The role of culture in literary acquisition: an interdisciplinary approach to qualitative research. *International Journal of Qualitative Studies in Education*, 3, 1, 1–14.

Trulson, M. 1986: Martial arts training: a novel 'cure' for juvenile delinquency. *Human Relations*, 39, 12, 1131–40.

Tyler, B. M. 1989: Black jive and white repression. *Journal of Ethnic Studies*, 16, 4, 31–66.

Udry, J. R. 1989: Biosocial models of adolescent problem behaviors. *Social Biology*, 1/2, 1–10.

Ullah, P. 1985: Disaffected black and white youth: the role of unemployment duration and perceived job discrimination. *Ethnic and Racial Studies*, 8, 181–93.

Ussher, J. 1989: *The Psychology of the Female Body*. London: Routledge.

Vance, C. S. and Pollis, C. A. 1990: Introduction: a special issue on feminist perspectives on sexuality. *Journal of Sex Research*, 27, 1, 1–5.

Varlaam, C. 1984: *Rethinking Transition: Educational Innovation and the Transition to Adult Life*. Lewes: Falmer Press.

Veness, T. 1962: *School Leavers*. London: Methuen.

Venn, C. 1984: The subject of psychology. In J. Henriques, W. Holloway, C. Urwin, C. Venn and V. Walkerdine, *Changing the Subject: Psychology, Social Regulation and Subjectivity*. London: Methuen.

Voight, L. and Thornton, W. 1987: Counselling joint custody adolescents: new problems for an old profession. Paper presented at Society for the Study of Social Problems conference, USA.

Walker, D. and Pendleton, B. 1987: The gender role and its consequences for investigation in adolescent female sexuality. Paper presented at North Central Sociological Association Conference, USA.

Walker, J. C. 1986a: Romanticising resistance, romanticising culture. Problems in Willis' theory of cultural production. *British Journal of Sociology of Education*, 7, 1, 59–80.

Walker, J. C. 1986b: *Lotus and Legends: Male Youth culture in an Inner City School*. Sydney: Allen and Unwin.

Walker, M. A. 1988: The court disposal of young males, by race, in London in 1983. *British Journal of Criminology*, 28, 4, 441–60.

Wallace, C. 1987: *For Richer, for Poorer: Growing up in and out of Work*. London: Tavistock.

Walvin, J. 1982: *A Child's World: A Social History of English Childhood, 1800–1914*. Harmondsworth: Penguin.

Warr, P. 1984: Job loss, unemployment and psychological well-being. In V. Allen and E. van de Vliert (eds), *Role Transitions*. New York: Plenum Press.

Warr, P., Banks, M. and Ullah, P. 1985: The experience of unemployment among black and white urban teenagers. *British Journal of Psychology*, 76, 75–87.

Warr, P., Jackson, P. and Banks, M. 1982: Duration of unemployment and psychological well-being in women and men. *Current Psychological Research*, 2, 207–14.

Watts, T. and Lewis, R. 1988: Alcoholism and Native American youth: an overview. *Journal of Drug Issues*, 18, 1, 69–86.

Weber, D. and Burke, W. 1986: An alternative approach to treating delinquent youth. *Residential Group Care and Treatment*, 3, 3, 65–85.

Weedon, C. 1987: *Feminist Practice and Post-Structuralist Theory*. Oxford: Basil Blackwell.

Weeks, J. 1981: *Sex, Politics and Society: The Regulation of Sexuality since 1800*. New York: Longman.

Weinberg, M. and Williams, G. 1988: Black sexuality: a test of two theories. *Journal of Sex Research*, 25, 2, 197–218.

Weiner, G. and Arnot, M. (eds) 1988: *Gender under Scrutiny: New Inquiries in Education*. Milton Keynes: Open University Press.

Weis, L. (ed.) 1988: *Class, Race and Gender in American Education*. Albany, NY: State University of New York Press.

Weiss, R. 1987: On the current state of the American family. *Journal of Family Issues*, 8, 4, 464–7.

Wells, E. and Rankin, J. 1986: The broken homes model of delinquency: analytic issues. *Journal of Research in Crime and Delinquency*. 23, 1, 68–93.

West, D. J. 1982: *Delinquency: Its Roots, Careers and Prospects*. London: Heinemann.

Westwood, S. 1989: Racism, black masculinity and the politics of space. In J. Hearn and D. Morgan (eds), *Men, Masculinities and Social Theory*. London: Unwin Hyman.

Wetzel, J. R. 1990: American families: 75 years of change. *Monthly Labor Review*, March, 4–13.

Whyte, W. F. 1943: *Street Corner Society: The Social Structure of an Italian Slum*. Chicago: University of Chicago Press.

Wiggins, D. K. 1989: 'Great speed but little stamina': the historical debate over black athletic superiority. *Journal of Sport History*, 16, 2, 158–85.

Williams, R. 1976: *Keywords*. Harmondsworth: Penguin.

Willis, P. 1977: *Learning to Labour: How Working Class Kids Get Working Class Jobs*. Farnborough: Saxon House.

Willis, P. 1978: *Profane Culture*. London: Routledge and Kegan Paul.

Willis, P. 1984: Youth unemployment: thinking the unthinkable. *Youth and Policy*, 2, 4, 17–36.

Willis, P. 1985: The Social Condition of Young People in Wolverhampton in 1984. Wolverhampton: Wolverhampton Borough Council.

Willis, P., Jones, S., Canaan, J. and Hurd, G. 1990: *Common Culture: Symbolic Work at Play in the Everyday Cultures of the Young*. Milton Keynes: Open University Press.

Wilson, M., Engels, D., Hartz, J. and Foster, D. 1987: The employability inventory: an overview. *Journal of Employment Counselling*, 24, 2, 62–8.

Wimbush, E. and Talbot, M. (eds) 1989: *Relative Freedoms: Women and Leisure*. Milton Keynes: Open University Press.

Winfield, L. A. 1991: Resilience, schooling and development in African-American youth: a conceptual framework. *Education and Urban Society*, 24, 1, 5–14.

Wolpe, A. 1988: *Within School Walls: The Role of Discipline, Sexuality and the Curriculum*. London: Routledge.

Wolpe, A. and Donald, J. (eds) 1983: *Is There Anyone Here from Education?* London: Pluto Press.

Women's Studies Group (ed.) 1978: *Women Take Issue: Aspects of Women's Subordination*. London: Hutchinson.

Wood, J. 1984: Groping towards sexism: boys' sex talk. In A. McRobbie and J. Garber (eds), *Gender and Generation*. London: Macmillan.

Wright, R. and Watts, T. 1988: Alcohol and minority youth. *Journal of Drug Issues*, 18, 1, 1–6.

Young, L. 1990: A nasty piece of work: a psychoanalytic study of sexual and racial difference in 'Mona Lisa'. In J. Rutherford (ed.), *Identity: Community, Culture, Difference*. London: Lawrence and Wishart.

Zuckerman, M. 1990: Some dubious premises in research and theory on racial differences: scientific, social and ethical issues. *American Psychologist*, 45, 12, 1297–1303.

Index